Interpreting the Religious Experience: A Worldview

John Carmody

Denise Lardner Carmody

University of Tulsa

Prentice-Hall, Inc.
Englewood Cliffs, New Jersey 07632

Library of Congress Cataloging-in-Publication Data

CARMODY, JOHN
  Interpreting the religious experience.

  Bibliography: p. 199
  Includes index.
  1. Religions. 2. Religion. I. Carmody,
Denise Lardner. II. Title.
BL80.2.C344 1987   291   86-91532
  ISBN   0-13-475609-6

For Jerry and Renée Unterman

Editorial/production supervision and
    interior design: Patricia V. Amoroso
Cover design: Ben Santora
Manufacturing buyer: Harry P. Baisley

© 1987 by Prentice-Hall, Inc.
A Division of Simon & Schuster
Englewood Cliffs, New Jersey 07632

Printed in the United States of America

10   9   8   7   6   5   4   3   2   1

ISBN 0-13-475609-6   01

PRENTICE-HALL INTERNATIONAL (UK) LIMITED, *London*
PRENTICE-HALL OF AUSTRALIA PTY. LIMITED, *Sydney*
PRENTICE-HALL CANADA INC., *Toronto*
PRENTICE-HALL HISPANOAMERICANA, S.A., *Mexico City*
PRENTICE-HALL OF INDIA PRIVATE LIMITED, *New Delhi*
PRENTICE-HALL OF JAPAN, INC., *Tokyo*
PRENTICE-HALL OF SOUTHEAST ASIA PTE. LTD., *Singapore*
EDITORA PRENTICE-HALL DO BRASIL, LTDA., *Rio de Janeiro*

Contents

Preface

For some time we have wanted to write a provocative theoretical book that would offer a radical analysis of the religious experience of humankind. Our main reason has been pedagogical. Some of the best learning occurs when professors take a position, lay out their data and arguments, and invite the students to probe, challenge, consult other authorities, and thereby themselves become passionate participants in the analytical and evaluative processes. Behind this pedagogical approach shines the verity that students tend to learn to the extent that they are active, engaged, and vitally participant. Further, to encourage discussion, we have tried to furnish at least some of the arguments against our own positions. We also assume that most readers of the book will have teachers guiding them through, demanding other readings, offering alternate interpretations, and the like.

The book is an introduction to the religious experience of humankind as a whole. Thus, its potential data are overwhelming and its sharp delineations are bound sometimes to be simplistic. We have used the most sophisticated philosophy of history we know, that of Eric Voegelin, but even so the result can only be considered a sketch: In his *Order and History* alone Voegelin has written at perhaps ten times the length we had available, and he had no need to simplify his language or repeat his argument. Readers therefore should not hold Voegelin responsible for the defects that follow from either our insufficient expositions or our biases. If readers will take themselves to his own writings, almost always they will find an amazingly subtle sense of the complexities that a full treatment would involve. We have not consulted Voegelin about the project (he died while this work was in progress). We make no claims that he would have approved it or been glad it was tried. The times we did talk with Voegelin he was completely gracious, but this was (from our side) a giant being magnanimous to pygmies.

What we have taken from Voegelin is the main design of the work as an analysis of religious history in terms of four main movements and the prime theoretical categories of myth, philosophy, revelation, gnosticism, differentiation, and the like. We have also taken a somewhat firm style, assigning credits and debits as the evidence seemed to warrant. We have not pretended that some insights are not better than others. We have rejected the notion that education or academic work should stay removed from either personal spiritual experience or public political consequences. The issues involved in religious history are too momentous to bow to fallacious notions of "objectivity" or "detachment." Our one aim throughout has been to present a clean, deep, provocative interpretation that would stimulate vigorous debate. To this end we have followed Voegelin's judgments, without much apology.

Our thanks to Emily Baker and Joe Heider of Prentice-Hall, who shepherded the project along; to Bill Thompson, Ken Keulman, Bob Kelly, and the late Bill Clebsch, with whom we have shared an enthusiasm for Voegelin's work; and to the following reviewers of the manuscript, who offered useful comments: Henry W. Bowden of Rutgers University and Stephen J. Reno of the University of Southern Maine.

Our last and greatest debt is to Eric Voegelin himself, a great mind and a great spirit, who has offered the most precious sort of encouragement and nourishment to hundreds the world over—may he rest content.

CHAPTER ONE

Introduction

ON THE STUDY OF WORLD RELIGION

It is commonplace nowadays to hear someone say that the world is growing smaller. Communications and transportation link us to victims of earthquake in Mexico or victims of French espionage in New Zealand. Ecological problems such as acid rain and polluted oceans tell us that the waste products of one nation easily become the smelly nuisances of another nation. When people riot in South Africa, stockholders around the globe meet to reconsider their investments. When the governor of Oklahoma considers the plight of his state's oil-based economy, he hits on a trip to China as a way to boost local business.

This sort of interconnectedness did not exist as recently as thirty years ago. It has come with communications satellites, advanced computers, and supersonic transport. And, whether we like it or not, it has forced all the advanced nations to begin rethinking their sense of the human race. No longer can any nation uncritically think of itself as either an isolated island or the center of history. No longer can Jewish, Christian, or Muslim assumptions that God chose a single people to reveal the divine nature and purposes expect to go unchallenged. If a new generation of telescopes and theoretical physicists is making us rethink the origins of the universe, a new sense of the unity of the earth's 5 billion people is making us rethink how Asians and Africans, Europeans and Latin Americans, can understand one another sufficiently to keep the earth from blowing up.

Such an understanding must, of course, deal with economic and military matters. It must keep in mind the history that has brought the different peoples to their current situations and the cultures or worldviews that they now possess. In this context, though, the understanding of one another that the peoples of the earth now require also spotlights **religion**.* For *religion* is probably the best word for the ultimate convictions, the deepest acts of faith, that finally shape a given worldview.

For example, if one considers the problems of the Middle East as they stem from the differences between Israelis and Palestinians, one finds that both peoples ultimately think they are special or chosen by God in a way that no other people is or can be. Thus Jews look at the Hebrew Bible as a record of their election by God to special status, whereas Muslim Palestinians look at the **Qur'an** as a similar record of God's unique revelations to the final, consummate prophet Muhammad. Christian Palestinians, for their part, think that Jesus and the New Testament have made the Hebrew Bible old news. They also think that Jesus, as the Word of God become flesh, is a far fuller revealer of God than Muhammad ever could be. These deep religious notions, to be sure, do not wipe away the significance of secular history, economics, and military matters. But they do symbolize a realm of difference and potential division that we very much have to take into account if we are ever to understand the happenings of the Middle East.

Much the same story is repeated in other parts of the globe. If we want to understand contemporary India, we have to grasp the historical and philosophical differences between Muslims and Hindus. If we want to understand dictatorship and revolution in Latin America, we have to grasp certain key notions of traditional Latin Christianity, as well as the changes being proposed by "theologians of liberation." Traditional (or tribal) African religion now mixes with Marxism, Christianity, and Islam throughout that large continent. Traditional (or Confucian) customs underlie many of China's peculiar obstacles on the road to technological innovation.

In both small matters and great matters, therefore, the major religious traditions that have shaped the past four thousand years or so of world history continue to leave their impression. As political scientists who have been trying to understand the fanatics of **Shiite** Muslim countries have finally come to realize, what people think about the final structures of reality very much influences how they live and how they are willing to die.[1] If we cannot see this in a war such as that between Iran and Iraq, we certainly should be able to see it in the hostilities between Protestants and Catholics in Ireland. To bring the matter home even more directly, we certainly should be able to see it in the history of racism and sexism in the United States. For example, the Ku Klux Klan, with its hatred of blacks, Jews, and Catholics, makes no sense except as a perversion of both Protestant Christianity and American patriotism. The current battles over evolution, abortion, and prayer in the public schools all arise from Americans'

*Terms in boldface are defined in the glossary.

quite different yet equally firmly entrenched religious or areligious convictions.[2]

Only when we begin to realize that other people might not at all believe what we take for granted, in terms of ultimate or religious outlook, can we start to make sense out of our current global culture. Only when the **Shema** of Deuteronomy 6, with its bold assertion of **monotheism,** becomes something to wonder about, rather than something to accept as obvious, do we start to realize how much of human history and culture could have developed quite differently. And only then, of course, do we begin to see, in a most positive way, that a great many of our current roadblocks and stalemates could be pushed away tomorrow, if first leaders and then whole peoples developed a new appreciation of world religion.

ERIC VOEGELIN'S *ORDER AND HISTORY*

The principal ideas driving our interpretation of world religion are not original with us but derive from the work of Eric Voegelin. Born in 1901, Voegelin fled Austria in the late 1930s because of disagreements with the Nazis. He taught at Louisiana State University for many years, directed an institute for political science at the University of Munich, and then returned to the United States to be a Distinguished Scholar at the Hoover Institute, on the campus of Stanford University. Although his doctorate had focused on law, Voegelin first made his scholarly reputation in political science. In later years he broadened his scope, more and more pursuing the philosophy of history. *Order and History*, his major work, comprises four volumes.[3] Because *Order and History* inspired our present effort, sketching its contents might provide some helpful background.

Voegelin began the first volume of *Order and History* with the sentence, "The order of history emerges from the history of order."[4] By this he meant that we best grasp the meaning history carries by studying how peoples have symbolized their understanding of the world, how they have tried to represent the whole. Volume 1 studies the symbols of several societies of the ancient Near East (Mesopotamia, Persia, and Egypt), but it devotes more space to ancient Israel, the society that produced the Hebrew Bible (what Christians call the Old Testament). Voegelin's basic finding is a development from a *cosmological* style of symbolization, which dominated Mesopotamia, Persia, and Egypt, to a new Israelite style of symbolization called *revelation*.

In most societies of the ancient Near East, people thought of reality in terms of an inclusive natural world. Nature—the physical span from heaven to earth—included everything that was real. Rocks and trees, plants and animals, human beings and gods were all citizens of nature. What made any of them exist was more like than unlike what made all the others exist. For the world was a living whole, a single organism. It had different realms and levels, different kinds of creatures, but they were all parts of one inclusive entity. Thus human affairs became clearest when one placed them in the perspective of nature's cycles. If human affairs moved harmoniously with nature, one could expect them to prosper. If they opposed the ways of the stars and the seas, the earth and the life force, they would come to grief.

We shall describe the cosmological orientation at length, showing how it clarifies a wealth of data about prehistoric, nonliterate, and early civilizational peoples. We should note here, though, that Voegelin found no society that had completely abandoned cosmological ways of picturing reality. Even in ancient Israel, where revelation meant that a personal God beyond the world was thought to have singled out human beings for a special role in the cosmos, the rhythms and inclusiveness of nature retained great force.

Still, the experiences recorded in the Hebrew Bible show a movement away from cosmological symbolization. As Israel tried to express its understanding of what had happened to Abraham and the patriarchs, to Moses and the prophets, it reconceived its sense of order. Its people finally came to feel that only by orienting themselves toward a God independent of the world, free of nature's cycles, could they be faithful to their best instincts.

Revelation, too, will occupy us at considerable length, so we only note here the great importance Voegelin accorded it. Like *philosophy*, the love of wisdom that is the main subject of Volumes 2 and 3 of *Order and History*, revelation was a "leap in being," a fresh understanding of reality that went beyond humanity's previous attainments. But Greek philosophy, which began with the probings of the early poets and dramatists, stressed the mind. Revelation stressed the underlying spirit or soul. Nonetheless, when philosophy reached maturity, with Socrates, Plato, and Aristotle, it too expressed something new, something more than the old cosmological symbols had conveyed. For Plato and Aristotle, human reason was a presence of divinity. The meaning that ran through nature became luminous, aware, in human beings, and this luminosity was divine. Ultimately, the philosophers saw that the light by which the ablest intellects found patterns, proportions, logic, or reason in reality was the presence of divinity—was the Godhead luring the human mind toward Itself.

Like Israel, Greece never completely abandoned the cosmological style of expressing its convictions. In fact philosophy placed less stress on divinity's independence of the world than revelation did. But with philosophy, a second dramatically new way of looking at things had arisen, a second dramatically new clarification of human awareness had occurred.

Volume 4 of *Order and History* represents Voegelin's reworkings or refinements of these findings in the context of modern struggles after order (from the seventeenth century on). For him much modern thought about reality had lost the experiences from which revelation and philosophy emerged and so had lost some of humanity's deepest truths. As we shall see, the reasons for this are complicated (and certainly other scholars challenge Voegelin's interpretation), but the charge implies that we will only regain a fully satisfying orientation to reality if we can restore revelation and philosophy for contemporary times.

Portrait of Old Parr. Peter
Paul Rubens. The eyes of
this old man might have
seen what makes for
Voegelinian wisdom.   *(The
Nelson-Atkins Museum of Art, Kansas
City, Missouri [Nelson Fund])*

A FIRST INTERPRETATION OF RELIGION

If cosmological symbolization, revelation, and philosophy are the main
categories Voegelin used to interpret world history and human consciousness, where does religion fit in? It fits in at the center, because most
peoples have considered their symbolic expressions of order sacred, holy,
most central, things that bound them to mysteries deserving awe and worship. This association with sacrality or holiness is what we shall mean by
religion. For us religion is the dimension of human life in which people
consort with mysteries deserving awe and worship.

Certainly the peoples of the ancient Near East, the Israelites, and the
Greeks pursued order, meaning, as though their rites, myths, and symbols
dealt with holy things, mysteries that excited awe. But so did virtually all
the other peoples of whom we have records. Prehistoric peoples left traces
of sacred ceremonies apparently designed to keep them in good standing
with nature's powers. Indians, Chinese, and other peoples of the East tried
to order social and personal life through sacral ceremonies and interior
exercises such as yoga. Christianity and Islam taught their adherents that
God is holy, to be worshiped with a clean heart.

Religion, then, has made humanity's search for order both exciting and daunting. Its mysteries have fascinated the best minds and hearts, but they have also made many people's hair stand on end. For whether we picture ultimate reality in cosmological or theological terms (as an inclusive nature or as a God independent of the world), ultimate reality is *both* beautiful and fearsome.

A case in point is the sea, which many peoples have regarded religiously, as a presence or symbol of ultimate reality. In good weather the sea is playful, energetic, soothing, a breathtaking mixture of blue and white. We authors stood one day for several hours watching a perfect sea swirl and pound off the coast of Bundoran, a small town of west Ireland. On the other hand, how many people have gone to their deaths in storms off the west coast of Ireland? How many typhoons and tidal waves have terrorized other coastal peoples? The depths of the sea are out of sight, as impenetrable to the mind as to the body. The source, or creator, of the sea is all the more impenetrable, all the more beyond our capacity to evaluate.

For Voegelin and the approach we are taking here, religion is highly ambiguous. On the positive side, it has been part and parcel of humanity's attempt to orient itself to reality and to prosper by thinking hard and with pure heart. On the negative side, religion has often resisted fresh thought, creative imagination, and profound cries for justice, becoming a prop of mediocrity and oppression. Any fair treatment of world religion must report both sides of the story. Any fully satisfactory treatment must explain how religion can have been both so good and so bad.

Where do the positive and negative effects of religion play in the main patterns that human history has shown? Where do they play in personal consciousness? These will be among our most central questions. As they suggest, we will be trying to be fair to religion but not neutral. Fairness means giving both sides of the ledger their due. Neutrality can mean bracketing the personal or social significance of religion, as though what one studied made no difference in the real world. That is bad scholarship, because religion has made an enormous difference in the real world. Historically, most societies have been religious and most mature personalities have been absorbed with religious mysteries.

Our first, orientational interpretation of religion therefore stresses its immense importance. The first significance we want *religion* to carry is "the awesome ultimate questions of human meaning." In due course we shall consider such secondary significances as temples and churches, stories and ceremonies, rules about what to eat and how to behave. Most of the time, people do not live in the curling depths of the awesome ultimate questions. Most of the time they are preoccupied with getting food and shelter, raising children, and healing pain. The ceremonies and rules of religion try to mediate between a people's understanding of the awesome ultimate questions and such secondary issues as getting food and shelter. They and the other paraphernalia of religion amount to a semipermeable shield, warding off the terror and utter absorption that the awesome ultimate questions can provoke while letting through enough energy, meaning, and beauty to make life endurable, even adventurous.

We need not contrast our interpretation of religion with all the others on the market, but you should know a little about the main competition. Sociologically orientated scholars lay primary emphasis on religion's role in popular culture, tending to see religion as a support for the status quo and tending to neglect religion's roots in individual human consciousness. Psychologically oriented scholars lay primary emphasis on the ways religious symbols shape individual consciousnesses, often neglecting religion's roots in the external realities of nature, society, and God. Analytic philosophers concentrate on the meaning of religious concepts, often underplaying religion's many other (paraconceptual, infraconceptual and supraconceptual) sides. We shall try to take the strengths of these other orientations into account and skate around their weaknesses.

A FIRST SKETCH OF THE HISTORY OF RELIGION

This introductory chapter is a series of warm-up exercises, a number of gross tunings. As we get into stride, the hard work of clarifying what the initially blurry outlines actually enclose will place considerable nuance on what we have said thus far. That hard work will be so much fine tuning of these initial concepts, so that they communicate the history of world religion more accurately.

Interestingly, this sort of progress from gross to fine tuning is a fair image for the history of religion itself. In our interpretation, human beings have made progress in their search for order by slowly clarifying, or *differentiating*, what their consciousnesses have reported. To clarify, of course, means to shed light, to bring from obscurity into understanding. To differentiate means to unpack something compact so that its different parts become more obvious, better appreciated. The basic movement in terms of which we find it most profitable to periodize human history is from a compact consciousness to a more differentiated consciousness.

The advantage of this focus is that it makes meaning or order history's main line. Then events and symbols become significant to the extent that they advance humanity's grasp of the world's order. For example, wars that merely move bodies back and forth across bloody plains are not themselves very significant. They become significant when a people reflects on their pathos and takes a quantum leap in understanding the human condition. The heroes of human history are the people, famous or anonymous, who have understood the human condition, fencing the way against chaos and building the towers of meaning. Zoroaster, Buddha, Jesus, and Muhammad are great heroes but so are countless mothers, poets, nurses, and craftspeople who defended and edified their tribes.

In *Order and History* Voegelin stressed two outstanding differentiations of consciousness. Through philosophy and revelation, human history made quantum leaps in understanding, and so, quantum leaps in being. Because this understanding potentially brought the whole race deeper into the mystery of reality, it belongs at the central plot line of the religious story. Before and after philosophy and revelation stand cosmological and modern symbols. Very roughly, the cosmological symbols represent an anterior stage of human understanding, from whose prior compactness philosophy and revelation differentiated fuller views. Equally roughly, modernity represents a posterior stage of human understanding, a subsequent compacting or confusion of the differentiated reality that philosophy and revelation disclosed. The central plot line therefore has three sections. First there is the cosmological symbolism, then there is philosophy and revelation, last there is modernity's retreat from philosophy and revelation (or modernity's qualifications of their views of reality).

However, history is much more than a simple story with a single plot line. Specifically, much more was going on to the side than the image of a linear arrangement suggests. During the phase of cosmological symbolization, people had many of the experiences and touched on many of the external realities that philosophy and revelation clarified. During the phase of philosophy and revelation, cosmological symbolism continued, keeping many people midway between the new awareness of the sages and prophets and the old awareness of the shamans. Even in the societies that philosophy and revelation shaped deeply, such as those of Europe, there was a constant tendency to retreat from differentiation to old or

The Arts—Music. Gaspare Traversi. The picture suggests the foolish complacency modernity has often indulged.   *(The Nelson-Atkins Museum of Art, Kansas City, Missouri [Gift of the Samuel H. Kress Foundation to the Nelson Gallery Foundation])*

new forms of compactness. Thus the challenges, regressions, and upsets of modernity were not unprecedented. They were distinctive enough, however, to demarcate a new historical era, with a new set of obstacles blocking the way to order.

COUNTERVIEWS

Voegelin's heavy marking of the main plot line and his many forays into what was going on to the side furnish a large measure of what one needs clearly to tell the story of world religion. Nonetheless, there are important areas that Voegelin neglected and serious challenges to his basic assumptions. For example, he wrote relatively little about Hinduism, Buddhism, Chinese religion, Islam, and the religion of nonliterate peoples past or present. His theories provide more than hints of how these peoples factor into the world historical picture, but anyone wanting to do justice to India, China, or Africa (for just three instances) has to develop such hints in connection with new data. One also has to take seriously such alternatives to Voegelin's basic assumptions as the shamanic stress on ecstasy, the Marxist stress on alienation, and the empiricists' stress on sensory experience. All three dispute Voegelin's understanding of *order*, and perhaps all three also dispute Voegelin's placing order at the center of history. Let us briefly develop these alternatives.

Eric Voegelin's favorite among the major personality types that have shaped world history is the philosopher (the lover of wisdom). The lover of wisdom, as Voegelin best found in Plato, comes to a balanced view of reality that centers on human reason. This reason is both unlimited and limited, and most of *wisdom* is knowing precisely how to handle the paradox of such a combination.

The shaman, in contrast, tends to stress the imagination. (Roughly, imagination is how we picture reality, and reason is how we extract or receive meaning.) The peak experience, for most shamans, comes through ecstatic journeys out to the gods or the animal-spirit forces. From such experiences, shamans tend to conceive of human life as mainly an opportunity for ecstasy. This is not to say that they or their people don't know enough to come in out of the rain or don't provide for eating and housing. It is to say, though, that a lot of what modern Western culture considers significant doesn't very much impress traditionally shamanic peoples— American Indians, native Australians, traditional Africans, or traditional Eskimos, for example. Such peoples have been more interested in feeling good—harmonious with themselves and the physical world—than in making money or accumulating a lot of possessions. They have thought that the inside of a person (the realm of images, thoughts, feelings, and silences) is at least as important as the outside. And they have sought to be whole or integral, fighting any tendency to set hard and fast boundaries between themselves and nature, or between the individual and the tribe, or between the forces of nature and the gods or the God. Consequently, such traditional peoples or the modern people who seem like them in psychological profile (some artists, ecologists, and feminists, for instance) would probably dispute Voegelin's high evaluation of rationality and order. In their view it is far more important to feel at one with the rest of the universe than it is to understand all of reality's main parts.

The objections of Marxists and empiricists would come from different quarters, but they would have the same effect of disputing Voegelin's criteria for staging progress and regress in human history. Many Marxists, for instance, take it as virtually given that we human beings will be alienated—cut off from and out of sorts with nature, other people, and ourselves—until we get finished with the class struggle between rich and poor and reset labor or work on a healthy basis. Many Marxists also think that "God" is the biggest of illusions and that we won't have full harmony until we stop projecting our best ideals and energies away from ourselves and onto "God." Thus they would tend to find Voegelin's talk of the divine mystery at the center of human consciousness alienating and destructive.

Empiricists, those who basically confine what is "real" to what can be sensed and verified in terms of experiential data, have somewhat related quarrels with Voegelin's basis for periodizing human history. In the view of most empiricists, modernity was a great advance over the classical culture developed by Greece and the medieval Christian culture that grew from Greek and biblical roots. The key to the development of modern science

Head of a Peasant. Vincent van Gogh. Van Gogh communicates the sobriety and dignity that peasant labor can develop. *(The Nelson-Atkins Museum of Art, Kansas City, Missouri [Nelson Fund])*

was empirical observation and critical testing, both of which put strict limits on previous views of human "reason." It was not by speculating in the sky, as Plato did, that modern technology and science arose, but by close work down to earth. So empiricists will not be happy with the high marks that Voegelin gave to classical philosophy and biblical revelation, both of which depend upon, and supposedly demonstrate, a human consciousness whose deepest levels go well below sensation. Relatedly, they will not be happy with the esteem that a follower of Voegelin can show for such spiritual phenomena as Hindu philosophy and Islamic prophecy.

In the long run, therefore, the argument that we are making will depend in good measure on the view of human nature with which it dovetails. In the long run, any view of how human history ought to be periodized (that of shamans, Marxists, empiricists, and Voegelinians alike) goes hand in glove with an anthropology or set of convictions about human nature. So our "argument" for this view of Eric Voegelin will face a great many questions (including those from people who think that all schematizations of history do more harm than good, and that one which can be read in terms of *evolution* or even *Western supremacy* is especially objectionable). Here we can only acknowledge that Voegelin was no divinity beyond the reach of criticism, and we can only demand, by way of fairness, that other views we entertain should provide (as space warrants) their counterunderstandings of human nature.

THE PROGRAM OF THIS BOOK

Our program begins with a study of peoples who have expressed their understanding of the world in stories and ceremonies that stress the inclusiveness of nature. Using Voegelin's terminology, we designate the first two chapters "The Cosmological Myth." *Cosmological* should be clear by now. *Myth* does not imply *untrue* but simply means *storied.* The people who symbolized their sense of order in terms of a harmony with nature tended to use stories. Were we to generalize their stories into an archetypal tale, we might speak of *the* cosmological myth, a story that begins, "Once upon a time we came from the earth," progresses in terms of various interactions with forces of nature, and ends, "and unto dust we shall return."

So described, the cosmological myth is applicable to many more peoples than those we treat in this first section. Nonetheless, the peoples we treat display the cosmological myth handsomely, one might almost say purely. In chapter two we consider prehistoric human beings from paleolithic times and Africans, American Indians, Australians, and Eskimos of recent times. The central religious figure in nonliterate cultures is the shaman, and the wisdom that many shamans have developed shows that the cosmological myth is far from a primitive human achievement. Also far from primitive are the early civilizational peoples we study in chapter three. In the new context of literacy and town life, they developed the cosmological myth, so that human society became a miniature of the heavenly society of the gods.

Chapters four through six deal with philosophy, what Voegelin called *noetic differentiation*. Noetic differentiation is the clarification of consciousness that stresses thought (**noesis**) or reason. Typically, it produces a society in which the ideal personality is the sage.

India often spoke as though its ideal personality were the sage, the Hindu or Buddhist come to **enlightenment**, so in chapter four we treat Indian religion as a species of philosophy. Our subject in chapter five is China, another culture that sang hymns to the sage. Whether Confucian or Taoist, the Chinese sage prescribed an order that made the individual and society harmonious with nature. Thus in China the continuing influence of the cosmological myth is clear. Chapter six takes us to Greece, the culture where noetic differentiation reached its greatest heights. In the heroic work of Plato and Aristotle, humanity greatly clarified the structure of reason. Indeed, it grasped the form of the light that discloses the full span of reality: nature, society, self, and God.

Chapters seven through nine study the second great leap in being, revelation. Revelation is a "pneumatic differentiation," a clarification of consciousness that focuses on the spirit (**pneuma**) rather than the mind. In revelational societies the ideal personality tends to be the prophet.

Chapter seven initiates our study of pneumatic differentiation with ancient Israel, whose patriarchs, prophets, and kings wrote variations on the experience of being addressed by a divinity free of the world. The upshot of this divinity's speech was that human beings are fit subjects for a divine-human communication. In chapter eight we move to Christianity, which owes its rise to Jesus and Paul, Jewish prophets with a slightly different understanding of the divine-human communication. Islam, the subject of chapter nine, offers yet another variety of prophetic religion. For Islam, Muhammad is the prophet par excellence and the Qur'an is revelation par excellence, offering human beings the divine blueprint for their order.

The last section deals with modernity. By modernity we mean the attitude, originating in seventeenth-century Europe and thereafter spreading throughout the world, that the cosmological myth, philosophy, and revelation are passé, rendered out of date by new science, exploration, industrialization, and the like. The archetypal personality that this attitude produces is the alienated intellectual, such as Freud or Marx.

In chapter ten we examine the rise of this attitude, trying to show both its good and bad causes. The last chapter is a summary, in which we review the whole exposition, to underscore the key points.

So the program has a beginning part, in which we deal with the cosmological myth; two middle parts, in which we discuss philosophy and revelation; and a concluding part, in which we treat humanity's modern states of consciousness. Superficially, therefore, the book uses the simple linear pattern of historical development mentioned earlier. To provide for the developments that took place to the side of this straight line, we try to invest the subsections of the chapters with considerable data from eras or movements that complicate the false simplicity that the linear arrangement could suggest. The result, we hope, is a tale clear enough to be followed easily, vivid enough to be enjoyed, sophisticated enough to give the past its due, and bold or opinionated enough to provoke spirited discussions of how the history of world religion could be better schematized.

We should stress, as our last introductory remark, that our program is not evolutionary. We do not look upon philosophy and revelation, let alone upon modernity, as moral progress over a "primitive" humanity mired in the cosmological myth. As we show throughout, all peoples contend with the constants of human experience, and so, all peoples have a certain equality of opportunity. There has never been a human society in which one could not grow wise and good. On the other hand, certain societies have offered sizable advantages to people wanting to grow wise and good, for in them occurred human developments that were indeed advances we should applaud. Thus revelation, philosophy, and modern science deserve special stress in the history of world religion, and we shall try to provide it.

SUMMARY

To launch this study of world religion, we first considered why one should bother about world religion in the first place. Mainly, we noted that it is impossible to understand world events such as the war between Iraq and Iran or the conflicts between Catholics and Protestants in Ireland, without an appreciation of their religious underpinnings. In a world growing smaller all the time, world religion is becoming increasingly significant.

To get a first sense of the whole of world religion, we suggested a plot line that would be both modest and comprehensive. In our view, this plot line is the development of consciousness from compactness to differentiation. Eric Voegelin's *Order and History* furnishes us this hypothesis, and it will be our main theoretical guide. Voegelin's view, somewhat simplified, is that humanity has passed through such discernibly different stages of consciousness as the cosmological myth, revelation, philosophy, and modernity. Religion, which we understand as the dimension of human life in which people consort with mysteries deserving awe and worship, is at the center of this story, for all four stages of consciousness centrally deal with the ultimate structures and values of human life. The history of religion therefore runs in tandem with the overall history of humanity, and one perhaps best plots it, too, in terms of the differentiations of consciousness.

The program of our book derives from these theoretical considerations and plots the history of religion in four sections: the cosmological myth, philosophy, revelation, and modernity. Within these four sections we shall deal with prehistoric humanity, nonliterate humanity, early civilizational humanity, Indian culture, Chinese culture, the Near Eastern cultures of Judaism, Christianity, and Islam, and modernity. Our hope is that this breadth of coverage, combined with bold interpretation, will stimulate an energetic and profitable study.

STUDY QUESTIONS

1. Why has an understanding of religion been essential for studying recent American politics?

2. What is the basic plot line of world history that we are proposing?
3. What does Eric Voegelin mean by a cosmological style of symbolizing order?
4. Why do we consider religion highly ambiguous?
5. What are the two main differentiations of consciousness that we use to structure our history of religion?
6. How does modernity figure in our program?

NOTES

1. See V.S. Naipaul, *Among the Believers* (New York: Random House, Vintage Books, 1981), pp. 4–82.
2. See Jerry Falwell, *Listen, America!* (Garden City, N.Y.: Doubleday, 1980), p. 13.
3. Eric Voegelin, *Order and History, Vol. 1: Israel and Revelation* (1956); *Vol. 2: The World of the Polis* (1957); *Vol. 3: Plato and Aristotle* (1957); *Vol. 4: The Ecumenic Age* (1974) (Baton Rouge: Lousiana State University Press).
4. See Voegelin, *Order and History, Vol. 1*, p. ix.

CHAPTER TWO

Nonliterate Peoples

ORIENTATION

For the Greeks, to whom we owe the word, the *cosmos* was the ordered whole of nature, human beings, and the gods. It signified all of reality, insofar as reality presented itself as a whole with discernible and coordinated parts. Opposed to the cosmos was *chaos*, an unformed or disordered alternative. Sometimes chaos appeared to be the counterpart of the cosmos, the other pole necessary to balance the tensions between flux and stability, creativity and achievement. Other times, chaos appeared to be the antagonist or enemy of the cosmos, the wild other option that threatened to tear the cosmos apart or swallow it up. Chaos, then, was quite real, but largely negative or privative. It named the darkness out of which the light of the sun and the light of reason arose somewhat miraculously. It was the watery unformed original stuff from which the earth and the heavens emerged and took shape. Insofar as it was like the womb from which life issues forth, or like the uneasy confusion that precedes creative insight, chaos was necessary, inevitable, even valuable. Insofar as it connoted the wildness of a nature that might at any time turn destructive, or the madness of a human reason that could become unhinged, chaos was fearsome, threatening, a power that had to be warded off and appeased.

The cosmos that the Greeks conceived of as an ordered or integrated whole other early peoples dealt with more intuitively or symbolically. So, for example, the uniformity of the landscape of ancient Egypt made nature the physical backdrop of singular living things that stood out in bold relief.

So the falcon that floated in the sky, like the sun that dominated the cloud-less heavens, became in Egypt an entity that evoked great interest, even wonder or awe. The same with the jackal that ran along the edge of the desert, the crocodile lurking near the Nile, the huge bull that represented the prodigious powers of fertility. The early Egyptians tended to rivet their senses and minds to these extraordinary features of their landscape and deal with them as though they were fellow persons. It was not as an "it" that the falcon or the bull lodged in the typical early Egyptian's mind but as a "you," a fellow center of consciousness.

It follows, therefore, that the cosmos was extraordinarily alive and spiritual. For the early Egyptians, the Mesopotamians, and the other peoples whose records leave us relatively well informed, human beings were fellow citizens of animals and natural phenomena, compatriots. They knew, of course, that great differences separated crocodiles from either rivers or human beings. They even speculated on the differences between jackals and crocodiles. But, more than we moderns, they were impressed by the sameness that ran through all existents, the single order that we all seemed to comprise and the single life force that we all seemed to exhibit.

We shall deal more with the early civilizational forms of the cosmological myth that formed such cultures as the Egyptian when we get to chapter three. Prior to that, we investigate the evidences of cosmological mythology that nonliterate peoples have left. By and large, both the peoples who lived before the rise of writing in Sumer about 3100 B.C.E. (Before the Common Era that other peoples share with Christians) and the non-writing peoples who have continued down to the present (although in quite small numbers today) have dealt with reality as though it were a cosmos. Thus for the Pygmies who have long lived in the Congo forest of what is now Zaire, the forest is the most powerful and comprehensive symbol of God. They owe their lives to the forest. It is their daily context or environment or milieu. So they sing to the forest many evenings to try to make it feel good. The forest provides their food and shelter. Many of them have never not lived under its branches and would not be able to grasp a perspective of rolling hills or wide open spaces. Quite literally, the forest has determined how the Pygmies see. It is impossible, therefore, for the Pygmies to conceive of themselves as apart from the forest.

The cosmological myth is the form within which early humanity, both nonliterate and literate, organized its sense of reality. By narrating stories of how the ordered whole (the *universe*, we might say) came into being and gained its present shape, early peoples oriented themselves in the world. One species of such stories are what scholars call *cosmogonic myths*. They deal with the birth of the cosmos, the beginnings of the ordered whole. Later we shall see some examples of the cosmogonic myth and some examples of the myths that explain the traits of different animals or the fate of human beings (for example, why human beings, or all animals, have to die). Here our main point is that these stories take for granted and spell out the basic early human assumption that the world constitutes a single living whole.

One of the problems modern students face in understanding early human cultures is the care with which people in such cultures transact their dealings with nature. When American loggers in the Northwest set out to fell tall trees they do not pause to apologize. They might feel a twinge when they start putting the axe to a spectacular redwood, or they might wonder about the intrusions of human beings into the delicate forest ecology, but they virtually never address a tree as a fellow citizen of a single natural community, virtually never think that the tree has rights they might be violating. When the American Indian chief Smohalla met this modern attitude it both confused and offended him. The whites were proposing to till the soil, to plow and plant and reap. For Smohalla, ripping up the crust of the earth with a plow was like plunging a knife into the bosom of one's mother. The stones that the plow would unearth were like the bones of the one who had borne him. In the spring, Smohalla's people would tread lightly, perhaps even removing their moccasins. Their mother was pregnant with new life, and they were taking care not to injure it.

Premodern peoples (even those quite changed because of philosophy and revelation) tended to venerate the earth and nature much more than we do. No doubt, this was a complicated attitude, and we should not approach it simplistically. For instance, it is much more than the aesthetic appreciation of nature that motivates many environmentalists to protest numerous forms of development. It was much less exactly informed than the fears of today's scientists, who increasingly appreciate the delicacy of the connections among the different strata of life. We perhaps best appreciate the psychological impact of the cosmological myth if we think of early human beings as democratic or egalitarian about their relations with nonhuman creatures. They of course realized that their ability to reason distinguished them, but their relative impotence in the face of the great powers of nature made them feel more like than unlike the birds and fishes who were subject to the sky and the sea.

If, for instance, you consider the place that human beings have in the landscape paintings of Sung dynasty China, you realize the priority given to nature and space. Certainly Sung dynasty China (around 1000 C.E.) was a sophisticated cultural complex, not at all something preliterate. Indeed, such powerful thought systems as Confucianism, Taoism, and Buddhism had all made a deep impact. The smallness of the human figures in a Sung landscape therefore expresses many different cultural ingredients. However, it is also a good example of the way that most human beings have pictured their position in reality (if one were to grant each generation equal space on a single time line). On the whole, nature has been the great matrix or context or system, and we human beings have been but tiny, vulnerable actors playing very subordinate parts.

Thus, the confident, even aggressive or exploitative, attitude toward nature that has come with modern science and technology is something of an aberration, when one considers the full human time line. Far more representative of most generations' experience has been a subordinate, almost a petitioner's, mentality.

PREHISTORIC RELIGION

We begin our schematic approach to the history of human culture and religion by focusing on what not so long ago would have been called *primitive religion*. The first scholars of both prehistory and the culture of nonliterate peoples almost unconsciously relegated both to a lesser state of human development. The evolutionary theories of Darwin and his followers in biology influenced this judgment but so did the Western (usually Christian) upbringing of most of the early theoreticians.

We should make it plain, therefore, that the view we are developing from the theories of Eric Voegelin is not evolutionary and does not think of prehistoric humanity or nonliterate peoples as primitive. Voegelin did think that philosophy and revelation were great leaps of progress. He would, of course, find in literacy a cultural development of enormous significance. But his final criterion for human health was right order: realistic and harmonious relationships among nature, society, the self, and divinity. A prehistoric individual or tribe could be more healthy through its version of the cosmological myth than a later individual or group is through a cultural complex shaped by philosophy, revelation, or modern science. In terms of artistic beauty and religious wisdom, what came earlier is often at least as impressive as what followed after. So the differentiations by which we distinguish later peoples from earlier cosmological peoples do not necessarily confer an ethical or anthropological superiority. That is always a matter of the actual honesty and love that any people shows. In this chapter we simply focus on the quite different way that early human beings seem in fact to have viewed the world.

The beliefs of the human beings who lived before the development of writing must be inferred from the material remains they have left. Sometimes scholars employ data from nonliterate people of much later, even present-day times, but the best such scholars only use apparent parallels among all nonliterate people very gingerly. The fact that nonliterate people of recent times have organized the world through stories and have reverenced striking natural phenomena as expressions of a single ultimate force raises intriguing possibilities about how human beings of long ago thought about the world, but it hardly allows us to say that early men and women also had cosmogonic tales and held in awe the equivalent of Wakantanka, the Amerindian Great Spirit.

Still, from the Mousterian period of prehistory (about 70,000–50,000 B.C.E.), there are unmistakable signs of human burial, and some scholars find similar evidence from much earlier eras (indeed, from as early as the Choukoutien era around 400,000–300,000 B.C.E.). Such burials often involved red ochre, perhaps to suggest blood, and so, the life force. The very fact that people would take the trouble to bury a person's body, instead of just leaving it exposed to the elements, argues that the act was significant, perhaps a way of testifying to a belief that something in the dead person might continue on.

The fact is, however, that most of the artifacts left by prehistoric people are mute or ambiguous. Lacking any explicit indication from the people who made them, we have to conjecture what they meant. Still, the presence of animals in such outstanding remains as the paintings on the walls of prehistoric European caves proves that animals were significant to the artists who bothered to make the paintings and to the people who bothered to contemplate them. Sometimes the paintings depict human figures wearing animal skins, horns, feathers, and the like. The dancing or ceremonial posture of such figures suggests that the depiction has to do with early people's rituals, but again we must be cautious in what we say about both the existence and the content of such rituals. By analogy with nonliterate people of later ages, one can conjecture that fertility, a successful hunt, protection against enemies, and protection against the possibly vengeful dead were prominent themes in such rituals, but conjecture is all that such analogies can yield.

Nonetheless, the indications we can soberly attach to prehistoric cultural remains, with the suggestions we get from later preliterate peoples and the inferences we can make from sure facts about the living conditions of prehistoric tribes, combine to make a strong case for something like the cosmological myth. The burial remains and the suggestions of rituals for hunting, giving birth, and the rest situate early human existence in the context of a very powerful and threatening natural world. The analogies from later peoples show us many stories about the sun, the storm, the sea, Mother Earth, and the animals that shaped a particular tribe's world. So, for example, the Eskimos of the coastal areas of Canada and Greenland have had many myths about the seal and the mistress of all the sea animals. The Indians of the American plains have had many myths about the buffalo and the beautiful maiden who gave the tribes that hunted the buffalo their rituals.

When one adds to these two strands of argument or suggestion the inferences one can make from a physical existence dependent on hunting animals and gathering edible plants, a physical existence often lived out in caves or other natural shelters, one can easily imagine that nature, its seasons and outstanding forces, must have been the dominant reality in early human beings' lives. The likelihood is that prehistoric peoples lived on average only about half as long as we and that their infant mortality rates were considerably higher. The large number of statues of pregnant females that have been found among prehistoric remains suggests a strong interest in fertility, and the indications of deliberate burial procedures (sometimes the skeleton has been placed in a fetal posture, suggesting a hope of rebirth) put this interest in counterpoint with a strong concern about death. Alexander Marshak has done detailed studies of prehistoric bone markings and argued that they imply thorough calculations about the cycles of nature.[1] All in all, then, the immersion of early humanity in nature makes it highly likely that the rhythms and structures of the cosmos provided the mental as well as the physical framework.

This is considerably different from our own mental framework today, of course, and it behooves us to reflect on the gap that consequently separates us from early humanity. We moderns continue to depend upon nature for our physical lives—the food we eat, the air we breathe—but our cultural world is much more than natural. Indeed, for a citizen of a developed country today *nature* can be confused with the supermarket. Electricity allows us the possibility of going counter to the natural rhythms of night and day. The technology of our housing, clothing, tranportation, and communication greatly decreases our direct dependence on sun and wind, water and earth. The earth remains our habitat, and we lose psychic balance and physical prosperity if we forget that fact, but perhaps the majority of our relations with nature are mediated, distanced, buffered. Only occasionally do we meet nature directly, nakedly, in such a way that nature could threaten us or thrill us to the bone.

By the simple assumption that early humanity existed in a considerably more immediate or direct relation with nature, we start a picture of prehistoric religion that is bound to make it come out markedly different from modern religion. Prehistoric humanity was dominated by the cycles and forces of physical nature. It had but the smallest capacity to shield itself from the seasons and storms, to make an artificial, hothouse environment. It had to understand nature's ways as a matter of life and death, mustering all its cunning. So in all probability, a sense of being out of phase with nature, inharmonious, was a perilous feeling indeed. Latter-day shamans often try to ritualize their people back into harmony with the cosmos. When a member of the tribe has broken the ethical code or fractured a tribal **taboo**, the shaman attempts to elicit a confession of this transgression and some act of atonement. Both the confession and the atonement tend to involve the tribe, or at least the immediate family, as well as the individual offender. The sense communicated, then, is that "we" are all in this matter of harmony or disharmony with nature together. Whether we generalize the powers of nature into one primary divinity or distribute them across many different divinities, it is crucially important that we fit ourselves to nature's patterns, not go against nature's grain.

Prehistoric religion, in Voegelin's terms, was an effort to integrate oneself with the cosmos. Much of the religion of historical humanity has been the same. Indeed, prior to modernity, virtually all peoples who had not made revelation or philosophy the soul of their culture retained as a primary religious goal harmony with nature. This included many groups that nominally were Jewish, Christian, or Muslim, because often only the elite had really taken to heart the notion of a God transcending nature. Certainly in prehistoric times the physical world was the overwhelming reality, and so, the overwhelming religious object.

HUNTERS

In the world of early humanity, animals were not just fellow citizens of the single living cosmic whole but sources of food. They remain sources of food for us today, of course, but we seldom meet them with the hunter's immediacy. So closely are the psyches of many recent hunter groups identified with the animals they hunt that the tribe's rituals regularly feature **shamanic** ecstasies in which a representative of the tribe portrays the game or travels to the keeper of the game to beg their release. In the same vein, the seal became a summary of the whole culture of the Eskimos who hunted it and used its skin for their clothing. The buffalo became a summary or epitome of the culture of the Plains Indians who depended on it for their meat, moccasins, tepees, and much more. The cave paintings that provide some of our best clues to the psychological world of paleolithic hunters conjure up a similar mentality. To find a dancing figure dressed with tokens of various animals and sexually aroused is to suspect a ritual that linked hunting and fertility in a tribal effort to petition the powers of life and ward off the forces of death.

Mircea Eliade has written extensively on shamanism and the religion of hunters, both paleolithic and more recent. Among the phenomena that he singled out are myths about the origin of the game; concern for the tribe's relations with a figure variously named but in effect the "Lord of Wild Beasts," who controls the beasts' availability; stories about the origin and mysteries of fire; and rituals and stories pivoting on sexuality or procreation.

According to Eliade, the phenomena of the sky and the atmosphere probably held special fascination for hunters. Somewhat in contrast with the fascination that the earth held for gatherers and farmers, the sky and the weather no doubt controlled the hunters' psyches. One has to remember the crucial impact of the Ice Age, when a long period of bitter cold dominated life in the northern hemisphere. The melting of the ice meant a change in the migratory patterns of the game, and therefore a great change in the lives of the hunters who followed the game. As much as later farmers, the early hunters had to follow the seasons and learn with considerable precision the seasonal habits of their prey. Remains of early hunters indicate a great interest in such phenomena as the spawning of the fish and the mating and delivery of the deer and the bear. Shamans of later ages have regularly taken "flight" to the heavens, the source of the weather, in trance, becoming identified with eagles, falcons, and other birds of prey.

Summarizing these indications that the religion of hunters probably focused especially intensely on celestial phenomena, Eliade wrote

> This is one of the few experiences that spontaneously reveal transcendence and majesty. In addition, the ecstatic ascents of shamans, the symbolism of flight, the imaginary experience of altitude as a deliverance from weight, contribute to consecrating the celestial space as supremely the source and dwelling place of superhuman beings: gods, spirits, civilizing heroes. But equally important and significant are the "revelations" of night and darkness, of the killing of game and the death of a member of the family, of cosmic catastrophes, of the occasional crises of enthusiasm, madness, or homicidal ferocity among members of the tribe.[2]

The sky, then, was not the whole paleolithic story. In those early days, as now, human beings were challengingly complex. Day and night, life and death, in their symbolic as well as their simply physical power, made the hunters' experience of the cosmos both intense and complicated.

Intrinsic to Voegelin's notion of the cosmological myth is the sense that all of the participants share in the same single substance of the universal whole. Simply by existing and having a place on the map of reality, they become partners, partakers, of the one stream of existence or being or life. Voegelin's principal historical sources for asserting this ground-level dimension of cosmological symbolization are peoples of the ancient Near East, but what he said about the experience of human existence in such societies bears on hunters and gatherers as well.

> Whatever man may be, he knows himself a part of being. The great stream of being, in which he flows while it flows through him, is the same stream to which belongs everything else that drifts into his perspective. The community of being is experienced with such intimacy that the consubstantiality of the partners will override the separateness of the substances. We move in a charmed community where everything that meets us has force and will and feelings, where animals and plants can be men and gods, where men can be divine and gods are kings, where the feathery morning sky is the falcon Horus and the Sun and the Moon are his eyes, where the underground sameness of being is a conductor for magic currents of good or evil force that will subterraneously reach the superficially unreachable partner, where things are the same and not the same, and can change into each other.[3]

This sense of the mutuality of all beings, their sharing in a single underlying or inmost reality, was sufficiently vivid among the early civilizational peoples that Voegelin analyzed to break down the walls between different species. Even today, hunting tribes sponsor shamans who "become" a bird or other animal. In ecstatic trance, such shamans fly to other realms and establish relations with the natural world and the spirits of ancestors that ordinary consciousness does not accredit. Michael Harner, in fact, described the shaman as one who can work in two different fields of consciousness, profiting from the strengths of each.[4] Typically, the shaman's tribe agrees with this dualism, observing the dance or drum beating that takes their functionary out to the special realm, listening to a narration of the shaman's adventures on the journey, and giving the shaman such faith that he or she may heal them with the power or knowledge that the journeys provide.

GATHERERS

In two recent popular novels, students of paleolithic culture have laid out what early men and women might have felt from their interactions with a vast and threatening nature. Bjorn Kurten's *Dance of the Tiger* focuses on the roles of male hunters, and Jean Auel's *The Clan of the Cave Bear* concentrates on the roles of female gatherers.[5] Both novels do a good job of plausibly reconstructing life in the Old Stone Age, but neither, almost in the nature of the case, is able to communicate the density, richness, and power that the cosmological myth probably possessed.

On the whole, nonliterate peoples past and present appear to distinguish the roles of men and women rather strongly. These distinctions can break down in times of special relaxation or of special stress, but for the middle 75 percent of the time, nonliterate men and women have fitted themselves to different yet complementary patterns. In the matter of economy or work, for example, there has been a rather clear distribution of tasks. Men have been the main hunters (women have sometimes hunted small game), and women have been the main gatherers of plants, berries, and herbs. As a result, men have been more directly involved in killing and more directly connected to animal life, whereas women have been more deeply immersed in the cycles and varieties of plant life.

Women have also been more associated with fertility and lifepower, through their pregnancies, births, and nursings. They have been the cooks and often the primary healers (herbalists). In the largest sense, then, women have had a closer connection with life, whereas men have been more directly confronted with death. This is not to say, of course, that women have not also been shaped by death. In tribes that suffered high rates of infant mortality or that practiced infanticide when there were too many mouths to feed, women must have experienced death as a sword piercing their hearts. But the material remains of prehistoric humanity and analogues from nonliterate tribes of recent times allow us to place femininity close to the early human consciousness of the awesomeness of creating life.

As gatherers, women's sense of the cosmos was shaped somewhat differently from men's. Whereas men had to learn the seasonal fluctuations of the game, women had to learn the seasonal variations of the plants. Most historians of early human culture speculate that women probably spearheaded the development of agriculture (the controlled production of cereals, fruits, and herbs), because they were the specialists in gathering. Even before agriculture, however, women probably provided the stable major portion of early families' diets. Adrienne Zihlman, in fact, has put the fraction of women's contribution at from 50 percent to 90 percent.[6] When one adds in women's production of children (it took some time for humanity to understand the more hidden male role in reproduction), one can see why the earliest personified divinity was a Great Mother Goddess. The men who provided the large game and protected the tribe against enemies might have been the political leaders (there are data suggesting matriarchal leadership for some early periods, but they are not conclusive), but the women, who were more closely identified with the earth and the power of human fertility, provided the nearer analogy for the personal face of the sacred.

The cosmological myth, being so basic to early human consciousness, could admit of many variations. For at least the later epochs of prehistory, however, where the archaeological remains are the richest, we can say with some conviction that the cosmos was mainly represented by a female deity. Across a wide swath of Old Europe, from the Mediterranean to the borders of Asia, a uniformity of artifacts argues for a pervasive cult of the Great Mother. By 7000 B.C.E., for instance, in modern Turkey, a veritable system of sanctuaries had developed, all of them focused on a female fertility figure. She had three principal facets: virginal young woman, mature woman giving birth, and old crone. Almost always she had associated with her, in an important but subordinate status, a masculine sacral figure in the form of a child or a young man. The usual scholarly conjecture is that this male figure was either the son of the goddess or her potent young lover. Other remains from paleolithic sanctuaries confirm the early preoccupation with fertility. The bull is frequently represented and probably stands for vigorous virility. The Goddess is often pregnant, and often she or other female figures have a superabundance of breasts. The sexuality portrayed is strong yet so impersonal that it clearly comes from a premodern mind. The accent is on the natural force, the power of regeneration that keeps the cosmos living. The impact of this force on individual tribal members is secondary, for the whole is much more prominent in early consciousness than the individual parts.

Gatherers, of course, could be somewhat more stationary than hunters. They therefore suggest a transitional psychic state between the nomadic mentality of the hunter and the stable mentality of the farmer. So long as hunting predominated over farming, the cosmological myth occurred mainly in a nomadic mode. People wandered with the elk or the buffalo, tied more to these primal game than to particular lands or rivers. As the advantages of cultivating grains, and then of domesticating animals, came home, in concert with the skill to accomplish such goals, early humanity went through a sizable revolution. No longer would it wander with the game, and so experience the cosmos in what later cultures might have called a **pilgrim's** mode. Gradually it decided to settle down, claim a particular area, and sink roots. This opened the way for the proliferation of divinities, insofar as each important locale was conceived of as having a protective god or goddess. It opened the way for a closer scrutiny of natural phenomena, especially the movement of the stars.

On the way to writing and early civilization, the culture sponsored by the large settlements of towns and cities, people foresaw the possibility of specializing in their labor. Hunters, farmers, people raising domestic animals, workers of stone, and later, workers of metal could all narrow their focus and learn more and more about less and less (become experts). As we shall see in the next chapter, this went hand in hand with the development of more specialized and complicated religious systems. People also began to specialize in religious functions and to organize the different sacral forces of the world into theological wholes. Sexuality continued to be an important theme, and divinities continued to symbolize the fertility of both nature and humanity. The cosmological myth remained in force, inasmuch as people considered reality a rather seamless living whole. But political or sociological factors grew in importance as larger social units replaced the wandering small tribe.

It was the gatherers, therefore, and the female side of the closely balanced early **androgyny** that were the bridge to later developments. The hunters continued to have a great influence, and the male side later became politically dominant again, but the first great revolution of human culture probably came from the people who identified most closely with mother earth. Thus, the first significant shift or beginnings of differentiation within the compactness of the cosmological myth led to a stress on female symbols of divinity. The later extensions of this shift or differentiation, in fact, appear in the highly ambivalent female divinities of such cultures as India, where a Great Goddess such as Kali is both gently maternal and the fiercest of destroyers.

AFRICANS AND NATIVE AMERICANS

The cosmological myth provides a framework for understanding the peoples who have kept closest contact with prehistoric humanity and preserved some of the earliest sensibilities. Thus, it is something of an umbrella to shelter all the peoples whose cultures either predated or fell outside revelation, philosophy, and modernity. This does not mean, of course, that we can make wholesale identifications between traditional African, Native American, or other nonliterate peoples and early humans of the paleolithic or even the neolithic age. Although traditional African or Native American tribes often remained essentially nonliterate well into the twentieth century, the more than five thousand years separating them from prehistoric humanity were not static or uniform. Indeed, sometimes there was considerable interaction among the different tribes of the African or the North American continent, and so indirect contact with literate peoples of those areas. Nonetheless, the basic myths, rituals, and orientations to reality that formed the consciousnesses of traditional Africans and North Americans made these peoples intimate with nature as no modern, and few revelational or philosophical, peoples could be. For the rest of this section let us simply illustrate how the cosmos functioned in traditional Africa and North America.

A cosmogonic myth of the Boshongo, a central Bantu tribe, pictures the origin of the world as beginning with a stomachache of the great god Bumba.

> In the beginning, in the dark, there was nothing but water. And Bumba was alone. One day Bumba was in terrible pain. He retched and strained and vomited up the sun. After that light spread over everything. The heat of the sun dried up the water until the black edges of the world began to show. Black sandbanks and reefs could be seen. But there were no living things. Bumba vomited up the moon and then the stars, and after that the night had its light also. Still Bumba was in pain. He strained again and nine living creatures came forth: the leopard named Koy Bumba, and Pongo Bumba the crested eagle, the crocodile, Ganda Bumba, and one little fish named Yo; next, old Kono Bumba, the tortoise, and Tsetse, the lightning, swift, deadly, beautiful like the leopard, then the white heron, Nyanyi Bumba, also one beetle, and the goat named Budi. Last of all came forth men. There were many men, but only one was white like Bumba. His name was Loko Yima. The creatures themselves then created all the creatures. The heron created all the birds of the air except the kite. He did not make the kite. The crocodile made serpents

and the iguana. The goat produced every beast with horns. Yo, the small fish, brought forth all the fish of all the seas and waters. The beetle created insects.... Thus from Bumba, the Creator, the First Ancestor, came forth all the wonders that we see and hold and use, and all the brotherhood of beasts and man.[7]

Now, one myth of one tribe hardly represents the traditional culture of a whole continent, but what one finds in this Bantu creation account is more like than unlike the other myths that get into scholars' collections. Generally, the impression given is that, way back, at some indefinite point or time of origin, the world was unformed, chaotic. By some process (usually the action of a creator god or an agent delegated by such a god), the different creatures that we now know were brought into being. This Bantu story gives little prominence to the watery darkness that (alone) coexisted in the beginning with the creator god. Other stories give the primordial chaos a more direct role in the process of creation, usually as a material cause (that from which the creatures were made). Here the implication is that all creatures were somehow in the Creator, perhaps lodged in his stomach. Why they began to give Bumba pain is not explained. The story, typically, isn't constrained to answer all logical, let alone what we would now call scientific (cosmological) questions. It is a general picture, an overall or holistic way of trying to symbolize the mystery of the world's origins.

A myth of the Salishan-Sahaptin peoples of the North American Northwest, although poorer in imagery than the Bantu creation account and probably somewhat influenced by Christian notions of the creation, displays the three-decker universe and cosmic pillar that many shamanic peoples hold.

The Chief above made the earth. It was small at first, and then he let it increase in size. He continued to enlarge it, and rolled it out until it was very large. Then he covered it with a white dust, which became the soil. He made three worlds, one above another—the sky world, the earth we live on, and the underworld. All are connected by a pole or tree which passes through the middle of each. Then he created the animals. At last he made a man, who, however, was also a wolf. From this man's tail he made a woman. These were the first people.[8]

The earth is pictured almost like a ball of dough that might be rolled out with a rolling pin. The implication seems to be that it is now flat. The connection of the three realms suggests why shamans can travel to the sky or the underworld (via the cosmic pillar), and it provides domiciles for the spirits of the natural forces and the dead. The animals precede human beings, which leaves the reader to wonder whether human beings are the climax of creation or the creatures of least importance. The fact that the first human being was also a wolf testifies to the fluid character of a cosmological consciousness (the Egyptian pharaoh at one and the same time could be a man, a falcon, and a god).

Indian Boy. Frank Wilkin.
The boy is a prince,
depicted by the somewhat
romantic artist as proud of
his traditional insignia and
culture. *(The Nelson-Atkins
Museum of Art, Kansas City, Missouri
[Nelson Fund])*

AUSTRALIANS AND ESKIMOS

Each nonliterate group has its own distinctive features, and certainly the distinctions among Africans, Native Americans, Australians, and Eskimos are not to be underestimated. Africans, for example, are markedly less shamanistic, overall, than Native Americans and Eskimos. The "magical flight" to the realm of the gods that is central to the Siberian tribal culture from which comparativists such as Eliade have drawn their paradigm or basic pattern of shamanism is hard to find among the leading religious functionaries of Africa.[9] Even when one finds that African **diviners** or healers are **ecstatic** or at least function while in trance, the motifs of flying like a bird, ascending the cosmic pillar, and the like are thin to the point of absence.

It is by their similar intimacy with the natural world, their similar sense that the universe constitutes a single organic whole, therefore, that nonliterate peoples as diverse as the Africans and the Native Americans, the Australians and the Eskimos, stand together as one discernible group and stand apart from revelational, philosophical, and modern peoples. Thus, for the gross distinctions that we are attempting in this generalist interpretation of world history and world religion, it is their similar acceptance of the cosmological myth that makes us treat these diverse nonliterate peoples as siblings.

An Australian story from the Wotjobaluk tribe, for example, says that once upon a time all animals were men and women. In addition, the moon used to resurrect these animal-people when they died, simply by ordering them to rise up again. However, because an old man once said that the dead should remain dead, this pattern of the moon's bringing creation back to life again ceased. Now it is the moon alone that dies and comes back to life again, tokening the old universal pattern.[10]

Note that this traditional Australian story, like the Native American myth we used, accepts the identification of human and animal life. Whereas the Native American tale coalesced the first man and the first wolf, this Wotjobaluk tale runs the whole animal and human worlds together: animals were men and women and, presumably, women and men were animals. The moon had a potent influence on this fused realm over which it rose. And the phases of the moon had a mirror image in the death and resurrection of earthly life. The Australian story does not say why the old man put an end to this pattern. It is more concerned to explain what now simply is so.

The dominant physical feature on which the story hangs, obviously enough, is the intriguing "death" and "resurrection" of the moon each month. In addition to their poetic appreciation of this phenomenon, which would not distinguish the Australians from even us moderns, we sense something considerably deeper. For the people who first coined this myth, the moon was as alive as any human or animal being. Indeed, it was a fellow citizen of one circuit that the life force ran. Why, then, should the moon alone be able to return from death? How is it that human beings don't possess this capacity? The intuition of the story is that in the past, at a time closer to the world's origins, human beings did possess this capacity. In the beginning they were much closer to the moon, and perhaps many other fellow creatures, much more palpably **consubstantial**.

The Central Eskimos, as represented in the classic study by Franz Boas, one of the most influential early cultural anthropologists, had a basic story of Sedna, mistress of the sea animals, by which they accounted for the present order of creation. In a rather complicated prelude to the portion of the story most significant for our purposes, Sedna was married to a bird called a fulmar because she pridefully rejected an Eskimo youth. She was miserable, and the relevant portion of the story picks up from the visit of her father, who determines to ease her sorrow.

> When a year had passed and the sea was again stirred by warmer winds, the father left his country to visit Sedna. His daughter greeted him joyfully and besought him to take her back home. The father, hearing of the outrages wrought upon his daughter, determined upon revenge. He killed the fulmar, took Sedna into his boat, and they quickly left the country which had brought so much sorrow to Sedna. When the other fulmars came home and found their companion dead and his wife gone, they flew away in search of the fugitives. They were very sad over the death of their poor murdered comrade and continue to mourn and cry until this day. Having flown a short distance they discerned the boat and stirred up a heavy storm. The sea rose in immense waves that threatened the pair with destruction. In this mortal peril

the father determined to offer Sedna to the birds and flung her overboard. She clung to the edge of the boat with a death grip. The cruel father then took a knife and cut off the first joints of her fingers. Falling into the sea they were transformed into whales, the nails turning into whalebone. Sedna holding on to the boat more tightly, the second finger joints fell under the sharp knife and swam away as seals; when the father cut off the stumps of the fingers they became ground seals. Meanwhile the storm subsided, for the fulmars thought Sedna was drowned. The father then allowed her to come into the boat again. But from that time she cherished a deadly hatred against him and swore bitter revenge. After they got ashore, she called her dogs and let them gnaw off the feet and hands of her father while he was asleep. Upon this he cursed himself, his daughter, and the dogs which had maimed him; whereupon the earth opened and swallowed the hut, the father, the daughter, and the dogs. They have since lived in the land of Adlivun [under the sea], of which Sedna is the mistress.[11]

This myth is considerably richer than the Australian story of the moon, in that it has manifestly psychological and cosmological interests. It was used to explain how the sea animals came into being and why it is that Sedna now rules under the sea (where shamans must go, if they want her to intercede for them concerning the sea game). However, it also casts a rather jaundiced eye at father-daughter or parent-child relations, expressing the murderous potential in these closest ties.

For our present interests, the intimacy between the human realm and the animal realm is perhaps the first feature to note. Sedna could in fact be married out of her own species, becoming the wife of a bird. Moreover, the sea animals stem from Sedna's human substance, arising from her lopped-off fingers. Finally, by a human word, which in many ancient or nonliterate cultures could have a powerful, even a magical, effect, the earth opens up to swallow Sedna and her father, as though they, like the hut and the dogs, were just pawns or bit players. The link between Sedna and the sea creatures that stem from her fingers continues from the aboriginal time of the myth to the present. She is now the mistress of the undersea realm. Thus, nonliterate peoples of even the recent past have continued to think of the cosmos as a system of rather fluid relations among the different living parts. We have to conjecture how closely this recent mentality approximates the mentality of prehistoric humanity, but we have many signs that the two are not far apart. For both, the world probably was one compact organism.

COUNTERVIEWS

Scholars who would contest this Voegelinian reading of prehistoric religion and the religion of more recent nonliterary peoples are, of course, beset by the same inadequacies in the data that we have faced. However, if they approached the remains of prehistoric peoples with the conviction that any of the four basic factors in reality (as we conceive it) should get a significantly different weight, they will probably come out with a different pic-

Mask. Eskimo, Alaskan. The mask depicts a spirit that the people want to tame or employ. *(The Nelson-Atkins Museum of Art, Kansas City, Missouri [Nelson Fund])*

ture. In other words, if they would omit nature, society, the self, or divinity from their analysis, of if they would have one or more of these factors absolutely determine the situation, they would come up with quite a different reading.

For example, materialists who deny the reality and influence of a realm aptly labeled *divinity* tend to give economic factors more play in determining early culture. Psychoanalytic scholars tend to give more play to the pressures of sexual maturation, especially the tensions between parents and children. On the other hand, scholars who find little "progress" in classical philosophy, biblical revelation, or modern science make less of the mythological character of early human culture. For them our current-day concern with nuclear weapons or space exploration is as fantastic as what we speculate preoccupied the early cave dwellers.

The notion that Voegelin has used to summarize much of the cosmological mentality, *consubstantiality*, would also prove offensive in many circles. "Substance," many would say, "is a term carrying too many overtones from early Greek philosophy to serve well in a broader context." Specialists in African or American Indian religion might be able to bring forward evidence that at least certain tribes distinguished a creative force from the rest of the natural world and so did not think of "God" and "man" as consubstantial. Specialists in other fields might well express a general dissatisfaction with any overarching theory, arguing that the data are both too vast and too incomplete for us to give much credence to fully comprehensive explanations.

All of these reactions, of course, have some merit and basis. All in fact remind us that we are proposing a sketch, a pedagogical prod, rather than a finished "system." In rejoinder, though, we would have to ask the dissenters to make clear their own sense of the links between later humanity and prehistoric or nonliterate peoples. Just how do both groups share and not share the same status as "human beings"? Is this name but a taxonomical or classificatory convenience, more a lie than a solid truth? Or do the earliest discernibly human beings in fact share with us a distinct niche in evolution, and is that niche finally a matter of having a similarly rational consciousness (the ability to reflect or be both subject and object of the same awareness) that different experiences and different stresses color quite differently? One can see, then, that a great deal of what one makes of the earliest human religion depends on what one makes of "human nature."

SUMMARY

Our topic has been nonliterate peoples, whom we have considered the first class of humanity structured in its consciousness by the cosmological myth. We dealt first with prehistoric humanity, admitting the opacity or ambiguity of the material remains they have left, confessing the shortcomings in arguments from analogies with more recent nonliterate peoples, but nonetheless proposing them, on the basis of such remains as their cave paintings and such grounds of inferential argument as their exposure to nature, to be deeply immersed in a world they felt to be living and unified. Unless they could integrate themselves with the cosmos, come to harmony with the whole and the other prominent parts, prehistoric humans risked both physical and psychic disaster.

Hunters confronted the interrelation of the living parts of the cosmos in the almost brutal terms of the need for life to take from life. Eliade has stressed the place of the sky in the symbolism of hunting peoples without neglecting the polar symbolisms of the earth. Voegelin's concept of consubstantiality suggests that hunting peoples did feel akin to the bear and the buffalo, were aware of a mysterious sameness coursing wherever blood flowed. Gatherers applied this sort of cosmological awareness to the cycles of vegetation. Predominantly they were women, so the cycles of the earth ran in phase with the cycles of human fertility. On the way to agriculture, this concern with cosmic fertility wrote the sacral force of the world largely in maternal terms. The first great personalized deity was a Mother Goddess.

Africans and Native Americans have lived by treasuries of myths that seem to display a similarly cosmological orientation. The Bantu myth of creation that we studied placed the origin of all species in Bumba's stomachache, whereas the Salishan-Sahaptin story we quoted merges man and wolf. The Australian story of the moon's previous power to resurrect dead human beings and the Eskimo story of the creation of the sea animals from the fingers of Sedna are variations on the theme of consubstantiality. Despite all the necessary qualifications and distinctions one must enter, prehistoric and recent nonliterate peoples all seem to have experienced the world as a single organism, a democratic society of quite different species quite alike in their similar dependence on the basic life force. The counter-views of materialists, psychoanalysts, or other theoreticians remind us that Voegelin's theory is far from being dogma, but even they suggest that the key to the distinctions among the stages of human religion probably lies in the various ways that different groups deployed the constant interaction between their experiences of nature and their reflective consciousnesses.

STUDY QUESTIONS

1. How much should our approaches to prehistoric religion stress early humans' very direct encounters with the forces of nature?
2. What is the probable connection between recent-day shamans' identi-fication with animals and early hunters' connection with the game?
3. What is the probable connection between the Great Mother Goddess and the gatherers' concern with vegetative fertility?
4. Of whom is Bumba the First Ancestor?
5. Describe the moral climate or ethical atmosphere you sense in the Eskimo myth of Sedna.

NOTES

1. See Alexander Marshak, *The Roots of Civilization* (New York: McGraw-Hill, 1972).
2. Mircea Eliade, *A History of Religious Ideas, Vol. 1* (Chicago: University of Chicago Press, 1978), p. 27.
3. Eric Voegelin, *Order and History, Vol. 1* (Baton Rouge: Louisiana State University Press, 1956), p. 3.
4. See Michael Harner, *The Way of the Shaman* (New York: Harper & Row, Pub., 1980).
5. Bjorn Kurten, *Dance of the Tiger* (New York: Berkley, 1981); Jean Auel, *The Clan of the Cave Bear* (New York: Bantam, 1981).
6. See Adrienne Zihlman, "Women and Evolution, Part II," *Signs*, 4 (1978), pp. 4–20.
7. Mircea Eliade, *From Primitives to Zen* (New York: Harper & Row, Pub., 1967), pp. 91–92.
8. Barbara Sproul, *Primal Myths: Creating the World* (New York: Harper & Row, Pub., 1979), p. 244.
9. See Mircea Eliade, *Shamanism: Archaic Techniques of Ecstasy* (Princeton, N.J.: Princeton University Press, Bollingen, 1972).
10. See Eliade, *From Primitives to Zen*, p. 140.
11. Franz Boas, *The Central Eskimo* (Lincoln: University of Nebraska Press, 1964), pp. 176–77.

CHAPTER THREE

Early Civilizations

ORIENTATION

Nonliterate humanity, dominated by the shaman, meets the world rather directly or immediately. Literate humanity, dominated by the priest, deals with the world indirectly or mediately, through scriptures or texts. In this chapter we consider some of the religious worlds that writing and humanity's coalescing into large social units generated. The word *civilization,* which comes from the Latin for town or good-sized social unit, implies both writing and at least a middle scale of social organization.

The examples of civilizational religion that we use, coming from both the ancient Near East and Old World America, can stand for the past five thousand years or so of human experience generally. Certainly before revelation and philosophy (including the analogies to Greek philosophy that we shall find in India and China), many peoples were living in cultural situations considerably different from that of the shamanic tribes. After the development of agriculture, many peoples possessed the wealth, stability, and density of population to diversify their work force and encourage literary specialists. These, both scribes and priests, regularly created impressive written collections of traditional myths and rituals, as well as archives of tax records and trading receipts.

In the process, they considerably expanded the people's sense of the complexity of reality, including the reality of the realm of the gods. Thus we find in the civilizational religions great rosters of gods and goddesses. Yet, in Voegelin's view, these rosters did not finally break the circuit of the cosmological myth. Despite strains here and there (which we shall indicate), the civilizational peoples continued to experience themselves as part of a natural whole of physical forces, human cultural forces, and divinities.

MESOPOTAMIA

Sometimes one comes across the slogan "Civilization began at Sumer." From about 8000 B.C.E. to 6000 B.C.E., humanity was in a period of intense creativity. Agriculture arose, the domestication of animals was achieved, and people began to congregate in settlements deserving the name *towns*. One of the first of these towns was Jericho, in the Jordan Valley. Extensive excavations have revealed a settlement there around 8000 B.C.E. that covered eight to ten acres and housed up to three thousand people. Although Jericho predates the making of pottery,

> . . . it was not a nomadic community's temporary settlement, for the houses the people built were substantial (made of bricks of sun-baked clay). They were laid out in lines both utilitarian and aesthetic, with such conveniences as a central courtyard for cooking, plastered walls and floors for easy washing, rush mats, storage bins, and utensils of limestone and flint. What appear to be temple remains indicate a cultic use of stone and also a fertility orientation toward the Mother Goddess. The people of Jericho must have revered their dead, for they preserved their skulls in a finely molded plaster that gave them a delicate, lifelike appearance. The walls of this town were built many times, a fact that suggests both a high level of community cooperation and the presence of external enemies. All in all, then, Jericho resembles a prosperous little medieval town, with rich fields outside and numerous amenities inside.[1]

As town life developed into city life, agriculture became more extensive and more specialized. People freed from concern for bare subsistence could also specialize in arts, crafts, and religious activities. Thus there arose in Mesopotamia, the land between the Tigris and the Euphrates rivers, civilizations: cultures at a level or power above what a town such as Jericho could sponsor.

At Sumer, around 3100, writing appeared. Probably it grew out of efforts to keep records of produce, taxes, and the like. At about the same time, Upper and Lower Egypt were unified, setting the stage for a great and long-lasting civilization along the Nile. These developments came after the discovery of bronze and the invention of the wheel. They predated the development of farming in central Africa and the rise of an impressive culture in the Indus Valley in India. For our purposes, their outstanding feature was the changes they rang on the cosmological myth.

The first impression one gets when stepping from the world of non-literate peoples into the written religious world of people such as the Sumerians is the proliferation of gods that has occurred. As a mirror image of the increased complexity that has come with urbanization, the "system" of the gods has similarly grown more complex. Nonetheless, the Sumerian sense that each phenomenon is controlled by an indwelling force, and the suggestion that these forces comprise a cosmic circuit, tells us that Sumer remained highly indebted to the cosmological myth. Helmer Ringgren has described the operation of the indwelling divine forces as follows:

> What is clearly attested, however, is the view that every phenomenon is controlled by an indwelling divine force (**me**) which determines its essential character and nature. There is a myth which tells how the goddess Inanna succeeded in wheedling out of the God Enki in Eridu all these mes and transferring them to her own city of Uruk. In this connection a list is given of a hundred or so cultural themes, of whose mes the goddess took possession. They included godship, the throne of kingship, the sceptre, kingship, various priestly offices, the flood, sexual intercourse, art, music, heroship, power, the destruction of cities, lamentation, the craft of the smith, the craft of the builder, wisdom, fear, peace, weariness, etc. It could almost be called a system of ideas, like those of Plato. The point, however, is that in this case Inanna, or in other cases other gods, are praised as the lords over these mes. In other words these are the indwelling laws of each phenomenon, as they are determined by the gods.[2]

This sense of proliferated gods occurs in an old Babylonian oracle, composed in Akkadian, that was found at the site of Uruk and dates from about 1850 B.C.E. It is hard for us to understand the full meaning of the oracle, but the likelihood is that it refers to the regeneration of the hero of the city, and that the forces mentioned are the equivalent of mes.

> The faithful shepherd, whose name is good, whose guardian angel is permanent, entered the temple Eanna—from now on well-being will be before him, vigor behind him. From a day Nanaya [a goddess of love] visited me and had me sit in the doorway of the god Sin, her father: She spoke, saying: "Until I have established a faithful shepherd and revived dead Uruk you shall grind

Gilgamesh. Gold plaque, Persian, about 700 B.C.E. Gilgamesh, King of Uruk, is the main character in *The Epic of Gilgamesh*, a moving Sumerian poem about death that dates from about 2000 B.C.E. *(The Nelson-Atkins Museum of Art, Kansas City, Missouri [Nelson Fund])*

the **sutu** ration of Uruk. Great Uruk will be given to me. Town and temple I will take over when the faithful shepherd has been designated for the land."[3]

EGYPT

Imperial Egypt, as we have mentioned, arose about the same time as writing. Because Egyptian culture lasted more than two thousand years, however, it developed a much more extensive cosmological mythology than that of any Mesopotamian realm. As many historians of ancient civilizations have noted, the Egyptians were remarkably constant, or conservative. Dynasties came and went, but basic attitudes toward the land, life, and death flowed on. To be sure, different theologies colored these basic attitudes differently in different ages, but such permanent features as the sun, the desert, and the Nile bound all the Egyptian ages together.

Henri Frankfort's influential work *Kingship and the Gods* captures much of the ancient Egyptian sense of creation.

> The imagery from the solar sphere deeply affected Egyptian thought and culture, and the Egyptian always dwelt with particular pleasure upon the emergence of the sun from the waters. There was something familiar in that thought which brought the mystery and the marvel of creation closer without annihilating it. Every year, after a hot summer, when the Nile had risen and covered the parched lands and renewed their fertility by the silt which it brought, some high piece of ground would emerge from the slowly receding inundation and herald the beginning of a new season of fruitfulness. With delight, they piled image upon image for this phase of the act of creation. Sometimes the sun-god was said to have appeared as a small child, seated within a lotus flower which had been mysteriously lifted above the water. Sometimes a large egg had appeared from which the sun-child emerged; or the goose of Amon-Re had flown from it, its honking the first sound in the waste of the water.[4]

Because it developed a full social hierarchy and a long imperial tradition focused on the pharaoh, Egypt manifested a pattern, still within the cosmological myth but nonetheless more differentiated than one finds in simpler societies, of what we might call political theology. The empire was considered a microcosm, or small world, that played out in miniature what the great world of nature accomplished comprehensively. The above of the gods was reflected in the below of human beings. Like other early cultures, the Egyptian had a three-decker universe. The heavens were the province of the gods, above all of the sun god Re. The earth was the province of human beings but also of natural forces and natural divinities that impinged directly on human beings. The underearth was the realm of the dead and the gods who judged them. Connecting these three realms was not a cosmic pillar as in Shamanic cultures, but the pharaoh himself.

For the Egyptians, the pharaoh personified the sun god (and other gods as well). The overriding conception was that a divine force (**maat**) ran through the world and that pharaoh mediated it to human society. Maat

Head of the pharaoh Sesostris III. Sesostris (Sen-Usert) III ruled about 1880–1840 B.C.E. *(The Nelson-Atkins Museum of Art, Kansas City, Missouri [Nelson Fund])*

was a principle of order, and therefore implicitly a justification for custom and law. To be out of phase with maat, disharmonious, was to violate an impersonal ultimacy or sacrality.

The greatest predictable crisis in Egyptian culture was the death of the pharaoh, so elaborate precautions were taken to ensure a smooth transition from old to new king. The death of the pharaoh could be assimilated into the death of Osiris, an important vegetative god whose dying and rising went in tandem with the annual recession and flooding of the Nile. Osiris held a central place in the underworld, and the pharaohs developed a massive preoccupation with death, as the pyramids (their tombs) testify. Each night the sun would pass through the realm of the dead on its way to rising again in the heavens. Thus those who reposed under the earth continued to be part of the holistic cosmos.

During the reign of the pharaoh Akhenaton (1375–1358 B.C.E.), Egypt came quite close to breaking the cosmological myth and confessing a divinity outside the natural whole. The king was particularly devoted to the sun god, under the name Aton, and he came to think that Aton might be the sole god, creator of all that exists. For Akhenaton, Aton was the beginning of life. He rose over all peoples, not just the Egyptians (a remarkable confession in an age when each people had its own gods). He was the sole God, like to whom there was none. The world was an expression of his creative desire, and it came forth when he was alone. The pharaoh seemed enthralled by this creative and universal light. He was on the verge of separating the creator god from the world, of making the god the sole possessor of the divine substance. But Akhenaton's "reform" perished soon after his death, because the powerful priesthoods of the old **polytheistic** order reasserted the traditional rights of their deities.

Some years after Akhenaton, during the XIX Dynasty when Ramses II was pharaoh (about 1301–1234 B.C.E.), a group of writings called the Amon Hymns carved another landmark in Egyptian theology. The distinctive note of these hymns is their sense that divinity, or the creative force, which Egypt almost always focused primarily on the sun (light and heat), is inevitably, one might even say intrinsically, mysterious. In saying this the hymns tried gropingly to express their intuition that the final or original cause of the cosmos exists at a level different from any of the levels of creation. To put things this way is probably to speak with more philosophical clarity than Egypt (a distinctly unspeculative culture) usually mustered. But when the hymns sing of the sun god creating his own beauty and having a nature ever unknown, they stumble toward what theologians sometimes call the *negative way* of dealing with divinity strictly so called: by stressing its mysteriousness.

PERSIA

The Achaemenian empire of Persia, which derived much of its sense of order from the Iranian prophet Zoroaster (about 628–551 B.C.E.), shows us another powerful factor that differentiated the cosmological style of symbolization. Zoroaster had spoken of a great god Ahura Mazda who summarized the forces of goodness and light. Opposed to Ahura Mazda was a destructive spirit, and Zoroastrianism developed into a **dualistic** religion that spent much of its energy trying to aid the forces of goodness and counter the forces of destructiveness. Zoroaster himself described a number of spiritual forces associated with divinity and seems in effect to have been extrapolating from experiences of his own powers of mind and will. At any rate, the rulers of Persia who reflected on their imperial expansion in Zoroastrian categories focused on the universal implications of Zoroaster's divinity.

Voegelin has summarized the gist of this movement in the following terms: "The Achaemenian expansion is characterized by the combination of a derailment from the cosmic analogue to the indefiniteness of pragmatic conquest with the spiritual movement of Zoroastrianism."[5] The cosmic analogue is the imagery, previously noted in the case of Egypt, that makes the local political realm a miniature of the cosmos. In the Persian case, before the great conquerors Cyrus and Darius embarked on their ventures to expand their empire, the sense had been that the Persian realm reflected on earth the order of the gods in heaven. This sense, or symbolism, derailed, got off the track, because in moving out of their relatively self-contained land and culture, the Persians encountered the meaninglessness of pragmatic conquest: war and the mere acquisition of territory. They were not certain how the gods, the realm of heaven, related to the new lands and peoples they were conquering. It was not clear, therefore, what their greater secular power and possessions meant. Pragmatically, in the world of simply military or economic might, possessing more seems progress. Spiritually, in the world of meaning and peace-through-harmony-with-the-ultimate-powers, possessing more can destroy the prior sense of reality that gave a people its order.

The Persians took their problems to their traditional Zoroastrian faith and came away emphasizing the universality of their prophet's "Wise Lord" (Ahura Mazda). In what is known as the Behistun Inscription, King Darius I (ruled 521–486 B.C.E.) linked his conquest of more than twenty countries to the will of Ahura Mazda, the divinity who presided in the heavens that overlooked all countries. The emperor's campaigns of conquest became a service to Ahura Mazda in the battle between the Truth of the Wise Lord and the Lie of the Evil Spirit. Conveniently, those who opposed Darius were considered representatives or servants of the Lie. The movement of the Persian empire into the territories of the peoples it conquered therefore took on the gratifying aura of the spread of truth into realms previously benighted or held in bondage.

Voegelin's analysis occurs in the fourth volume of *Order and History*, where his topic is the ecumenic age. This is the time of the great multinational empires, such as Persia, Greece, and Rome, where lands and peoples traditionally rather self-enclosed were forcibly set into new, more comprehensive patterns. In other words, no longer could rulers or people think of their realms as self-contained. No longer could they virtually disregard other peoples. The old sense that foreigners were not fully human, did not represent humanity, and so the ties of here-below to heaven-above completely adequately, shattered on the rocks of pragmatic history. In this context, the pattern of microcosm to macrocosm, the human realm as miniature of the cosmic realm, unraveled rapidly.

The result was a new sense of universalism that extended both the sense of divinity and the sense of humanity. Persia and Rome certainly did not break the cosmological myth through their extension of divinity and humanity. Like the Egyptians who groped after a single creator god Aton or sensed the mystery of the sun god Amon, the leading Persian and Roman thinkers did however differentiate their sense of the cosmic whole. "Humanity" had to be something transethnic, and so did "divinity." Today, we take this transethnicity, or universality, for granted. To us moderns, *human* and *divine* apply essentially equally to all members of the species **homo sapiens** and all varieties of monotheistic power (Yahweh, God, Allah, and so on). We forget that this sense had to develop or be discovered.

In the age of the first ecumenical empires, the first politico-spiritual realms that thought of themselves as worldwide in principle, the cosmological myth moved from essentially local overtones to nearly universal overtones. The rise of civilizations had changed the connotations of *reality* from the prehistoric human beings' sense of the force field of nature, the system of plants-animals-humans-gods, as experienced in one's local geography, to the more political field of one's enlarged social context, one's urbanized and then imperialized land-and-group. The new ecumenical empires, whose impetus to expand and conquer had no natural limitation, considerably extended this politicization of reality. In their new horizon of the whole inhabited world, the system of plants, animals, human beings, and gods grew dramatically more vast.

The differentiation one can see takes the line from small tribe, dominating and naming a small patch of territory; to larger city unit, dominating more territory and developing a richer culture; to empire potentially universal, enlisting or conscripting very diverse lands and people, with their perhaps new species of plants, animals, and gods. The compact sense of reality that we found good reason to suspect has dominated nonliterate peoples had to unfold or unpack to accommodate a richer and more numerous citizenry. *Plant, animal, human being,* and *god* all became more complicated or sophisticated conceptions. Indeed, each word now pointed to or covered many more instances, as the range of human experience greatly extended. What originally had been a compact little ball of meaning was in each case rolled out, extended, to serve many more instances. The pressures of experience were like a great rolling pin.

Despite this differentiation, Persia and the other ecumenic realms remained outside the perspectives of revelation, philosophy, and modernity, with the partial exception of Greece, where philosophy essentially broke the comprehensiveness of the natural cosmos. Designations at this point are not hard and fast, but in Persia, Rome, and much of Greece, nature or the physical world continued to appear as a single living whole. The differentiations we have mentioned had diversified this whole considerably. People now had to think about humanity and divinity with considerably more sophistication. But the consubstantiality so prominent to the consciousness of earliest humanity continued to persuade most people in the ecumenic empires. Despite their new horizon of conquest and transethnicity, they continued to think that animals and divinities were fellow parts of an ordered or holistic totality. No "beyond" escaped the cosmos. No realm of transcendence stood outside the living world.

THE OLMECS AND AZTECS

While ecumenical realms were being differentiated in the Near East and the Mediterranean, sizable empires were growing in the Americas. The Olmec culture of Mesoamerica (about 1200–400 B.C.E.) has been described as the mother civilization of that area. Especially in religious matters, it shaped much of what was to follow in Mexico and Central America. Archaeological remains suggest that the Olmecs fashioned a **theocracy** and that they built large ceremonial centers, pyramids, and tombs for their priestly kings. They sculpted giant stone heads, experimented with hieroglyphics, and roughed out a calendar system. Among the sculptural remains, a group of animal-human figures stands out. Apparently they represented gods of forces such as fertility or of striking places such as mountains. The Olmecs used the symbolism of the cross, perhaps as a **mandala** signifying totality: the whole indicated by the four directions. Their most famous divinity, however, was a being that merged a jaguar and a human, creating what is sometimes called a *were-jaguar* (parallel to a *were-wolf*). Despite the scholarly disputes about the significance of this figure, it is clear that the Olmecs, like the North Americans whose myths we studied, felt quite free to merge the animal and human species. In their world, human beings were not so singular that they could not be fused in imagination (dreams, rituals, shamanic flights) with striking animals.

Indeed, Ignacio Bernal, one of the leading authorities on the Olmecs, has made the fusion of the animal and the human a linchpin of Olmec religious thought.

> Throughout the Olmec period the idea of animal-men is present, or of fantastic men-animals in which human traits are associated with those of one or more animals. Two or more animals are also found combined, thus forming a monster. With time this mythical beast was to embody religious concepts and would even become an anthropomorphic god. All these variations revolve around the complicated concept of the **nahual.** This can be an animal mythically associated with a certain man so closely that his life depends upon that of the animal; if the animal dies, the man will surely die also. Or it can be the symbol of something harmful and dangerous, although at other times it can be only mischievous, like a poltergeist. Even today the sorcerer continues to be, as he was in ancient times, capable of endless witchcraft, the one who steals things, who roams by night, and who lives surrounded by darkness.[6]

The nahual introduces us to the impersonal quality of the ultimate cosmic force. We might call it a "localization" of the impenetrable and more-than-human power by which the world runs. In the form described by the quotation, such power attaches itself to particular persons or functionaries: a given tribal member, a shaman, or a witch. The conception seems to stress the irrational quality of natural power. It is not something willing to fit itself to tidy human mental tracks. This conviction of the Olmecs, and of most other cosmological peoples, reminds us that the orderliness introduced by revelation and philosophy constituted a considerable revolution. No doubt there were trade-offs (for instance, a diminution of awe), but the valuable new thing that the prophets and sages offered was a strong psychic protection against a world that could easily seem more chaos than cosmos. If nature really was amenable to rational inquiry and control, as the Greek Pre-Socratic natural philosophers argued with increasing effectiveness, or if the world actually did depend in all its being and patterns on a benevolent, liberating God, as the biblical prophets argued with increasing cogency, then the weird, the irrational, the psychically dark side of reality no longer was in the driver's seat. It certainly remained—too much evidence existed to contradict that—but now it had lesser status, was subordinate to the Logos (reason) or God (Yahweh, Father) that gave the world an intrinsic order.

The Olmecs apparently focused the nahual of the jaguar on the supreme ruler, and so integrated their rather shamanistic sense of the world with an impressively imperial political structure. The roots of the jaguar's symbolic power probably lay back in jungle life, when it was a terrifying summary of the destructive violence that could spring out at any time. It was beautiful, dazzlingly swift, and deadly. To this animal symbol of ultimate danger and thrill the Olmecs added features of birds, as though to fill out its land-based powers with the powers of flight. Precisely how this fitted into the calendar system, the custom of renovating their buildings every 104 years, and the impressive sacrificial rituals, including human sacrifice, that the Olmecs developed is hard to say. We may speculate, however, that even when their social structures had moved well beyond tribal simplicity, they continued to venerate the raw forces of nature and to strive mightily to integrate themselves with the cosmic flow of potentially deadly power.

The Aztecs, who flourished almost two thousand years after the Olmecs, have been compared to the Romans. As the Romans drew much of their higher culture from the Greeks, so the Aztecs drew much of their higher culture from the Mayans. As the Romans' distinctive genius was organizational and military, so was the distinctive genius of the Aztecs.

> In the beginning the Aztecs constituted a small group among many others in the Valley of Mexico and they were at times held in submission to stronger peoples of that area. About the year 1325 [C.E.] they settled on some small islands in the Texcoco lake, where they had taken refuge from their hostile neighbors, and here they founded the city of Tenochtitlán, upon whose ruins the modern capital of Mexico is built. According to their own traditions, they settled in a place that had been assigned to them by Huitzilopochtli, the patron god of the Aztecs. Huitzilopochtli is said to have led his people the long way around through the Mexican deserts. In a vision he told the priests that their new home was to be built on the place where they saw a gigantic eagle kill and devour a snake. The legend tells that this vision became reality on the island in the middle of the Lake of the Moon, the lake of Texcoco. The eagle was a representative of the sun god, Huitzilopochtli, and the scene with the eagle fighting the snake is in motif identical to a myth known throughout North America: the combat between a celestial bird, the eagle, the thunderbird, and the monster of the underworld or of water, often a double-headed or horned serpent.[7]

The Aztecs' efficiency and military prowess soon made them rulers of their region. By 1500 C.E. the Aztec rulers Moctezuma I through Moctezuma II, his grandson, had solidified a huge kingdom that stretched from ocean to ocean and contained 5 to 6 million people. The capital city of Tenochtitlán had become a metropolis with canals, palaces, and temples. Around 1480 the Aztecs erected a huge pyramid-temple that commanded a view of the entire city. At the inauguration of this temple they sacrificed twenty thousand prisoners of war. (One theory is that the Aztecs were so warlike because their religion regularly required human victims. Another theory lays more stress on population pressures.)

The Aztec empire was connected to the heavenly realm of the gods through the king, who functioned much like a pharaoh. At his enthronement ceremony he did penance before the gods, pledged to maintain their ceremonies of worship, and took office as the "father and mother" of his people. In fact, the Aztec rulers seem to have cared well for their own

Funerary Urn. Mexican, about 500–650. Death, like other significant features of ancient Mexican life, was served by personified spirits. *(The Nelson-Atkins Museum of Art, Kansas City, Missouri [Nelson Fund])*

people, and the Aztec culture developed a love of flowers, dance, poetry, and the like to balance its militarism.

For our interests, the main quality that stands forth from a survey of both the early Olmecs and the late Aztecs is the immersion of traditional Central American culture in the cosmological myth. Both the shamanistic basis of that culture and the imperial superstructure that came with large-scale social organization situated the people within a self-contained system dominated by the gods. That the extreme of human sacrifice might be necessary to keep that system going shows the power of the myth.

THE COSMOLOGICAL MYTH EAST AND WEST

To speak of the cosmological myth is to imply a holistic relationship with nature. The peoples we have glanced at stand for countless generations of premodern human beings whose basic outlook was holistic. They thought, felt, worried, exulted, and all the rest without dividing themselves into an intellectual part and an emotional part, without dividing nature into widely separated strata of plants, animals, humans, and gods. This is not to say, of course, that they recognized no differences between dispassionate analysis and ecstatic joy, between the king and the jaguar. Especially concerning the different natural species, and sometimes concerning the different components of the human personality, their descriptive differentiations could be extremely precise and detailed. But they continued to treasure the wholeness of the human personality, of the human group, and of the cosmos. They continued to think of the gods as forces to whom one should dance and sing.

Thus, when we say that the Olmecs worshiped a were-jaguar, or that the Aztec king was the mediator of the gods, we should not imply anything simplistic. There are no signs that earlier human beings were significantly less intelligent than we. They simply applied their intelligence differently, with different major foci, goals, and presuppositions. The major focus, East and West, was harmony. Prior to modernity, and with significant qualifications for revelational and philosophical peoples, fitting into the cosmic whole, being in tune with the cosmic force, was the matter to which most people turned their attention. The basic goal of cosmological peoples, in other words, was being true to, living out, their deep conviction that the world was a living whole.

The priests who arose when tribes were absorbed into larger social units retained many of the earlier shamanic instincts for wholeness. They too thought of the world as a living whole, and their rituals and sacrifices were efforts to maintain the people in harmony with this whole (or to reestablish harmony after any sort of breach). In the grisly case of human sacrifice, we see a priestly concern with sacral harmony that has lost balance, fallen away toward mental aberration. Preoccupied with the sense that the divinities demand the substance of human existence, love and dedication from the heart, Aztec priests, for example, could think that their gods required great hordes of human victims.

Harmony and power, then, nail down the corners of the cosmological religious map. In India, China, and other Eastern cultural areas, the Hindu, Buddhist, Confucian, and Taoist religious complexes rose atop an older cosmology. Indeed, Voegelin thinks that the Eastern sages, for all their acuteness about human psychology, never really broke with the cosmological myth. We shall take up that thesis in the next chapters, but it is useful at the present juncture. Nature has always been so comprehensive or atmospheric a reality that the notion of living within nature as part of an all-embracing system of vital forces has never receded very far. The Indian yogis might learn the pathways to deepest inner self-possession (**samadhi**). The Chinese social thinkers might work out the intricate relations between goodness (**jen**) and ritual (**li**). But seldom if ever did they move away from their assumptions about the cosmic whole to let the transcendent possibilities in these achievements fully flower. Seldom, in other words, did they articulate what the creative power might be in itself, apart from its embodiment in this specific, perhaps **contingent**, world.

The Western peoples, prior to the influence of revelation and philosophy, thought about the cosmos in much the same way. They had different gods, myths, and traditions, of course. Their ceremonies were their own. But, as the Olmecs and Aztecs suggest (and Germanic, Celtic, Slavic, and other peoples could confirm), nature was the fullest embodiment, perhaps even the fullest **sacrament** of the ultimate, mysterious power of existence and life. Like the Eastern shamans, the main functionaries of the Western tribes greatly prized ecstatic power and harmony. They had techniques for achieving ecstasy, sensitivities to dreams and visions, that showed them how to walk through the dangerous yet thrilling world. The forces upon which they depended, whether in hunting or agriculture, regularly received their petitions.

What, then, is our heritage from this longest portion of human existence? How should it stand between the cosmological myth and us today? First, it should stand on a plank of appreciation. Whatever the qualifications we might want to place on certain practices of cosmological peoples (for example, human sacrifice), we have to recognize from the outset that cosmological religion was ingredient in, essential to, an amazing story of survival. By their myths, rituals, symbols, and other ways of dealing with cosmological power and harmony, our ancestors managed to transmit life, even joy and happiness, generation after generation.[8] When one looks at the record of past species that became extinct, this achievement is not to be underestimated. When one looks at today's threats of annihilation by nuclear arms, the defects of the cosmological cultures can seem minor.

Second, the cosmological myth offers us many suggestions about the way back to wholeness, the way out of modern alienations. As Huston Smith has suggested, sanity and fuller wisdom now appear to lie beyond the postmodern, the modern-pushed-to-the-point-of-realizing-its-deficiencies, mind.[9] This "beyond" no doubt cannot be a simple-minded return to a consciousness undifferentiated by revelation, philosophy, and modern science. It cannot be the sort of naiveté that went into the paleolithic cave paintings. But perhaps it can and must be a reverent, integrating view of nature that can curb our present destructiveness by showing us treasures worth more than money or political power. For tens of thousands of years, human beings measured their prosperity in terms of beauty they had seen, exaltation that had filled them. Compared to these, possessions were baubles.

COUNTERVIEWS

Among scholars less interested in or impressed by cultural "consciousness" than Eric Voegelin was, the notion of an ecumenic age probably would not seem persuasive. Voegelin depends on famous texts or inscriptions whose meaning is far from absolutely certain, so other authorities tend to grant Akhenaton or Darius less grandiose visions. Sometimes this counterposition cloaks an assumption that people living several thousand years ago could not have had conceptions of reality that seem to rival a Hegel or other modern philosopher of world history. Other times the opposition seems to represent an unwillingness or an inability to meditate or muse imaginatively on the symbols that the texts do in fact sprinkle as clues to their author's cast of mind. (Another possibility, of course, is that the more constrained interpretation is in fact the more accurate one.)

Once again, perhaps the sharpest bone of contention would be the notion of consubstantiality. When it comes to the ecumenic empires of Persia and Greece, Voegelin wanted to diversify or differentiate this concept considerably, yet he continued greatly to depend upon it. For his desire seemed to be to say at one and the same time that the most sophisticated citizens of the new multiethnic realms developed a new appreciation of the universal aspects of *humanity* (people from many different tribes showing that they share the same essential human traits) and that these citizens still lived within a cosmic whole. To be sure, their cosmos was richer, more complicated, or more layered sociologically than that of the earlier tribes. Through their kings and priesthoods they possessed a great hierarchy, mediating heavenly power to their earthly zone, that simpler peoples did without. Yet they in fact still could not conceive of a reality that didn't fit into the span of the natural universe (that wasn't finally physical or able to be represented by a spatiotemporal form).

Interpreters who think that everything real can be represented by a spatiotemporal form will of course dispute Voegelin's way of setting up this matter. This, or other factors, such as different readings of historic texts and religious symbols, might then lead them to deny that there was any such thing as consciousness of an ecumenic age (a new era of transtribal or transethnic awareness). On the other hand, interpreters from the monotheistic traditions might wonder why Voegelin made so much fuss over the civilizational religions, because in the final analysis they remain polytheistic paganisms. Specialists will have to pass judgments on the particulars of the debates latent in these counterviews. Our general response to such opposition would take an interrogative form: If you do not like Voegelin's basis for characterizing what happened to religious awareness through the growth of cities and empires, what alternative basis does your analysis rest upon and why do you claim that it better organizes the data?

SUMMARY

Humanity broke out of prehistory in the ancient Near East. At Sumer writing arose around 3100 B.C.E., and Mesopotamia was the site of an extensive early mythological literature, one of the most distinctive features of which was a proliferation of divinities (to keep pace with the proliferation of culture). We hypothesized that this proliferation was connected to the mediated character that the Mesopotamian mythology took on when it was committed to writing.

In Egypt a long and stable civilization fostered a rich mythology. The Pharaoh mediated maat from heaven to earth, and the rhythms of life were set by the sun and the Nile. The monotheistic reform of Akhenaton, along with the Amon Hymns, shows the pressures this put on cosmological consciousness, but on the whole Egypt happily kept the realms of heaven, earth, and underearth well connected if not compact.

The differentiations in the Persian imperial realm brought similar pressure to cosmological consciousness. As the conquerors Cyrus and

Darius fashioned a multiethnic population of subjects, they drew out the universalistic qualities of Ahura Mazda and the truth. This meant breaking with the cosmic analogue, in which the political realm was a miniature of the natural whole. It also meant confronting the potential meaninglessness of pragmatic expansion and thinking about a source of meaning that transcended the past ethnic realms and maybe even transcended the ecumenical humanity of the known inhabited world.

The Olmecs and Aztecs showed us imperial culture on another continent and with quite different symbolisms. Close to their shamanic foundations, yet shaped by a more developed social order, these peoples both continued the old **symbiosis** of animal and human life and made their rulers connections to the gods. Thus in them, too, the conviction that the cosmos was a living whole determined the basic patterns of culture.

Generalizing about the cosmological myth East and West, we stressed this priority or originality of the natural cosmos. Even in India and China, where "higher" cultures flourished, harmony with the cosmos was compelling. In the West, prerevelational and prephilosophical cultures were mainly shamanic. Overall, then, the cosmological peoples show us the potency of nature's invitation to harmony and nature's treasury of powers. Because their ways helped humanity survive for millennia and could hold the key to our own future prosperity, we have good grounds for viewing them appreciatively.

In considering views of the civilizational religions counter to Voegelin's, we again noted his dependence on consubstantiality, which both empiricist and monotheistic interpreters might dispute, and we then asked for such opponents' alternative theories of the shifts in religious consciousness that the new empires provoked.

STUDY QUESTIONS

1. Relate the Sumerian notion of *me* to life within a cosmic circuit.
2. How could the Pharaoh link the gods and his people?
3. What is the significance of the Persian emperors' conceiving of their conquests as advancing the realm of Ahura Mazda?
4. How might the jaguar and the nahual fuse with the Olmec ruler?
5. What has been the relation in cosmological cultures between power and harmony?

NOTES

1. Denise Lardner Carmody, *The Oldest God* (Nashville: Abingdon, 1981), p. 55.
2. Helmer Ringgren, *Religions of the Ancient Near East* (Philadelphia: Westminster, 1973), p. 5.
3. James B. Pritchard, ed., *Ancient Near Eastern Texts*, 3rd ed. (Princeton, N. J.: Princeton University Press, 1969), p. 604.
4. Henri Frankfort, *Kingship and the Gods* (Chicago: University of Chicago Press, 1978), p. 134.

5. Eric Voegelin, *Order and History, Vol. 4* (Baton Rouge: Louisiana State University Press, 1974), p. 149.

6. Ignacio Bernal, *The Olmec World* (Berkeley: University of California Press, 1976), pp. 98–99.

7. Ake Hultkrantz, *The Religions of the American Indians* (Berkeley: University of California Press, 1979), p. 244.

8. See John Bowker, *The Sense of God* (Oxford: Clarendon Press, 1973), pp. 44–65.

9. See Huston Smith, *Beyond the Post-Modern Mind* (New York: Crossroad, 1982).

CHAPTER FOUR

India

ORIENTATION

The cosmological myth, we have argued or hypothesized, massively shaped the reality of prehistoric, recent nonliterate, and early civilizational peoples. In the case of the two leading religious functionaries one finds in such societies, the shaman and the priest, natural power and harmony were the main preoccupations. Shamans and priests continue to function in what we are calling *philosophical* cultures, but they no longer hold pride of place. A new personality or social type comes to the fore: the sage. To be sure, the sage is a rather ideal type, almost an achievement that one can only hope to approximate. For the mass of people within the philosophical cultures, shamans and priests probably had more day-to-day influence. Yet the sagacious ideal had greater dignity or status, and if we investigate why this was so, we venture upon the changes that differentiated the philosophical cultures from the cosmological.

First, it is typical of the shaman to focus on the imagination. The ecstasy or stepping out of ordinary consciousness that the shaman achieves depends on a fluid notion of reality in which anything vividly experienced must be taken seriously. It does not matter, therefore, that the vivid experience comes in a dream, or a waking vision, or an ecstasy induced by drugs. If one confronts a god, an ancestor, or an evil spirit vividly one has had a noteworthy experience, has been given a happening that one is foolish not to ponder.

Second, priesthood generally entails a step away from this fluid consciousness and sense of reality. Priests focus on rituals and sacrifices, which generally multiply when a people becomes literate. In a relatively leisured society, the priest can specialize in the ceremonies and perhaps arcane lore that the people believe are their passports to harmony with the sacred cosmos. This encourages priests to become masters of ritualistic information and theory, and so it can be a step toward disciplined education. Shamans, of course, often have been put through quite disciplined initiations. In many tribes, there are definite signs by which to distinguish good shamanic candidates and definite steps by which to educate them. But a literate priesthood can generate whole libraries in which prior ritualists have squirreled away their experiments and insights. So the priestly mentality, in negative stereotype, becomes arid and **rubrical**. Male or female, members of the different priesthoods have had the reputation of being more interested in their moldy texts and endless rituals than in either individual suffering people or the wonderous cosmic whole.

Individual members of the priesthood often broke this stereotype, of course, and the proximity of religious rituals to medical healings and commonsense counselings regularly made priests people who heard a lot of society's laments. Still, by and large, priests are conservative, loyal servants of the status quo. In the cosmological cultures they preserved the myths about the origins of the world, the sources of the seasonal ceremonies, more than they criticized those sources or transformed them creatively. Priests of imperial cultures tended to become one of the important blocs of political power, as we saw in the case of Egypt (it was the priests who frustrated Akhenaton's monotheistic reform, because it ran counter to the interests of their local gods and ritualistic systems). Rarely do members of the important power blocs spearhead any culture's self-criticism or creativity.

As we shall see in the case of India, the sage arose as an antagonistic alternative to the priest. The priest, or **Brahman,** was at the top rung of the social system, but Brahmanism (the religious system spun out by the Indian priests) failed to satisfy deeper spirits. So the Mahavira (the founder of **Jainism**), the Buddha, and the thinkers responsible for the **Upanishads** attacked the Brahmanical establishment. From their ascetical practices and reflective musings they made bold to proclaim a more interior and better way.

The sage, then, in the somewhat simplistic sketch that we are presently attempting, is first distinguished by reflectiveness. If the shaman develops a powerful imagination, the sage develops a powerful intellect. Sages want to know the ultimate causes and structures of things. Typically, they want to rise to the most comprehensive viewpoint, to judge things "under the aspect of eternity." This does not mean, however, that sages have no ambitions for daily life. On the whole, they go at their ascetical practices, their studies, their psychological or political experiments with a will to make them bear practical religious fruit. Thus the Buddha and the Mahavira are honored as religious founders, sages who plotted out pathways to peace and deliverance. The Upanishadic seers have functioned in much the same way, for traditionally Indians have read the Upanishads to

improve themselves, to make progress toward enlightenment and liberation. With proper qualifications, we can say the same about the motivations
of Chinese and Greek sages and about the uses to which their people
traditionally put them.

The "philosophy" that we are postulating has lain at the core of several highly significant cultures therefore is not merely academic. For the
Buddha, Confucius, Lao Tzu, Socrates, Plato, and the rest, the love of
wisdom has been wholehearted, practical, and political. To go to school to
one of these leading sages has been to enter upon a comprehensive way of
life. Because the founder's path has claimed to take one to the heart of a
numinous reality, it has been hard to distinguish such pathways from
religious schemata for salvation.

How, though, does the wisdom of the great sages move their cultures
away from the cosmological myth sufficiently to justify our placing such
cultures apart from prehistoric, recent nonliterate, and many early civilizational cultures? What differentiations and corresponding alterations in
worldview make our case for their advancement or distinction?

The main achievement of the great sages has been their intellectual
penetration of reality. They were the ones who fashioned (or at least began
the process that eventually fashioned) a comprehensive understanding of
nature, society, the self, and divinity and who pointed such understanding
toward the solution of humanity's most radical problems. In so doing, they
gained a considerable measure of control over reality, enough in fact to
make them masters of the cosmological myth. One could say, of course,
that many shamans and priests were masters of the cosmological myth, but
that would be a different thing. The shamans and priests mastered techniques and lore by which to maneuver profitably within the cosmos. The
sages gained a qualitatively different sort of control, because they at least
verged upon perspectives that challenged the cosmos's supremacy.

So, for example, the Buddha, nearly obsessed with the problem of
human suffering, finally sat himself under what has come to be known as
the Bo tree and vowed that he would not leave until his meditations had
brought him release from the cosmic circuit of suffering, from endless
birth and death. His victory, when articulated, set forth an intellectual
mastery of the world. If one did what he prescribed, fully absorbed what he
taught, the world would no longer dictate the script. The Buddha's
enlightenment professed to be a liberation from the cosmic prison, a flooding with light that set all the interactions of the world in a new, tamed
perspective. One may debate, as Buddhists do among themselves, how best
to lay nuance on the Buddha's **Dharma**, or "teaching," and just where the
victory over traditional cosmology centers. But the Buddhist teaching of
conditioned coproduction clearly claims to be an intellectual mastery of at
least the moral effects of the interactions of the elements within the cosmos,
and the Buddhist convictions about **nirvana** lay claim to a realm free of the
cosmos's control. For reasons such as these, the mastery of the Buddha and
other sages seems qualitatively ahead of what the shamans and the priests
achieved.

India is one of the world's richest religious treasuries. For well over four thousand years, people on the subcontinent have passionately pursued freedom from life's miseries, illumination that would wash away life's confusions. And at the center of this cultural passion has sat the guru or religious master. Part yogi and part scholar, he (only occasionally have women been leading gurus) exemplifies very well the type that we have called the *sage*. In this chapter we consider a few of the most significant stages in the long-playing effort of India's sages to clarify reality and show people how to gain full freedom.

Our study, true to India's own evaluation of what the center of a religious culture should be, will stress ultimate or metaphysical questions. India has been a land where *ultimacy* has preoccupied a great many religious practitioners (even though many of them, by stressing the dropping of all desires, have seemed to go forward almost casually). To understand this preoccupation, one must realize that Indians have almost always had to witness great amounts of suffering. Because they usually could not fully solve their bodily problems of food, housing, and disease, they tended to seek a spiritual realm relatively free of bodily concerns. In addition, the typical Indian, as we shall see, has thought of the human life span as but a tiny portion of either cosmic or personal time. The universe has existed for unimaginable eons, and each individual is but passing through one of what will probably be very many lifetimes.

However, **reincarnation**, determined by one's karma or previous moral momentum, strikes the typical Hindu guru as more a curse than a blessing. To keep going round the circuit of death and rebirth only multiplies one's sufferings. So the gold ring most Hindu masters have sought is freedom from the entire realm of **samsara**, or death and rebirth. To gain this freedom, the majority have thought, one must penetrate the true nature of reality and align oneself with something imperishable, something stronger than samsara. That is the conviction that makes most sense of the descriptions we now offer of some of the principal stages in Indian religion.

THE TESTIMONY OF THE VEDAS

The Vedas are the closest thing to an official Hindu **scripture**. For Indian belief, they present the wisdom distilled from the visions of the wise ancients. To an outside, academic analyst, they comprise mainly myths and ritualistic lore that testify to ancient India's full submersion in the cosmological mode of existence. The primary stratum of gods, historically, is a collection of divinities associated with natural powers: the storm, the sun, the fire. Most of the rituals for healings or good fortune deal with the cosmos as a living field of interconnected beings. The blurring of lines between plants, animals, human beings, and gods that we have witnessed in the cosmological societies occurs again and again.

Nonetheless, the Vedas also contain the beginnings of a revolt against this kind of thinking. In the main, it takes the form of **skepticism** or

Yakshi Figure. Sculpture, Indian, second century. Popular Indian religion has honored many demigods, some of them seductive and mocking as well as auspicious. *(The Nelson-Atkins Museum of Art, Kansas City, Missouri [Nelson Fund])*

agnosticism about the cosmic gods. For example, Rig Veda 10:129 is a famous reflection that shows a mind groping after the mystery of creation. The thinker responsible for it is not irreligious so much as impatient, almost irritated with the pretensions of the tradition to know with certainty about such ultimate things as creation. So after proposing, in a questioning way, the deepest explanations of creation that tradition could offer, the thinker admits to running into a blank wall. Implicit in the concluding confession that no one knows about these matters for certain is an intuition of the limitations of the cosmological tradition of infraworldy divinities.

To quote the text in full:

Then was not non-existent nor existent: there was no realm of air, no sky beyond it. What covered it, and where? and what gave shelter? Was water here, unfathomed depth of water? Death was not then, nor was there aught immortal: no sign was there, the day's and night's divider. The One Thing, breathless, breathed by its own nature: apart from it was nothing whatsoever. Darkness there was: at first concealed in darkness this All was indiscriminate chaos. All that existed then was void and formless: by the great power of

Warmth was born that Unit. Thereafter rose Desire in the beginning, Desire, the primal seed and germ of Spirit. Sages who searched with their heart's thought discovered the existent kinship in the non-existent. Transversely was their severing line extended: what was above it then, and what below it? There were begetters, there were mighty forces, free action here and energy up yonder. Who verily knows and who can here declare it, whence it was born and whence comes this creation? The Gods are later than this world's production. Who knows then whence it first came into being? He, the first origin of creation, whether he formed it all or did not form it, whose eye controls this world in highest heaven, he verily knows it, or perhaps he knows not.[1]

The mode of the reflection takes us away from myth. To be sure, it is still symbolic and indebted to the traditional stories of creation. But one senses at work a probing intellect that will stop at nothing less than adequate explanation, the attainment of a cause that will make sense of creation. The beginning state of the creational process probably was dark, voidlike, a sort of womb from which new life could issue. The later distinctions of existent/nonexistent, day/night, had yet to appear. The reflector's best intuition of what might have started the creational process is desire: the wanting, for weal or woe, that is proper to spirit. Sages have worked over these primal relations, sensed the kinship of what is with what is not. But who can know these primary things for sure? The gods are not the answer, for they came after creation (a sure sign of cosmological convictions). If there was a single origin, that person or thing would know, if only in the mode of seeing it all from above. But maybe even such an origin doesn't know (maybe creation is intrinsically unknowable, intrinsically **mysterious**).

This sort of inquiry, however modestly, defeatedly, or disconsolately it ends, signals a mentality that will no longer be satisfied with illogical or less than ultimate stories. It takes a hammer to the solid cosmological myth and starts trying to break through to something intellectually more satisfying. Relatedly, it grows disgusted with the ritualistic activities of the priests who preside over the mythological religious structure. Just as their stories do not go deep enough, so their ritualistic chantings become a burden to the awakened human spirit. The awakened human spirit is hungry for genuine nourishment, actual illumination. The priests but croak along like frogs.

We see this disgust, and find this figure of frogs, in Rig Veda VII:103.

They who lay quiet for a year, the brahmins who fulfill their vows, the frogs have lifted up their voice, the voice Parjanya [god of the rain-cloud] hath inspired. What time on these, as on a dry skin lying in the pool's bed, the floods of heaven descended, the music of the frogs comes forth in concert like the cows lowing with their calves beside them . . . as brahmins, sitting round the brimful vessel, talk at the **soma** rite of Atiratra so, frogs, ye gather round the pool to honour this day of all the year, the first of the rain-time.[2]

The depiction of the Brahmans could hardly be less flattering. Clearly the person describing them in this way has lost all reverence, even all respect, for what they do. In the world of things that matter, their activities are as ineffectual as the croaking of frogs by a pond. Real life, real significance, lies in other directions.

Insofar as the Brahmans could symbolize the entire Indian cosmo-mythic structure that had grown up by 1000 B.C.E., this satiric description of them was at least a step toward a radical revolution. When people are content with a religious structure, their descriptions of the human foibles of their religious leaders tend to be mild. Indeed, they might virtually veto any such descriptions if the leaders stand for a system or order that brims with sacredness, actually persuading them that it is utterly real. The writer of this satire has no such mildness or inhibitions. So far has the writer's disaffection gone, in fact, that the Brahmans are of little account. If they still had a strong hold on the writer's psyche, there would be palpable anger or bitterness. The tone of this satire is more one of boredom, unconcern. The Brahmans are about as important to the business of finding a satisfying explanation of things as frogs are to life as a whole.

The love of wisdom that gives philosophy its name lures people to a level considerably deeper than ritualistic information or routine ceremonial performance. This love, in fact, instinctively knows that spiritual nourishment is not a matter of facts or tidy actions. It suspects that the light by which to travel, the warmth that lets one create, comes from a movement of the deepest part of the person out or down or up (the love of wisdom has to express itself in space-bound figures, but it is tied to none in particular) to the source of such light and warmth. We shall see this more clearly in the fuller Indian philosophy that emerges in the next sections and most clearly in the classical Greeks (as Voegelin interprets them), but we can prepare the thought right now. In the rather agnostic and disaffected passages we have studied from the Rig Veda, we find spirits hungry for genuine wisdom, ready to make the loving move.

THE UPANISHADS

The movement of revolt against Brahmanism came to flower in the Upanishads. These writings, which technically are at the end of the Vedas and so may also be considered scriptural, combine poetry, mysticism, philosophy, and indebtedness to the cosmological myth. They are not a pure type or genre. Still, they represent some of India's deepest traditional musings about the ultimate constitution of reality. By the time that the Upanishadic seers had played out their suspicion that a single basic stuff is responsible for everything that exists, India had developed one of its most distinctive religious characteristics.

Perhaps this is the juncture at which we should introduce the notion of **yoga**, which might make the Indian tendency toward **monism** more intelligible. Etymologically, *yoga* simply means "discipline." Generally, however, it calls to mind the precisely mental discipline that serious Hindus have followed in an effort to penetrate ultimate reality and come to both enlightenment and liberation from **karmic** bondage. The essential note of this yoga has been the practictioner's efforts to still the mind and settle the consciousness so that his or her whole being rests at its foundations or inmost core. Often the road to this goal begins with the practice of regulating and following one's breathing. The breath is taken as a link between the material and the spiritual parts of the personality. Following the intake and the outflow of the breath can help one unify, simplify, get all of one's aspects together.

The main significance of yogic interiority for the philosophical achievement of the Upanishads that is our main interest here is the way it prepared potential sages for the realization or conviction that the inmost part or dimension of themselves was coincident with the basic stuff of reality as a whole. The **atman**, as the tradition often called the quintessential self or personality, was one with the Brahman that gave being or reality to the world as a whole. (Brahman here refers to *ultimate reality* and should not be confused with the same word for priest.)

In the Chandogya Upanishad (VII: 1–14) there occurs a dialogue between the sage Uddalaka and his son Shvetaketu that brings the Indian monistic tendency to a famous conclusion. The question of the dialogue is, What ultimately constitutes reality? The sage's final answer is that the subtle essence of the self is the same as the subtle essence of the whole world.

> "Bring hither a fig from there." "Here it is, sir." "Break it." "It is broken, sir." "What do you see there?" "These extremely fine seeds, sir." "Of these, please break one." "It is broken, sir." "What do you see there?" "Nothing at all, sir." Then he said to Shvetaketu: "Verily, my dear, that subtle essence which you do not perceive—from that very essence, indeed, my dear, does this great fig tree thus arise. Believe me, my dear, that which is the subtle essence—this whole world has that essence for its Self; that is the Real; that is the Self; that subtle essence art thou, Shvetaketu."[3]

The movement of the dialogue is plain. By setting the inquiry on the track of the ultimate constituent of the fig tree, and then of the world as a whole, Uddalaka has put the spotlight on the mind and its need for explanation. More precisely, he has focused on material causality: that from which something is made. The immediate goal, therefore, is no longer holistic: harmony or power that makes one right with the cosmos. That might be the ultimate goal, but to the forefront here is understanding, explanation. Uddalaka casts the pursuit of understanding in a framework of causality. What is it that will satisfy the mind as the reason why things (the fig tree, the world as a whole) are as they are? One could bring forward other candidates for the material cause of the fig tree or the world (sap, atoms). One could deal with different kinds of causality (efficient: the ultimate agent; final: the ultimate goal) or even recast the sense of *causality* so that it became more **relational** or **dialectical**, and so did a better job at dealing with the great variety of interlocking influences that modern ecology, for instance, suggests. But one would still be seeking a rational explanation, a patterning of the elements of the question that would bring the light of understanding, the "click" that makes one say, "Aha! So that is how it works."

Now, what distinguishes the Upanishadic quest, as we extrapolate it from this text and could exemplify it in many others, from either idle speculation or modern science is its quality of loving movement. Idle speculation is simply curious. It wants to know why, but scarcely deeper than the level of titillation. Modern science specifies its methods and understanding of causality much more carefully than we see in the Upanishads, and its assumption is materialistic or empirical (the causes it deals with are measurable). Moreover, modern science does not move the investigator by a love of the mystery of being. This love might exert some implicit influence, but the characteristic focus of modern science falls on the patterns or arrangements of things, not their underlying or inmost being.

In our Voegelinian interpretation, then, the Upanishadic achievement is a species of philosophy, because it reaches the level where the love of wisdom, the desire to experience the light and warmth of the whole and gain some intellectual appreciation of it, specifies the quest. The Upanishadic answer seems more or less adequate, depending on one's criteria. Certainly, however, it is an estimable answer, one that any analyst willing to deal with the full needs of the human spirit must greatly respect. For the Upanishads say, in effect, "Find the inmost portion or state of yourself and you will find the key to an adequate understanding of reality as a whole. When you have come to appreciate your own being, you will appreciate what it is that makes all reality be."

This conviction is expressed in a form that most modern Westerners find strange, and it depends on experiences that most modern Westerners have not had. The form, which we might call **metaphysical** or willing to call entities such as the *self* and *being* explanatory, is different from our modern common sense and our materialistic bias. The experiences, which summarily we might call yogic, take one below the level of sensation, below even the level of thought and feeling, toward an ideal point where consciousness is pure, where awareness is awareness of nothing particular.

Perhaps returning to the dialogue of the Chandogya Upanishad will make our analysis clearer. After giving Shvetaketu the example of the fig seeds, Uddalaka gives him an example using salt.

> "Still further may the venerable sir instruct me." "So be it, my dear," said he. "Having put this salt in the water, come to me in the morning." He did so. Then the father said to him: "That salt which you put in the water last evening—please bring it hither." Even having looked for it, he did not find it, for it was completely dissolved. "Please take a sip of water from this end," said the father. "How is it?" "Salt." "Take a sip from that end," said he. "How is it?" "Salt." "Throw it away and come to me." Shvetaketu did so thinking to himself: "That salt, though unperceived, still persists in the water." Then Aruni [the father] said to him: "Verily, my dear, you do not perceive Being in this world; but it is, indeed, here only: That which is the subtle essence—this whole world has that essence for its Self. That is the Real. That is the Self. That art thou, Shvetaketu."[4]

The bent of the dialogue therefore is clear. The Upanishadic seers want to know the ultimate essence of reality, and they think they gain such

knowledge by equating the being of the human self with the being of reality
as a whole (the atman with the Brahman). Moreover, they are conscious
that their movement departs from the Brahmanism of the past, and they
make no bones about their conviction that focusing on being is superior to
focusing on rituals. So, for example, the beginning of the dialogue we
studied has the father sending the son off for a traditional Vedic schooling.
The son returns home quite conceited, thinking he has mastered true
wisdom. The father's questions are designed to show him that he has
learned nothing of actual significance. He is stiff in his self-satisfaction, and
the father would unbend him so that he could learn about things hitherto
unheard or unthought—the world of mind and spirit. That is the world the
Upanishadic seers explored and treasured. So doing, they greatly differentiated the cosmological myth, venturing upon an order or reality that transcended the cosmos.

SHANKARA

The Upanishads were written over a period of perhaps five hundred years,
so it is not surprising that they contain a great variety of materials and
points of view. Nonetheless, the overall impact they made on Indian
thought was in the direction of what we have called monism. This is the
conviction that reality finally is one, unified and seamless. Correlated with
this conviction is the view that the apparent complexity or diversity of
reality is superficial or illusory. The Indian thinker who took the monistic
impulse of the Upanishads to its greatest heights, thereby becoming the
most revered Indian philosopher, was the sage Shankara (roughly 788–820
C.E.). By briefly considering his metaphysics, we can glimpse how far India
advanced toward the noetic differentiation that finally looked upon the
world as the limited product of an unlimited transcendent Being.

Rudolf Otto, one of the pioneers who founded the comparative study
of religion, came to the United States in 1923 to give the Haskell Lectures
at Oberlin College. The book that resulted from these lectures, *Mysticism
East and West*, compares Shankara with the Western medieval mystic
Meister Eckhart. At the outset of his study, Otto offers a succinct sketch of
Shankara's metaphysics.

> Shankara is the classic teacher and interpreter of "Advaita" in its most strict
> and subtle form. Advaita means non-duality or "secondlessness," and the
> doctrine of "secondlessness." (The usual translation is monism but non-
> dualism is more exact.) This monistic doctrine can be summed up in general
> terms as follows: "True Being is Sat alone, Being itself, the eternal Brahman,
> unchanging and unchanged, undivided and without parts, Ekam eva
> advitiyam." That is (a) the multiplicity of things exists only through "Maya"
> (which is usually translated as "mere appearance"). Sat itself is the One only,
> ekam eva; (b) in itself Brahman or Being is absolutely and immutably "One
> only," without parts, without any multiplicity, and therefore without the mul-
> tiplicity of differences and delimitations. Hence it is necessarily without any
> distinctions at all: nirgunam, nirvisesham. Therefore it is "advitiyam," non-
> dual, both outwardly and inwardly, and is opposed also to all alteration

(vikara) and to all change: Change rests simply upon a word. It is a mere name. Thence it is also opposed to all being (utpada) and becoming (sambhava).[5]

The quotation is perhaps more difficult than materials usually given to undergraduates, but bear with it. *Advaita* ("nonduality") is the name by which Shankara's philosophy or school has come to be known. It is also the characteristic most central to his description of ultimate reality (Brahman). The gist of his position is that there can be only one ultimate reality. Therefore, the Brahman can have no parts, cannot change, cannot have come into being at a particular time or be destined to pass out of being in the future. It simply is, simply exists, and for Shankara it must be the fullness of being or existence, the whole reality. From this it follows that when we apprehend reality as dual or multiple, we are failing to appreciate Brahman or give it its due. Maya is the realm of this failure, is reality as we conceive it when we fail to give Brahman its due. Maya clearly has a connection with sense-knowledge (here we are going beyond the quotation to other parts of Shankara's thought), because sensation is the main way that we perceive the world as changing, multiple, divided, and the non-Brahmanic rest. True knowledge, it follows, comes from something other than the senses. It stems from the spiritual portion of the human personality (and so, we note, would be nourished, at least remotely, by yogic exercises that made this portion more prominent or better known).

Let us try to make this more concrete. Shankara is not saying that there are not many different beings: men, women, cats, dogs. He is not denying that we all perceive that there are various kinds of trees, snakes, clouds, fishes. All of us constantly receive testimony from our senses that there is this external variety, just as all of us know from the inside that we have different moods, thoughts, pains, joys as we move from week to week, year to year. What Shankara denies is the ultimacy of any of these limited, diverse, changing beings. None of them, we might say, is an independent agent. None of them is, exists, self-sufficiently. Thus none of them answers the sort of question that the Upanishadic seers were posing: What is the ultimate cause or foundation of reality? None of them can accomplish the task of explaining to the mind how the world can be as it is, of proposing to the heart what it should love if it would be fully wise.

Shankara's way is to move from the limitations of the beings one finds in the realm of Maya to an unlimited Brahman, and vice versa. Brahman and Maya exist in two different realms, correlate with two different kinds of knowing. But only the realm of Being or Brahman is fully real, gives ultimate knowledge. The question, then, is how to relate Being and beings, the fully real and the merely partially real. Shankara's answer is that Brahman alone is real, if one wants an ultimate, utterly wise judgment. From this it follows that everything else is (a) illusory, insofar as we grant it a solidity or reality that, from an ultimate perspective, it doesn't have or deserve, and (b) but a manifestation of Brahman.

This latter inference brings us to the punch line of the dialogue between Uddalaka and Shvetaketu: "That are thou." In the context of most of the Upanishads, the "thou" is a human self and the equation being made is: The most real aspect of human self (atman) equals the most real aspect of reality as a whole (Brahman). By the time of Shankara, this equation has expanded, in fact has become universal. Shankara says that the most real aspect of *anything* is the Brahman in it, or present to it, or manifest through it. The only Reality, with a capital *R*, is Brahman. Other things are real to the extent that they express Brahman. (Why Brahman should choose to express itself in this way, to ground the discrete, multiple world we human beings sense and deal with, is never made fully clear.)

So far, then, we have seen the extremity to which India's leading philosophy took the philosophic movement in search of a firm ground for ultimate reality, a full explanation or illumination of the human mind. Does this extremity, though, finally break with the cosmological myth? Is it a noetic differentiation parallel or equal to that which Voegelin finds in classical Greek philosophy? Probably the answer should be no. People speaking from outside the culture in which an eminent religious achievement has occurred must always proceed cautiously, because almost surely they have missed something important, but by the criteria that Voegelin has established and we are using to structure this analysis of world religion, Shankara seems more to have transposed the cosmological viewpoint than to have broken with it.

We shall reflect on these criteria as we proceed, so we are not saying that Voegelin's or our own reasons for making a classification such as this should go unchallenged. At the moment, though, let us simply indicate our sense that Shankara's Brahman is not free of the world as the Creator or divinity or ultimate reality discerned in the classical Greek noetic differentiation is. To be sure, Brahman goes beyond the manifest, material, and even humanly spiritual world in several ways. There is an unmanifest Brahman, much more Reality than human observers can chart. In addition, whatever is, is Brahman—the sort of claim that the various **pantheisms** make. But the tie between Brahman and lesser beings, Brahman and the world, suggests the central cosmological notion of consubstantiality. Brahman is the one stuff that moves through the world, in a way that Voegelin's noetic differentiation would deny to the Creator. A physical inclusiveness seems to make Brahman the new "container" of whatever exists. We shall have more to say on this question when we get to the classical Greek achievement, and no doubt the distinctions will always remain both difficult and arguable. But at this juncture the identification that Shankara makes between Brahman and all things' reality, or the insistence Shankara makes that reality is nondual, seems more to replace the cosmological notion of a living whole with a more sophisticated, radical, and spiritual alternative than to break with its key conviction that all beings are consubstantial.

TRADITIONAL INDIAN COSMOLOGY AND THE LITTLE TRADITION

The Advaita philosophy developed by Shankara and his followers, for all its prestige, was actually appropriated by only a few, an intellectual elite.

More people probably were influenced by its popularizations, so that when they meditated or thought about the world, its monism was a directive factor, but on the whole the average Indian lived in a more mythic, compact, and less spiritualized world.

The place of the cosmos as a living whole is suggested by the following description from A.L. Basham's marvelous book, *The Wonder That Was India*.

> Hindu cosmology was slow in evolving, and in its final form was perhaps later than the cosmology of the Buddhists and Jains. According to this system the cosmos passes through cycles within cycles for all eternity. The basic cycle is the **kalpa**, a "day of Brahma" [a leading god, not to be confused with Brahman, the ultimate reality], or 4,320 million earthly years. His night is of equal length. 360 such days and nights constitute a "year of Brahma" and his life is 100 such years long. The largest cycle is therefore 311,040,000 million years long, after which the whole universe returns to the ineffable world-spirit, until another creator god is evolved. In each cosmic day the god creates the universe again and again absorbs it. During the cosmic night he sleeps, and the whole universe is gathered up into his body, where it remains as a potentiality. Within each kalpa are fourteen **manvantaras**, or secondary cycles, each lasting 306,720,000 years, with long intervals between them. In these periods the world is recreated, and a new Manu [first human being, equivalent to the biblical Adam] appears, as the progenitor of the human race. We are now in the seventh manvantara of the kalpa, of which the Manu is known as Manu Vaivasvata. Each manvantara contains seventy-one **Mahayugas**, or aeons, of which a thousand form the kalpa. Each mahayuga is in turn divided into four **yugas** or ages, called Krta, Treta, Dvapara, and Kali. Their lengths are respectively, 4,800, 3,600, 2,400 and 1,200 "years of the gods," each of which equals 360 human years. Each yuga represents a progressive decline in piety, morality, strength, stature, longevity and happiness. We are at present in the Kali-yuga, which began, according to tradition, in 3102 B.C., believed to be the year of the Mahabharata War.[6]

The Mahabharata is the greatest Hindu epic poem, within which occurs the Bhagavad Gita, perhaps the most influential Hindu religious text (which we shall consider shortly). The huge numbers of this traditional Hindu cosmology suggest the context for the doctrine of karma: immense time was available for the life force to accomplish its passage through various entities on the way to **moksha** or full liberation. The pulsating character of the kalpas fits the cosmological mythology and insinuates that the world is a rhythmic organism having day and night, intake and outflow. Like Shankara's notion of Brahman, the traditional notion of moksha suggests that Indians could think of a "beyond" even to this vast cosmological time frame, but most of Indian religion occurred within a consciousness that was infracosmic and tended to identify reality with the consubstantial whole of this vast universe.

The *little tradition*, as anthropologists sometimes call it, is the folk stratum of a given culture. In contrast to the official orthodoxy of the intellectuals or the establishment, the common people often have their own psychological world, in which gods and goddesses, ritualistic practices verging on the superstitious, and belief in occult forces are very influential. So,

Vishnu in the Avatar of a Boar. North India, ninth-tenth century. The "logic" of the cosmological myth permits the highest divinity to move in lowly, even humorous forms. *(The Nelson-Atkins Museum of Art, Kansas City, Missouri [Nelson Fund])*

for example, in certain areas where Christianity has been the official religion, among the common people the cult of the saints, or of the Virgin Mary, whether pure or mixed with local pre-Christian beliefs, has actually been more powerful than the official doctrines of the **Trinity** or the **Eucharist**. In traditional India, gods such as Vishnu and Shiva, goddesses such as Kali and Durga, astrological practices, spells, sacrifices, mandalas, **mantras**, and the like have shaped the common people more than even the Upanishads, let alone the refinements of Advaita philosophy. Sometimes the word given to the theistic portion of this popular Indian religious complex is **bhakti**: devotional love. Focusing on a personal god such as Krishna (an **avatar** or manifestation of Vishnu), the devotee would dedicate himself or herself in terms of a warm, emotional love. This love has probably been the outstanding characteristic of popular Hinduism, and so bhakti sometimes stands duty for the popular Hindu religious life as a whole.

Because women tended to be excluded from higher education and elitist religion, most of their religious lives focused on bhakti. We see a recent example of this in the report of a woman named Tila Sahu, the wife of a confectioner. She is a follower of Krishna, and she practices the **habisha** ritual, a devotion peculiar to postmenopausal women and designed principally to secure a long life for their husbands. (Traditionally in India the lot of the widow has been grim.) Tila Sahu says

"Ten years ago during the month of Kartik I went to [the town of] Puri to see a dance in the temple of Lord Jagannatha [a local name for Krishna]. I hardly saw it because of the thousands of people there. Although I had traveled to Puri with relatives, I stayed alone that night in the temple. I watched how different habisha people worshiped. They became ecstatic, and in their devotional fervor they forgot all about the world. They tried to merge their souls with that of the deity. When morning came, I returned to my uncle's house in Puri. Then I bathed in the temple's tank. Afterward I went with my relatives to the Gate of Heaven on the beach where the dead are cremated. I saw several women doing their **puja** [ritual]. I joined in and sang for them a habisha song that the milkmaids [associated with Krishna in mythology] sang when Jagannatha and his brother went to help the king of Puri fight a war against the king of the south. All the habisha people were surprised at how much I knew. They happily pulled me into the center of their group, dressed me as Radha [wife of Krishna], and dressed another woman like Krishna, while the others became milkmaids for the drama. We danced and sang on the beach, and the others praised me. Many groups of women were singing and dancing; one after another they invited me to dance and sing with them. I continued for twelve hours. I returned home by bus. In the village we dance and sing but not like in Puri. Men and women in the village criticize habisha people because, they say, it is improper to sing and dance publicly. Those villagers are wicked. They have no power of devotion.[7]

The power of devotion, excited by singing and dancing, is most important in the Indian little tradition. It has evolved into what Indians call a **marga**, or religious pathway. Just as yoga or study can be a pathway, so can devotion. If one loves a god such as Krishna wholeheartedly, one can grow pure, and the god will take care of one's liberation from karma,

Dancing Krishna. Indian, twelfth-thirteenth century. In contrast to Shiva, whose dance keeps the world spinning toward destruction, Krishna dances in mischief and joy. *(The Nelson-Atkins Museum of Art, Kansas City, Missouri [Nelson Fund])*

suffering, and the rest. For the little tradition, then, philosophy was at best a remote background. Up front stood devotional love. Probably this has been the case in most, if not all, other religions.

THE HINDU ACHIEVEMENT
AND BUDDHIST VARIATIONS

If by *Hinduism* we mean the Indian religious complex, historically derived from the fusion of native peoples and Aryan invaders, that arose after the challenges of Buddhism, Jainism, and other **heterodox** movements and was shaped by them, then the great Hindu achievement was to weave an umbrella under which all sorts of people could shelter. Philosophy and strict yogic regimes catered to the intellectuals and the spiritual elite. Bhakti and a wealth of gods catered to the common people and those who sought union with ultimate reality by way of personified love. What was called *karma-yoga* ("work-discipline") offered yet another popular religious pathway, teaching that people could stay in the world, trying to accomplish the responsibilities, or dharma, imposed on them by their families or their places in society, and yet gain purification, even salvation, by performing their obligations purely, without attachment.

The Bhagavad Gita, which probably was compiled between 500 and 200 B.C.E., summarized many of these different Hindu strains and offered ordinary people an almost biblical collection of prior wisdom. The Gita therefore is **eclectic**, stitching together different traditional strands. Concerning karma-yoga, for example, the Gita (3:3–9) says

> In this world there are two roads of perfection . . . Jnana Yoga, the path of . . . wisdom . . . and Karma Yoga, the path of the action of the Yogis. Not by refraining from action does man attain freedom from action. Not by mere renunciation does he attain supreme perfection. For not even for a moment can a man be without action. Helplessly are all driven to action by the forces of Nature. He who withdraws himself from actions, but ponders on their pleasures in his heart, he is under a delusion and is a false follower of the path. But great is the man who, free from attachments, and with a mind ruling its powers in harmony, works on the path of Karma Yoga, the path of consecrated action. Action is greater than inaction: perform therefore thy task in life. Even the life of the body could not be if there were no action. The world is in the bonds of action, unless the action is consecration. Let thy actions be pure, free from the bonds of desire.[8]

Hindu culture therefore came to look upon desire, untoward motivation, as close to the heart of the human problem. People stay stuck in karma, forced to endure endless deaths and rebirths, because of their impure desires. By summarizing matters so neatly, Hinduism gave all people—philosophers, yogis, common people of devotional bent, and common people of activist bent—a central target and explanation round which to organize their spiritual lives. If they would rid themselves of desire, they could gain complete liberation.

The Buddhist variations on this theme, as they began with the Enlightened One and developed in India (after about 80 C.E. Buddhism declined in India, and the Buddhist momentum moved toward East Asia through missionary ventures), did not dispute the overwhelming significance of desire. After all, the Buddha's diagnosis of the human situation, as summarized in the first two of his "four noble truths," said that all life is suffering and that the cause of suffering is desire. But when Buddhists went to work on solving this problem or removing this cause, they finally emerged with a significantly different sense of reality from what Hinduism taught.

First, the Buddhists tended to downplay the whole Hindu system of caste and social stratification. Perhaps this was due to the Buddha himself having been born into the second-ranked warrior class, rather than into the brahmanical priesthood. Whatever the social motivation, the doctrinal explanation came to be the irrelevance of social standing compared with one's central task of gaining enlightenment. Second, when the Buddhists bored into the problem of gaining enlightenment they found the core difficulty to be the notion of the self. Where Hinduism tended to focus on the atman, as we have seen, and to think of the atman as identical with or part of the world-pervasive Brahman, the Buddhists said that the atman was an illusion. There is no such thing as a permanent, reliable self, because the self, as much as everything else that we experience, is changing and therefore painful. Thus the Buddhists came to speak of what they called **anatman**, the doctrine that there is no substantial, unchanging self.

This in turn led to a different conception of reality as a whole. Whereas a radical monist such as Shankara finally spoke as though only Brahman were real, Buddhists denied that there was anything behind or at the foundations of the sensible reality that constantly changes. No Brahman lay within or as the realist portion of the elephants and bears, children and trees, dancers and bankers who populated daily life. The most the Buddhists would say is that the whole physical world was a flux of interlocking, interconnecting, selfless or insubstantial realities. With time the deeper Buddhist thinkers came to speak of nirvana, a realm of unconditionedness, where none of the limitations of sensible reality—change, painfulness, and the rest—obtain. Eventually **Mahayana** Buddhists, a more speculative, lay-oriented, and devotional branch that developed out of the conservative beginnings, even went so far as to identify nirvana with samsara, the realm of flux and suffering. By this they meant that flux and suffering depend on an unconditional aspect, if they are even to survive. Precisely how this teaching differed from the Hindu notion of a Brahman finally explaining all limited atmans or other beings is hard to say. By now we are at the point where specialists in Indian philosophy are needed. But it does seem clear that the Buddhists consistently spoke up for the interconnectedness of reality, the constant flux or changingness, and that they always were suspicious of the notion that the really real lies behind or underneath the flowing outer appearances of things. Rather, for them reality as a systemic, flowing whole is empty or impermanent.

These two connected Buddhist teachings—the doctrine that there is no self and the doctrine that reality as a moving and interlocking whole is empty or self-less—were not just esoteric philosophical doctrines but key elements in the practical Buddhist religious program. What Buddhists call *wisdom* (right doctrine as developed by Buddhist philosophy) has always undergirded meditation and ethics. Indeed, these three practices—study, meditation, and morality—form a tripod, each leg supporting the others. So one finds Buddhists describing their enlightenment experiences, in which they perceive in a flash of light the true arrangement of things, in terms of an empty personal reality (a sense of having no permanent self) and an interconnected cosmic reality.

For example, a Japanese businessman described his enlightenment experience as follows:

> As the train was nearing Ofuna station I ran across this line: "I came to realize clearly that Mind is no other than mountains and rivers and the great wide earth, the sun and the moon and the stars." I had read this before, but this time it impressed itself upon me so vividly that I was startled. . . . At midnight I abruptly awakened. At first my mind was foggy, then suddenly that quotation flashed into my consciousness: "I came to realize clearly that Mind is no other than mountains, rivers, and the great wide earth, the sun and the moon and the stars." And I repeated it. Then all at once I was struck as though by lightning, and the next instance heaven and earth crumbled and disappeared. Instantaneously, like surging waves, a tremendous delight welled up in me, a veritable hurricane of delight, as I laughed loudly and wildly: "Ha, ha, ha, ha, ha, ha! There's no reasoning here, no reasoning at all! Ha, ha, ha!" The empty sky split in two, then opened its enormous mouth and began to laugh uproariously: "Ha, ha, ha!" Later one of the members of my family told me that my laughter had sounded inhuman.[9]

In Zen Buddhist enlightenment, there is reason but no reasoning. Probably one should not speak of the basis of this conception as consubstantiality, because the doctrine of anatman denies that there are any substances at all. Nonetheless, something of the seamlessness of the cosmological myth seems to remain. If one may speak of Mind as the only reality, even though this speech does not mean to treat Mind as a substantial thing, one is blurring the borders between the cosmos and the whole of reality.

COUNTERVIEWS

In our foregoing descriptions of Hinduism and Buddhism, we have of course had to simplify. That is perhaps even more regrettable here than it would be with other traditions, because India above all is a very colorful and sensual religious realm. As anyone who has visited India can testify, the smells and spectacles linger long after the words and thoughts have faded. Many scholars of Hinduism therefore object to schematizations such as ours, arguing that the genius or special character of religious life on the subcontinent is its teeming untidiness or confusion. Here we can only note the validity of this argument and commend it to your consideration.

A second wave of negative reaction might come from the way we have dealt with Buddhism. To be sure, Buddhism will reappear in our treatment of Chinese religion, but we have indeed given a major tradition rather short shrift. The reason is that, for the story line we are developing, the main contributions that Buddhism has made seem to us best set in the context of the development of Hinduism. We have made rather clear our sense of how Buddhism differs from Hinduism on the related questions of the self and the best conception of ultimate reality. In their general effort to drop desire and gain an unconditioned state of freedom, however, the two native Indian traditions seem to us quite similar.

A third potential quarrel with our presentation concerns our judgment that neither Hinduism nor Buddhism finally breaks with the cosmological myth. We have placed some qualifications on this judgment, of course, and if we had more space at our disposal we could place several more. The counterview that would attack our position most cogently probably would stress the unconditionedness of moksha and nirvana. Searching for the experiences that generate the conviction that there is a *beyond*, or transcendent realm, students of Hinduism and Buddhism would take us into the same realm from which Western thinkers have derived their sense of creation from nothingness or of a God independent of the world. We would have to note that Buddhism, especially, has been reluctant to talk about nirvana, thinking that most of such talk is a distraction from the more important work of achieving nirvana. We would also have to agree that many Western religionists who profess a strict monotheism, confessing a God absolutely transcending the world, in fact have not broken through the cosmological myth to a purely spiritual or mystically cleansed understanding of such **transcendence**. The debate, then, could be quite evenhanded, and through its development we might find our Voegelinian perspective being forced to burn away not a few Western biases.

SUMMARY

We have been exploring Indian religious culture as a philosophical venture. From the Vedas we drew testimony to the development of dissatisfactions with a purely **animistic** view of reality, or one in which the gods and human rituals would remain potent but uncoordinated forces. Rig Veda 10:129, for example, suggests a deeper and more agnostic spirit, a mind that has probed the foundations of creation and glimpsed something of the ultimate mystery entailed. Similarly, Rig Veda 7:103 displays a disgust with the priests and the sacrificial system.

The Upanishads represent the massive, more positive or constructive movement that these dissatisfactions generated for the intellectual elite. In the dialogues between the son Shvetaketu and the sagacious father Uddalaka, the Chandogya Upanishad demonstrates the monistic direction that Indian thought followed and the identification of atman and Brahman to which many Indians concluded.

The Advaita Vedanta of Shankara, as we found it in Rudolf Otto's explanation, took this Upanishadic monism to its ultimate conclusion. For Shankara, only Brahman ultimately is real, and the knowledge by which we perceive a world of multiple different beings is seriously flawed. One may debate whether the ultimacy that Shankara accords to Brahman constitutes a break with the cosmological myth or a noetic differentiation, but our impression is that probably it does not.

Traditional Indian cosmology and the little tradition, which certainly shaped the nonelitist majority, spoke of the world as a great living whole that passes through huge and regular pulsations. The common people also made their way largely by devotion to gods such as Krishna. In the devotion of the contemporary Hindu woman Tila Sahu we saw a concrete example of bhakti.

The Hindu achievement, overall, has been to offer Indians a rich diversity of paths toward peace and enlightenment. Focusing on the removal of desire, the highly revered Bhagavad Gita offers such diverse ways as philosophy, yoga, bhakti, and karma-yoga, which have led millions toward ultimacy. The principal Buddhist variations from this program have stemmed from the Buddhist teaching that there is no stable self, and from the Buddhist tendency to think of reality as a system of fluctuating, connecting beings. Because of this holism, Buddhism too probably remained more within the cosmological myth than broke with it.

The counterviews that likely would challenge our interpretation of Indian religion include a stress on the teeming richness of Indian religion (which defeats any tidy schematizations); a plea for a fuller and more independent treatment of Buddhism; and an argument that the Indian concepts of moksha and nirvana suggest a break with the cosmological myth at least as profound as that of Western philosophy and revelation.

STUDY QUESTIONS

1. What is the desire that the Rig Veda thinks arose in the beginning?
2. Explain the analogy of salt that Uddalaka uses to explain the "subtle essence" of reality.
3. Explain the verse quoted by Rudolf Otto: "Change rests simply upon a word. It is a mere name."
4. How would bhakti help a woman such as Tila Sahu?
5. Explain how karma-yoga could function as a spiritual regime for people working in business.

NOTES

1. Ninian Smart and Richard D. Hecht, eds., *Sacred Texts of the World: A Universal Anthology* (New York: Crossroad, 1982), p. 182.

2. Sarvepalli Radhakrishnan and Charles A. Moore, eds., *A Sourcebook in Indian Philosophy* (Princeton, N.J.: Princeton University Press, 1957), p. 36.

3. Ainslie T. Embree, ed., *The Hindu Tradition* (New York: Random House, Vintage, 1972), pp. 60–61.

4. Ibid., p. 61.

5. Rudolf Otto, *Mysticism East and West* (New York: Macmillan, 1970), p. 19.

6. A.L. Basham, *The Wonder That Was India* (New York: Grove Press, 1959), pp. 320–21.

7. James M. Freeman, "The Ladies of Lord Krishna," in *Unspoken Worlds,* eds. Nancy A. Falk and Rita M. Gross (San Francisco: Harper & Row, Pub., 1980), pp. 56–57.

8. Juan Mascaro, trans., *The Bhagavad Gita* (Baltimore: Penguin, 1962), pp. 56–57.

9. Philip Kapleau, ed., *The Three Pillars of Zen* (Boston: Beacon Press, 1967), p. 205.

CHAPTER FIVE

China

ORIENTATION

China is the second world-historical culture that we are proposing was structured by a central reverence for the sage. But where India's traditional passion has been metaphysical and dictated by a desire to escape from the sufferings of samsara, China's traditional accent has been this-worldly. For example, *immortality* for the traditional Chinese has meant a long and vigorous life in the body, followed by the continuance of one's substance in numerous healthy offspring. Even when Buddhist notions of karma and rebirth came to color the Chinese religious synthesis, a here-and-nowness instructively different from the spiritualism of India made such notions discernibly East Asian.

Because the Chinese bent was practical and this-worldly rather than metaphysical and otherworldly, the "wisdom" of China focused more on order than on liberation. To be sure, Confucian and Taoist sages worked from deep spiritual experiences and sometimes spoke of flights of fancy and intellect and soul that challenge any narrowly empiricist worldview. When they reflect on the implications of the **Tao** ("Way"), whose movement gives the world its natural patterns, they enter upon realms of consciousness and reality alike that point to the outer limits of the cosmological myth. Yet even less than Shankara and the Indian Buddhist philosophers do the Chinese lovers of widsom let the no-thing-ness of ultimate reality (of what they might call "the Tao that cannot be named" or "suchness") lead them to a being or creative existence that has no essential relation to the cosmos. Their interest rather is the spiritual illumination of a path through

Standing Bodhisattva.
Chinese, twelfth century.
The Budda-to-be is
composed yet benevolent,
patiently postponing nirvana
to work for the liberation of
all creatures. *(The Nelson-Atkins
Museum of Art, Kansas City, Missouri
[Nelson Fund])*

given physical reality that will bring both individual and group to harmony and prosperity. In the final analysis, then, they are social ethicists rather than solitary metaphysicians. Because the world never can have too much wisdom about how to keep people from going to war and killing one another, the wisdom generated by traditional China continues to be highly relevant today.

CHINESE FOLK RELIGION

We postulated that India set the sage on a pedestal and consequently may be considered a *philosophical* civilization. The people who knew the solution to life's central problems of suffering and desire, such as the Buddha and Shankara, set the standard of human achievement. They might not have clarified noetic consciousness so radically as the Greeks nor fully broken with the cosmological myth, but they set the complex history of rituals and myths, popular devotions and huge kalpas for transmigration, in the ultimate perspective of atman and Brahman.

The situation is quite parallel for traditional China. While the vast majority of the (vast) population have been peasants who lived close to the earth and worshiped with a folk-religious mentality, the exemplar or model of human achievement has been the sage: the person who knew the Tao of the ancients that could bring harmony with nature and social prosperity. Confucius has been the paramount Chinese sage, and we shall consider his teachings and achievements shortly. Before doing so, however, it will be wise to sketch the Chinese version of the cosmological myth by which the majority have always lived.

In the earliest times of which we have records, the Shang dynasty (about 1751–1112 B.C.E.), life was organized on a tribal scale. The rise of the Chou dynasty in 1111 B.C.E. brought a shift to a more feudal social organization. Wing-Tsit Chan saw this first great social change as the basis for the *humanistic* stress that characterizes Chinese philosophy overall.

> If one word could characterize the entire history of Chinese philosophy, that word would be humanism—not the humanism the denies or slights a Supreme Power, but one that professes the unity of man and Heaven. In this sense, humanism has dominated Chinese thought since the dawn of history. Humanism was an outgrowth, not of speculation, but of historical and social change. The conquest of the Shang (1751–1112 B.C.) by the Chou in 1111 B.C. inaugurated a transition from tribal society to feudal. To consolidate the empire, the Chou challenged human ingenuity and ability, cultivated new trades and talents, and encouraged the development of experts from all levels of society. Prayers for rain were gradually replaced by irrigation. **Ti**, formerly the tribal Lord, became the God for all. Man and his activities were given greater importance. Humanism, in gradual ascendance, reached its climax in Confucius.[1]

This did not mean, however, that the common people lived in a fully humanistic, let alone modern secularized, world. Whereas the emperors were concerned to develop technological expertise, the people who lived close to nature continued not only to pray for rain but also to fear evil spirits, wear **amulets** to protect themselves, consult astrologers, set out food and gifts to placate ghosts, and perform many other rituals characteristic of folk religions everywhere. To the present day one can find diviners and **mediums** working the streets of Hong Kong. Throughout Chinese history the cultured sage has stood in tension with the village shaman or the local shrine to Kuan-yin, the Buddhist "Mother-Goddess."

The cosmological slant of traditional Chinese folk religion is especially manifest in such ancient practices as **geomancy** and such ancient beliefs as the polarity of **yang** and **yin**. Geomancy is concerned with the forces of the earth. Traditionally, it has gone by the Chinese name **feng-shui**. So, for example, one would always consult a practitioner of feng-shui before building one's house. Otherwise, one might not situate the house in the most propitious direction, so as to take advantage of the most helpful flow of the local spiritual forces. (One probably would also consult an astrologer to be sure the construction took place at the most favorable time.) The theory of yang and yin essentially held that all of reality is composed of two complementary elements. The degree to which each element is present determines much of the character and force of any thing, person, foodstuff, or whatever. Yang stands for the aspects of light, masculinity, and dryness. Yin stands for the aspects of darkness, femininity, and wetness. Theoretically these two elements were equally valuable or value free. In practice, the patriarchal structure of traditional Chinese society made yang the more desirable quality.

By the time that Buddhism had made a strong impression on China (from perhaps 300 C.E.), Buddhist notions of karma, **bodhisattvas**, meditation, selflessness, and the like had entered into the general religious mix. The common people often turned to Buddhist monks to conduct their funeral rites, probably because the Buddhist notions of karma and **transmigration** were more cogent than traditional Chinese views of death. The Chinese custom of venerating one's ancestors and keeping alive a strong sense of one's clan lineage could be fitted to the new Buddhist notions. Children came to be expected not only to mourn their parents elaborately (three years was the traditional period, during which at least the eldest son was supposed to withdraw from all business and normal social life) but also to send them money, food, and supplies (usually by burning paper equivalents) for their life in the hereafter.

The bodhisattva was a Mahayana Buddhist development. Early Indian Buddhism had spoken of the saint or **arhat** who was destined for enlightenment and represented Buddhist "success." Mahayana Buddhists found the arhat too self-contained. Their bodhisattva was a being equally destined for enlightenment, equally on the verge of nirvana, but so compassionate for the rest of suffering creation that he or she would postpone nirvana to labor for the deliverance of creation as a whole. Kuan-yin was the motherly figure who became the best-loved Chinese bodhisattva. In popular piety she often functioned as a goddess, receiving the people's petitions for help in time of sickness, childbirth, money troubles, and the like.

In traditional Chinese folk religion the world was densely populated with spirits. The recently deceased kept a shadowy existence near their old haunts. Eerie or striking places were thought to have their own good or evil spirits. The forces of rain, sunshine, grain, animals, birds, and the rest had a lively presence. The earth and the sky were comprehensive powers, to be reverenced and petitioned. Running throughout the cosmos was what the ancient sages (at this point the folk tradition linked up with the elitist tradition) called the "Way of Heaven." At one time heaven had been conceived of as the ancestor of the head of the ruling clan. In later times heaven became an impersonal force somewhere between *nature* and *fate*. The key notion, though, was that a Tao or Way made both heaven and earth (that is, the whole cosmos) somewhat intelligible. Human beings might never be able to grasp the full mystery of this Way, but they could gain sufficient sense of it to walk a behavioral path that would keep them in relative harmony with the cosmos.

We shall see more of this behavioral path in the next sections. Here the main point is the cosmic backdrop. When the Confucians spoke about ritual, or the Taoists spoke of meditative exercises, they presupposed the interaction of natural and social forces. The emperor's enactment of the spring rituals, for instance, was thought to have a marked effect on the fertility of the crops (and perhaps also of the people). At death a Taoist such as Chuang Tzu expected to return to "the Great Clod."

CONFUCIUS

The traditional dates for Confucius are 551–479 B.C.E. Thus he was a contemporary of the Buddha (536–476 B.C.E.). China reveres Confucius as the model sage, and most of his wisdom was concerned with social relationships. Confucius held the idea that the Tao that would bring political prosperity was the Way that directed nature. His great interest, however, was politics: how to make the people prosper through virtuous rule. His own life was an effort to learn and enact the teachings of the ancient rulers, whom both Confucius and tradition glorified as the heroes of a golden age. Thus we have the famous saying from the *Analects* (2:4):

> At fifteen I set my heart upon learning. At thirty, I had planted my feet firm upon the ground. At forty, I no longer suffered from perplexities. At fifty, I knew what were the biddings of T'ien [heaven]. At sixty, I heard them with docile ear. At seventy, I could follow the dictates of my own heart; for what I desired no longer overstepped the boundaries of right.[2]

The learning that Confucius esteemed was practical, traditional, and ritualistic. He was not interested in speculative matters, as we might now call them, so much as what the wise ancients had found to work. In part this was a question of human nature: How are people liable to act in given situations? In part it was a question of customs or traditional practices: How have "our" kind of people treated their elderly, greeted the spring, and so on. And in part this was ritualistic learning, because China, like many ancient cultures, thought that the proper performance of religious rituals was essential to the people's full health.

Confucius's ideal was what translators sometimes call the *gentleman*. This was a person of learning, refinement, experience, and discipline. Going to school to the past sages, the gentleman took to heart the traditional lore and ideally became a master of the customary rituals and etiquette. As a result, he (Confucian China gave little public influence to women) knew what to do in any circumstance that might arise, and he could offer judicious counsel to any ruler shrewd enough to consult him. Confucius himself wandered many years looking for a ruler who might put his theories into practice. He attracted a circle of disciples, who referred to him as the Master, and the *Analects* are somewhat secondhand records of the remarks Confucius made in discussion with his disciples.

The main virtues that Confucius stressed were goodness (**jen**) and ritual propriety (**li**). Ritual propriety, or decorum, or etiquette, involved knowing and gracefully doing what a stated occasion required. The rites entailed might be civic ceremonies for days of state, funeral ceremonies for a friend, or the simpler interactions between teacher and student, manor lord and serf. The gentleman strong in li was smooth in these matters, able to move through the social forms as though they had been tailored just for him. As a result, he contributed to the successful and helpful execution of the social interactions, large and small, on which his society depended. If society was to work well, it needed people who could embody its traditions and execute its customs persuasively and beautifully.

Ritual propriety therefore implied more than simply one's external behavior. Ideally, one would carry out the rituals, be they exceptional or humdrum, from the heart, with conviction and generosity. Nonetheless, rituals alone were but the outer casing of the Confucian ideal. Deeper, more interior, even more mystical was the goodness that Confucius set at the pinnacle of human development.

This goodness, or love, or humaneness—all three words are necessary to suggest the range of the Confucian jen—could not be programmed. Solid schooling in the tradition could set it up. Personal discipline and practice could pave the way. But it only came in rich, ideal measure when there occurred what Confucius says happened to him by the age of seventy. At that time, his own will and the dictates of the Tao (as tradition interpreted them) had come to coincide. He did not desire anything that the Way of Heaven forbade or frowned upon. So there was virtually no tension or conflict between what he wanted to do and what his public role required of him. He had so fitted himself to his people's customs, so grown into the role of teacher and gentleman, that everything seemed perfectly tailored.

Neither Confucius nor the other classical Chinese sages who solidified the high Chinese cultural ideals concerned themselves very much with **epistemology**. Consequently, one does not find in their records much discussion of how it is that human beings can know either the natural ways of the Tao or the dictates of traditional wisdom. It follows, therefore, that the noetic side of the Chinese achievement was relatively undeveloped, compared with the explorations in Greece or even India. The Chinese genius was practical organization and social relationships. The Confucians elaborated a hierarchical code, complete with rituals, that made it clear how one ought to treat both one's superiors and one's inferiors. For example, parents deserved great deference. For a child to disobey a parent was scandalous. Similarly, old people had more honor than young people, males than females, rulers than underlings. The eldest son had a special place in the family, with both more honors and more obligations. The other children were to respect his position and could in turn expect his aid. Rites for honoring the ancestors linked the present generation to the past, and the greatest boon was children, especially sons, who would carry on the clan line. So the Confucians carved out an impressive human order, but quite within the cosmological circuit.

LAO TZU

Confucius promoted what might be called the *anthropological factor*, meaning by this, human affairs. He and his followers, therefore, differentiated the compact cosmological culture that they had inherited. This differentiation did not focus sufficiently interiorly to clarify adequately the noetic and pneumatic domains, and it did not distinguish a precisely divine reality with rights independent of the cosmos, the social group, and the individual person. Nonetheless, the Confucians greatly enhanced the store of prudential wisdom about **homo politicus**, human nature insofar as it has to work out the immense variety of tasks that being social, living together cooperatively, imposes. After them tribal life seemed rude and terribly unsophisticated.

The Taoists strongly criticized the Confucian sophistication, arguing that it took humanity away from a rudeness or primitivism that was vigorous. For Lao Tzu, the legendary sage whose writing, the *Tao Te Ching*, became something of a scripture for both Taoists strictly so called and Chinese literary people generally, human nature is at its strongest when it is an "uncarved block." After we have whittled away its original solidity and glossed it over with social conventions, it is but a remnant of its pristine self. Thus Lao Tzu had his own version of a golden age, when giants lived as humanity was intended to live. He did not venerate the legendary rulers that Confucius quoted so much as the simple people of yore who were fully in tune with nature and themselves.

Another way in which Lao Tzu stands apart from Confucius is in his much more explicit preoccupation with the cosmic or natural Way that was China's best candidate for the localization of sacred power and order. The Tao that Lao Tzu venerated is the source of the 10,000 things, as he called them, that comprise the variety of creation. This source has a hidden side, much like the Brahman that is unmanifest. But it is sufficiently manifest that one can grow attuned to it, as though it were a music that played through the universe. Figures of speech abound, but the basic Taoist sense is that reality has a pattern or grain. Go with it, and your life will run smoothly. Go against it, and you will constantly suffer splinters and grief.

The Tao often appears in rather paradoxical form, as though it had to cry out for our attention or shake us awake. For example, it is the infant who has most power in a household and whose form of power most resembles the Tao. The apparent helplessness of the infant is deceptive, for it makes the whole household revolve around its needs. So, too, the water that wears away the rock and the female who indirectly maneuvers the male are better symbols of the Tao than their initially more prominent counterparts. Along the same paradoxical line, it is the emptiness that makes a house useful, not the walls that enclose the emptiness. It is the gnarled, ugly tree that survives to old age, not the attractive tree with the desirable grain.

In political matters, Lao Tzu's paradoxical approach can seem to verge on dishonest manipulation. So, for example, chapter 3 advises

> Do not exalt the worthy, so that the people shall not compete. Do not value rare treasures, so that the people shall not steal. Do not display objects of desire, that the people's hearts shall not be disturbed. Therefore in the government of the sage, he keeps their hearts vacuous, fills their bellies, weakens their ambitions, and strengthens their bones. He always causes his people to

be without knowledge (cunning) or desire, and the crafty to be afraid to act. By acting without action, all things will be in order.[3]

Lao Tzu was very conscious of the relative quality of the value judgments that can stir so much social activity. His ideal was a peaceful society where people can be content, feel solidly at home with nature and their tribe without a lot of strife. At the risk of cutting off invention and striving, he would have had all talk of goals, ideals, and competition cut back. At the risk of lessening appreciation of beauty, good craftsmanship, high quality, and the other things that make objects treasured, he would have diminished all talk of rareness to aim at a situation in which no one felt there was anything to covet. Better by far than a context in which people lusted for good things would be a context in which their hearts lay at peace. Better by far, to Lao Tzu's mind, than a state in which people boiled with ambitions or resentments or even ideals would be a simple state of physical sufficiency, robust good health. The ideal Taoist ruler would move the people away from the kind of cunning or craftiness that foments so much social unrest. Were it necessary to keep the peace, he would threaten such crafty people with dire consequences should they attempt disruptive actions.

The last lines of the chapter are perhaps the most important, for they are not only Lao Tzu's summary of how the sagacious ruler proceeds but also the tip-off to the cosmological basis for his political outlook. To act without action is almost a technical Taoist term (**wu-wei**). When one is attuned to the Tao, moving in the flow of the Tao, one acts effortlessly, more as a matter of responding to the initiative of the Tao (as presented by the coming together of natural or social forces) than of starting something on one's own. Things are in order when people do not push other people or natural things around. The touch that makes interactions go smoothly and profitably is gentle, indirect, dexterous. This is how Lao Tzu sees the Tao running the world. Little is overt, constrained, or forced. The violence of warfare and bullying, in contrast, is gross and ineffective. It is as though Lao Tzu could speak volumes on the dangers done by ham-handed rulers or interveners, who win battle after battle but lose the war for the people's hearts or the overall flourishing of nature.

The Taoists, like the Confucians, developed meditative regimes to help people enhance their connection with the Way. After the rise of Buddhism in China, such meditative regimes became almost commonplace, part of every cultured or well-educated person's set of resources. For the Taoists the general result was a powerful sense of the way that the Tao or the cosmic whole relativizes all human undertakings. As Chuang Tzu, the second most influential Taoist writer, often reflected, things simply move in the patterns of Tao and at the end of their appointed time return to the Great Clod, the earth that is the single matrix of us all. How silly we are, therefore, to lament at so natural a happening as death or to make much of social distinctions, which are so puny and short-lived compared to the natural whole. It is better to live simply, in contentment, than to chase after riches and honors and lose one's peace. It is best to love and enjoy Tao.

"Ink Bamboo" *Mo-chu*. Li K'an. Handscroll, Chinese. The bamboo just is, calming human turmoil by its unconscious perfection. *(The Nelson-Atkins Museum of Art, Kansas City, Missouri [Nelson Fund])*

THE ANALOGUE OF HEAVEN
AND BUDDHIST DEVELOPMENTS

Both the Confucians and the Taoists thought of political rule as an extension of the power of heaven. This rather vague, overarching force overlapped with Tao. Together, heaven and Tao supplied the sense of ultimate power, sanction, and order that a people needs to situate itself meaningfully in the world. The implications of this connection between the rule of human leaders and the direction or approval of the ultimate powers became clear when a dynasty lost "the mandate of heaven" and suffered ouster through revolution.

W.A.C.H. Dobson, a noted translator of Mencius, the second leading Confucian sage, has commented on the mandate of heaven as follows:

> The early Chou kings had appealed to a doctrine they called "receiving the Mandate of Heaven." The Mandate (**ming**) was a charge given to fief-holders. Heaven conferred its Mandate, so the Chous alleged, upon one designated by Heaven as its Son (**T'ien-tzu**). The Son of Heaven, as the viceroy of the deity upon earth, enfeoffed his subjects and vassals in their turn with "charges." This Mandate, it was further alleged, was not held in perpetuity, but upon lease. It was surrendered when the incumbent "lost virtue" and brought down upon his head "the punishment of Heaven." Such "punishment," the Chous

said, Heaven had charged them to bring down upon Shang, and Heaven, they averred, had placed thereafter the Mandate of Heaven in their hands.[4]

One sees, therefore, that imperial China bore considerable likeness to imperial Egypt and other cosmological regimes. The emperor, like the pharaoh, was the point of connection between heaven and earth. Moreover, somewhat the way that the pharaoh mediated maat to his subjects, the Chinese emperor was the conduit of **te**, the power by which nature and society alike moved along. One of Voegelin's few studies of Eastern societies focused on the way Chinese historians understood the passage of te from dynasty to dynasty. The pattern they discerned was cyclical, and they even tried to determine the regular length of time that the power, and so the Mandate of Heaven, could be expected to rest upon any group of rulers. The Confucians settled upon 500 years as the regular period, and Voegelin argued that this schema had as much to do with the periodizing of traditional Chinese history as the actual empirical facts of how long each dynasty flourished.[5]

We see Mencius struggling with this schema and somewhat indirectly revealing the high opinion that a Confucian sage could have of his potential benefit to a kingdom, in the famous text 2B.13.

> When Mencius left Ch'i, on the way Ch'ung Yu asked, "Master, you look somewhat unhappy. I heard from you the other day that a gentleman reproaches neither Heaven nor man." "This is one time; that was another time. Every five hundred years a true King should arise, and in the interval there should arise one from whom an age takes its name. From Chou to the present, it is over seven hundred years. The five hundred mark is passed; the time seems ripe. It must be that Heaven does not as yet wish to bring peace to the Empire. If it did, who is there in the present time other than myself? Why should I be unhappy?[6]

Classical Chinese political science therefore retained a distinctively cosmological flavor. Despite its penetrating analyses of both individual and group psychology, it held as its ideal a people moving smoothly to the rhythms of the natural cosmos. One of the strongest differences between the Western cultures that arose in the wake of Israelite revelation and Greek philosophy and the traditional Eastern cultures such as the Chinese was the Western move into a different sense of history. Generally, Chinese culture fitted human events—dynasties, fluctuations in political power, and the like—to the cyclical rhythms of the cosmos. It certainly made provision for a more linear movement of human developments, but the cycles of nature provided the comprehensive backdrop. The Western societies made the linear movement of human developments more central. They could never deny the cosmic backdrop, of course, but they could situate the meaning of time most crucially in free human events. Indeed, in modern times they could so concentrate on the human capacity to make history that they could neglect the cosmic rhythms to the extent of setting in motion forces of ecological devastation. We shall see more of these matters in the section on modernity, but the gross distinctions are worth noting here.

The Buddhists, who came to have great influence in later periods of Chinese history, for example, during the T'ang dynasty (618–907 C.E.), when North and South China were unified, generally exerted a humanizing influence. Their doctrines of compassion and nonviolence did not always prevent even Buddhist emperors from warfare, but they did serve as a brake. For Voegelin, the problem with the Buddha's own analysis of reality was that it leaped too quickly to the "divine void" behind the world. The Buddha perceived that the many infracosmic gods of the Hinduism of his time were not equal to the task of bringing human beings salvation. So he emptied the cosmos of these gods, so far as any genuine significance went, and concentrated on the experience of divine mystery that cannot be captured in cosmic symbols. This was a radical move, indeed, and it finally resulted in the powerful Buddhist symbolisms of nirvana and emptiness. But the Buddha did not have to factor in the cosmological empires, which demanded an acute analysis of the relations between divine, cosmic, and human political power. And he did not have to contend with the noetic and pneumatic breakthroughs of Israel and Greece, which demanded a considerable refinement of human consciousness and historical meaning. As a result, the Buddhist contributions, both in India and East Asia, did not greatly clarify the overall problem of understanding social order.

In China, Buddhism itself was changed because the Chinese insisted on molding it to their own cultural traditions. The most useful vocabulary that translators had available, when they wanted to render Buddhist philosophy into Chinese, came from the Taoists, so many interpreters see Chinese Buddhist thought as a fine blend of native Taoist ideas with Indian Mahayana notions. The general cultural difference between China and India boiled down to China's preference for the concrete, compared with India's preference for the abstract. This meant, for example, that Chinese Buddhists took physical nature more seriously than did Indian Buddhists. It led, as well, to such new Buddhist schools as Ch'an (which in Japan became Zen), which downplayed speculation or discursive thinking and stressed holistic regimes that fully engaged both mind and body.

JAPANESE VARIATIONS AND MAO TSE-TUNG

In the periods crucial to the formation of its historical culture, Japan greatly depended on China. The native Japanese tradition, which came to full expression as Shinto, was a naturalistic religion that stressed the great variety, indeed almost the omnipresence, of the **kami,** or sacred forces. Any striking tree, rock, lake, mountain, or the like would have its peculiar kami. Clans, imperial regalia, animals, and outstanding individuals all were apt to be shaped or empowered by kami. The Japanese love of natural beauty made the native tradition aesthetic as much as religious.

When Chinese culture gained prestige in Japan, Confucian social thought took hold. Before long, Japanese family life and politics became imprinted with a Confucian hierarchical design. Taoism influenced the Japanese philosophy of nature, and Buddhism greatly shaped Japanese conceptions of individual destiny and art. Most of the Chinese Buddhist schools developed Japanese equivalents, and in addition, Japanese masters created new schools of Buddhist thought precisely adapted to the Japanese character. Some of these schools were meditational. For example, the Japanese gave Ch'an a favorable reception and then worked out its implications for the warrior class (for instance, in swordsmanship and archery). The Japanese tea ceremony gained a Zen foundation, as did flower arrangement. Other Buddhist schools were more devotional and lay oriented. The followers of Shinran, for example, were taught that the Buddha's compassion is such that simply calling upon his name in faith can bring one salvation. In other devotional schools one chanted praise of the Lotus Sutra, a very important Indian Buddhist scripture, or one chanted greetings to Amida, the Buddha or Bodhisattva of light. Similarly, Kuan-yin, the Chinese Buddhist Mother Goddess, became Kannon, a parallel Japanese figure of mercy.

Throughout this adaptation of Chinese cultural imports, Japan retained its distinctive traditional emphases. From time to time a burst of patriotism or nativism would rouse resistance to all foreign cultural entities, and Shinto would gain both political and religious ascendency. From the sixteenth century on, Christian notions were part of the Japanese mixture, for, even after the missionaries were ejected, their Western views remained. The strongly Shinto core of Japanese culture meant, as one might suspect, the continuance of cosmological interests. The emperor was associated with Amaterasu, the sun goddess who reigned in earliest times, and the imperial shrine at Ise represented the Japanese conviction (quite reminiscent of Lao Tzu) that a simple, almost rough life close to nature was the most healthy and desirable. Thus the park at Ise is quite naturalistic, with trees and groves that are little pruned. The shrines have relatively little adornment, and one is supposed to walk mindful of the presence of the kami. Traditional Japanese culture had strong taboos about death and a passionate concern for cleanliness. These were somewhat transformed under Buddhist influence, insofar as the Buddhist priests or monks became the virtual custodians of funeral ceremonies, and Buddhist meditational exercises tended to make cleanliness a more interior notion.

For millennial Japan as much as millennial China, the cosmological myth held firm. Japan developed a marvelous art, strong family clans, great loyalty to the Shinto emperors, and other differentiations that took the people to a level quite above the other members of the cosmos. But the basic sense of time, prior to the most recent generations, was the rhythmic pulse of the cosmos. Buddhist views of karma and transmigration offered a religious philosophy that fit in with the cosmic cyclicism. The Japanese sense of ethnic solidarity under the emperor meant something approximating a cosmological culture living by the natural force that the emperor mediated.

Mao Tse-tung was the figure in whom China, and thereby all of East Asia, confronted the precisely modern mentality of Marxism and so had to come to grips with the traditional cosmo-mythology. Whereas the Japanese made rather ingenious accommodations, taking considerable amounts of

Western technology and political thought while trying to cling to the substance of their traditional Shinto aesthetic, the Chinese under Mao undertook the huge experiment of trying to adapt Marxism so as to bring China into the league of modern nations. Since Mao's death many of his theses have been rejected, but he remains the one who most decisively broke with the Confucian traditions and tried to root political change in the proletariat.

Critics of Mao have an easy task when it comes to pointing out his inconsistencies. His genius for mobilizing the will of the peasantry, for example, was not matched by a careful analysis of the technological skills that a modern economy needs. The swings in mood, accompanied by purges and bloodbaths, that dominated his later years were extreme to the point of mental imbalance, and the cult of Mao himself gave the lie to any pretensions that the new China would be a completely secular, this-worldly political entity.

Indeed, for some observers, Mao had a period when he embodied Chinese desires not just for renewed prestige in the world but also for new forms of an age-old sense of immortality. In the past the clan and the nation had stretched so far back in time, and could be expected to continue so far forward into the future, that physical immortality—the continuance of one's bodily substance, in some form—seemed guaranteed. Robert Jay Lifton, for instance, has analyzed Mao's extraordinary charismatic effectiveness in terms of his having come to represent "the life power of China" itself.

> It becomes clear that from the time of his youth Mao has felt himself deeply involved in a struggle to restore national pride—which over the years became nothing less than a heroic quest to reassert the life power of China. Hence, Mao came to associate communism with the timeless virtues of the peasant masses and of the Chinese earth. And his relentless pursuit of the thought reform process has been an effort to cement this association, especially within the minds of intellectuals. Mao once described his Communist movement as "passionately concerned with the fate of the Chinese nation, and moreover with its fate throughout all eternity." And one recalls Mao's ringing declaration, upon his victorious assumption of power in 1949, that China had "stood up" and would "never again be an insulted nation"—an expression of national resurgence which was as authentically Maoist as it was Chinese. **Rather than speak of Mao as a "father figure" or "mother figure" for his countrymen (no doubt he has been both), we do better to see him as a death-conquering hero who became the embodiment of Chinese immortality.**[7]

As much as India, therefore, East Asia developed the cosmological myth in impressive, often highly influential directions. Literally billions of people took their orientations to reality from this varied cosmological story, thinking that their small lives poured into a greater whole, whether that of the cosmos as a living natural organism, or that of the nation-clan. What few experienced was a clear sense of the freedom, intellectual and moral, to live by a measure or personal relationship that transcended the physical cosmos.

COUNTERVIEWS

Among the likely objectors to the reading of Chinese religious culture that we have offered, a quite pragmatic or empiricist group probably would immediately step forward to claim that our whole slant is inappropriate. In their view, China has traditionally been even more practical, this-worldly, political, ritualistic, and concerned with harmony than we have indicated, and this should simply be accepted or described as accurately as can be, without trying to fit it onto a prefabricated grid such as Voegelin's. The response, of course, would entail several distinctions.

First, if greater attention to the social determination of traditional Chinese religious culture would improve the accuracy of our description, by all means let such attention flourish. Second, the grid that we are developing from Eric Voegelin is not precisely "prefabricated," although spatial limitations sometimes leave the impression that it is. On his own turf—the more leisurely expanse of the four volumes of *Order and History*—Voegelin makes it plain whence he derives his view of human consciousness and why he thinks that this view is normative (applicable to all beings who have a reflective awareness like our own). As the best methodologist would require, his theory can point to definite origins or data (primarily the noetic and pneumatic experiences and clarifications suggested by classical Greek philosophy and biblical revelation) and definite reasons for the judgments it makes about other configurations of religious consciousness (for example, that of traditional Confucians or Taoists).

The point, then, is that our grid is not prefabricated, in the sense of fashioned arbitrarily. Moreover, we have no wish to do violence to any specimen that we are laying upon it. In the measure that people can point to definite texts or self-interpretations of Chinese or any other culture that we seem to bend out of shape, we certainly want to discuss this dissenting viewpoint with them. But the cavalier dismissal of Voegelin's (or any theoretician's) schemata, simply because they presume to make comparisons across cultural areas and even to make judgments based on a view of consciousness that they claim applies wherever human beings function, will not do. Too often one hears this sort of dismissal from specialists, whose very expertise has overly immersed them in a single area and so rendered them unable to see the forest of world historical human experience for their own beloved trees.

SUMMARY

We began our study of Chinese religious culture with folk religion, noting that, as in India, the common people lived more deeply immersed in the cosmic myth than did the sages who had the greatest cultural honor. Such traditional notions as feng-shui and yin-yang reflect a sense of consubstantiality with all other creatures. The Buddhist influences that later shaped Chinese culture added metaphysical depth and more personal focuses for prayer. Arching over the Chinese whole, however, was a "heaven" that kept reality in a relatively compact embrace.

Confucius and Lao Tzu are the two great sages who contributed the most to China's "humanistic" differentiations of the folk cosmo-mythology. Confucius embodied the gentlemanly ideal of ritualistic learning and inner goodness. In his view the main requisite for good politics was ethical integrity, and supporting this view was a little-expressed but nonetheless potent belief in the final powers of heaven. Lao Tzu stressed the Tao that runs through nature, meditating on its power to relativize most of one's spontaneous assumptions. For him the best life was simple and close to nature, and the best power came from wu-wei: not-doing. By linking the power of human wisdom with the Tao running the physical world, Lao Tzu kept his political astuteness in harmony with the cosmos.

The traditional Chinese doctrine of the Mandate of Heaven inserted the entire imperial system into the cyclical patterns of cosmic time. Voegelin has shown the importance of such cosmological thought to traditional Chinese historiography, and Mencius linked it with the Confucians' sense that they were the people who could bring a new, better age to flower. Chinese Buddhism, different from Indian Buddhism in preferring concreteness, brought many humanitarian reforms but finally did not radically alter the traditional cosmological patterns.

The Japanese variations on the Chinese pattern mainly derived from Shinto, the native Japanese tradition. The traditional Japanese love of beauty and association of the kami with natural and clan phenomena contributed to a distinctively aesthetic religion, whereas the Japanese domestication of Buddhism produced some distinguished new schools. Mao Tsetung was the great figure who forced all of East Asia to confront modern political thought, but in his complicated personality and teaching commentators such as Robert Jay Lifton have seen the continuance of many perennial Chinese themes, for example, physical immortality.

Last, we considered the objections to our view of Chinese culture that many a specialist might put forward, trying for the sort of balance that would open us to correction on matters of detail or emphasis without agreeing with the methodological attack that would deny the validity of any universalizing scheme such as Voegelin's.

STUDY QUESTIONS

1. In what sense has traditional Chinese philosophy been humanistic?
2. How might contemporary Western culture benefit from Confucian ritualism?
3. Why did Lao Tzu consider female action more like Tao than male action?
4. What is the significance of the Confucian expectation that a true king should arise every five hundred years?

5. What did traditional Japanese culture borrow from China?

NOTES

1. Wing-tsit Chan, *A Source Book in Chinese Philosophy* (Princeton: Princeton University Press, 1963), p. 3.
2. Sebastian de Grazia, ed., *Masters of Chinese Political Thought* (New York: Viking, 1973), p. 116.
3. Wing-tsit Chan, *The Way of Lao Tzu* (Indianapolis: Bobbs-Merrill, 1963), p. 103.
4. W.A.C.H. Dobson, trans., *Mencius* (Toronto: University of Toronto Press, 1963), p. xiv.
5. See Eric Voegelin, *Order and History, Vol. 4: The Ecumenic Age* (Baton Rouge: Louisiana State University Press, 1974), pp. 272–99.
6. D.C. Lau, trans., *Mencius* (Baltimore: Penguin, 1970), p. 94.
7. Robert Jay Lifton, *Revolutionary Immortality* (New York: Random House, Vintage, 1968), pp. 84–85.

CHAPTER SIX

Greece

ORIENTATION

In this chapter we focus on one of the two major sources for Voegelin's way of viewing order and history. By sifting through the classical Greek texts, Voegelin discovered or recovered the movements of the intellectual spirit that seemed to him the clearest delineations of the structure of human awareness. Because human (rational or reflective) awareness is the source of all culture, to think that one has found its self-constituting forms, its in-given or naturally generated patterns, is to think that one has found the key to how peoples all over the world have gone about constructing meaning (their sense of how the world hangs together and of what is truly valuable).

It is important to say here (because our focus in the expository sections themselves will be directed to the Greek noetic differentiation) that Voegelin didn't think that their intellectual advances made the Greeks better human beings than shamanic or Eastern philosophical peoples had been. It is also important to recall that the Greeks did not invent or create a new human consciousness. Rather, they "merely" differentiated or made more explicit what previously had been present in more compact form. Last, as we will make clear in the last five chapters of the book, Voegelin thought that the Greek noetic differentiation needed the complement of the biblical pneumatic differentiation before it could be considered a complete appreciation of human awareness, and he also found much to praise, as well as much to blame, in the cultural changes that distanced modernity from classical (Greek and biblical) Western culture.

THE HOMERIC WORLD

For Eric Voegelin, noetic differentiation was a phenomenon that we owe to classical Greece. Voegelin held that everywhere human beings enjoy or suffer essentially the same range of experiences. All must deal with nature, society, the self, and divinity. All participate in the remorseless flow of time. *History*, in the sense of remarkable, meaningful existence in time, derives from the clarifications, the differentiations, that particular individuals and groups achieve. The general movement, then, is from a more compact state of consciousness, in which the different participants in existence and the different dimensions of awareness are little appreciated, to a more differentiated state of consciousness that better gives a complex yet integrated reality its due. Precisely why given individuals (the Buddha, Jesus) or given cultures (Greek, Israelite) accomplish given differentiations is mysterious. Nonetheless, once a differentiating insight has come into history, it is the potential property of all human beings. In the case of the noetic differentiations that we owe to Greece, the clarifications of worldwide significance that were accomplished by the classical philosophers began with the earlier poets, the first of whom was Homer.

Homer is the figure to whom the Greeks traditionally ascribed their two great epics, the *Iliad* and the *Odyssey*. Certainly these poems were treasured because they preserved memories of the people's beginnings, including especially the long war with Troy. More than self-defining memories, however, were involved in the Homeric literature. The tales that Homer told became in effect mirrors in which the Greeks could study their traditions and culture. That Homer found this culture seriously flawed, indeed on the point of decline and ruin, made the singing of his poetry much more than entertainment.

For Voegelin, Homer's great interest was political order. From the mythical age of Achilles and Odysseus, when human beings were sufficiently larger than present life to make their actions like billboards shouting forth a moral message, Homer described situations that place the puzzling aspects of human nature in stark relief. The uncertainties of human conduct and the mysterious influences of divine forces led Homer to rivet his stories onto the interplay of mortal, passionate human beings and immortal, almost equally passionate divine forces. Essentially, the poet wanted to deny the common human tendency to blame the caprice of the gods for disasters that human beings' own follies have wrought.

In Voegelin's summary view,

> The primary concern of Homer is not a vindication of the gods but the interpretation which men put on their own misconduct. The tendency of his aetiological interest [his concern with the chain of causes] can, therefore, be circumscribed in the following theses: (1) Man is in the habit of making the

Cycladic Idol. Greek, about 3000–2500 B.C.E. The figure expresses the somewhat blank, unselfconscious concern with divine forces that preceded the Homeric anthropomorphism. *(The Nelson-Atkins Museum of Art, Kansas City, Missouri [Nelson Fund])*

gods responsible for his misdeeds, as well as for the evil consequences engendered by his misconduct. (2) Theoretically, this habit implies the assertion that the gods are the cause of the evil which men do and suffer. This assertion is wrong. It is man, not the gods, who are responsible for evil. (3) Practically, this habit is dangerous to social order. Misdeeds will be committed more easily if responsibility can be shifted to the gods. (4) Historically, a civilizational order is in decline and will perish, if this habit finds general social acceptance.[1]

At this point, we are focusing on a nest of problems that would have been quite congenial to Confucius. The principal question troubling Homer was why human passions so frequently are allowed to erupt irrationally and cause great social suffering. The Homeric world differed from the Confucian world (Homer, at least as written down, precedes Confucius by about two hundred years: 750–551 B.C.E.) in that the Homeric deities were forces much more personified than those in Confucius's writings. Nonetheless, the search for inner order, a balanced and rational human spirit, is parallel in both cases. Later, Plato would enunciate the basic political principle that the polis or city-state is but the individual psyche writ large. Confucius agreed, insofar as his struggle was to find a prince who would enact the wisdom of the ancients as that wisdom resided in the soul of a sage such as Confucius himself. The Greek advantage, if such we may call it, probably relates to the more human (**anthropomorphic**) depiction of divinity that Homer could employ. In Greece it was easier to search the human psyche for the dimension that seemed called or oriented to an ordering communion with the gods and to make that dimension the crux of the peace necessary for social justice.

> Homer astutely observed that the disorder of a society was a disorder in the soul of its component members, and especially in the soul of the ruling class. The symptoms of the disease were magnificently described by the great poet; but the true genius of the great thinker revealed itself in the creation of a tentative psychology without the aid of an adequate conceptual apparatus. Without having a term for it, he envisaged man as having a psyche with an internal organization through a center of passion and a second center of ordering and judging knowledge. He understood the tension between the two centers, as well as the tricks which passion plays on better knowledge. And he strove valiantly for the insight that ordering action is action in conformance with transcendent, divine order, while disruptive action is a fall from the divine order into the specifically human disorder.[2]

Voegelin set out this interpretation in light of the later developments in Greek political thought, above all the insights of Plato. We shall deal with these more fully later. Here the topic is the beginnings of the Greek movement from mythology to logic. *Mythology*, in our current meaning, is a traditional, storied way of talking about the world and teaching people how to orient themselves. *Logic*, for our present purposes, is something more analytical. The Greeks were the ones who developed analytical intelligence to the extent that they could quite dispassionately break problems down into their component parts and work through their implications. Indeed, by the time Aristotle developed the syllogism to articulate and discipline logical reasoning, the Greeks had advanced their intellectual control from dispassionate common sense to the threshold of science.

Homer certainly was still working with his people's storied traditions, but Voegelin saw in the *Iliad* and the *Odyssey* the clear beginnings of the Greek discovery of the human mind, or rational spirit. This was a discovery, a making plain of something that had been at work everywhere but nowhere else was understood with sufficient clarity to let it transform human beings' self-understanding. The particular points most important for our purposes are the purification of divinity that Homer launched and his gropings after the transcendent orientation of humanity's "ordering and judging knowledge." It took some time for this purified appreciation of divinity to penetrate Greek philosophy, but when it had, the gods clearly stood as far from human beings in their morality as in their being. Because the gods were deathless, immortal in their being, they had long been considered quite beyond mere humans. Now Homer was denying that the gods, whom the old stories certainly portrayed as capricious, were responsible for human moral disorders. Rather, human passions had to come under the control of a reason that aimed at genuine goodness. Implicitly, this said that the gods themselves had to be good. It also said that the crux of good social order was forming a people oriented toward transcendent divinity, dominated not by unruly passions for temporary advantage but by the stable goodness of the best holiness and creativity the world could suggest.

THE PRE-SOCRATICS

Between Homer and Plato a number of Greek thinkers advanced Homer's beginning analysis of human interiority, of the relation between the center of passion and the center of ordering and judging knowledge. The trage-dians Aeschylus, Sophocles, and Euripides, for example, dramatized the interior search for justice. And the natural philosophers who sought the **logos** or rationality of the physical world certainly made a great contribu-tion. It is these forerunners of Socrates and Plato that Hans-Georg Gadamer had in mind when he wrote of the "whole way of human civiliza-tion" that opened in the seventh and sixth centuries before Christ. To his mind, the decisive move of the Pre-Socratics was from mythology to cos-mology (in the sense of a rational investigation of the physical world).

> I will begin with a short description of the role of this movement, which began in the seventh and sixth centuries before Christ, and which undeniably opened the whole way of human civilization down to today. One can debate about the wealth and the depth of many other great cultures of the past, but until this culture no culture in the Western world really covered the whole globe with its achievements and with its impoverishments. And so a question which really should be asked is, what is this way of investigation which so much changed the surface of our globe and of our soul? To give a formal indication, what the first thinkers of Greece did was obviously to replace mythology by cosmology. This is what we see in all the documentation of this early history, and it fulfills in a way the formulation which we know from Aristotle—the distinction between mythikos and apodeiktikos, where apodeiktikos obviously does not mean demonstration in the technical sense of Aristotelian logic, but the more natural meaning of demonstrating by point-ing to something which proves what we are saying, in opposition to mythikos, which itself is defined by being nothing else than the tradition: narration, repetition, and transmission of narratives—the only valid definition of myth.[3]

We may say, then, that the Pre-Socratics advanced the Greek inquiry into the nature of the human mind, or the Greek discovery of the nature of the human mind, by asking for a demonstration, a proof, that was more persuasive than the simple repetition of traditional stories. When this inquiry into rational grounds developed momentum, the Pre-Socratics found themselves trying to understand what reason or mind is in itself. Parmenides, for example, studied the part of consciousness that can ascend to the vision of being—the light of Isness—that he himself had experi-enced. He called this part *nous* (mind), and he called the human ability to analyze the content of our vision of being *logos* (reason). For Parmenides, the great insight was the connection between mind and being. In the light of understanding, for something to exist and for it to be known were one and the same. At this point we may recall the Buddhist conviction that all reality is intrinsically enlightened or possessed of a buddha-nature (knowledge-nature).

Parmenides himself was especially concerned with the ultimate foundation of all existence, what Voegelin called the divine "ground." Other Pre-Socratics concentrated more on the intelligible structure of reality, not so much on the mysterious font of being as on the forms or patterns one can discern in both the cosmos and the human mind. Anaxagoras, for example, decided that nous was what gave the cosmos intelligibility, what made it capable of being understood. The Pre-Socratics kept working at this cluster of problems about the relationship between mind and reality, and the clarifications they achieved, especially their skill at delineating the forms or structures (for example, mathematical ratios) that made at least aspects of the material world intelligible, took them beyond the Eastern cosmological developments.

The combination of keeping close contact with empirical investigations (those informed by data received through the senses) and attending to the movements of the human spirit to transcend the empirical and reach out to the divine ground made Pre-Socratics such as Heraclitus powerful probers of human consciousness. So, for example, in fragments B 54 and B 55, Heraclitus made a twofold affirmation. On the one hand, he most prized the invisible harmony that the mind, the more-than-sensible human spirit, alone can find in the world. In other words, Heraclitus found humanity's greatest gift to be the reason that can discern a logic or intelligibility in nature or human events. On the other hand, Heraclitus did not want to downgrade what came to him through the senses. That too is highly valuable, although not so valuable, finally, as human reason. The distinction between these two realms of interior experience, sensation and intellection, already shows a considerable sophistication. To differentiate what comes from the mind and what comes from the senses is no mean accomplishment. Later Aristotle would correlate these two aspects of human understanding, showing how insight—the act of understanding—is precisely grasping the form or pattern of something (the structure that explains it to the mind) in the sense data of that thing, as memory and imagination have made such data **immanent** (present to or within the knower).

The search of the Pre-Socratics such as Heraclitus was not, however, an arid, scientifically detached affair. However much they wanted to gain a deeper understanding of the rationality of the human knower and the reasonableness of what is to be known (nature and human affairs alike), they were not unexcited by this problem. Indeed, they felt the problem took them into the heart of what it meant to be human and that their discoveries were preparing a new era of civilization. We must remember that writing was a relatively recent phenomenon and that most of human culture remained both traditional and mythic. Shamans and interiorly directed mystics had long explored human consciousness, but the Pre-Socratics were going about it in a disciplined way, guided by their central intuition that the luminosity of being and the light of the human mind held the key to human beings' position in the universe.

The passion and ultimate significance of the Pre-Socratic quest comes through in Heraclitus's discussion of faith and hope. Without the proper sort of commitment, trust, or positive anticipation, one will not find the disclosures of the invisible truth that are possible (the revelations of the divinity that is present to the world in the luminosity of being). The sense Heraclitus suggests is that one is involved in a search, a quest, a movement, and that only by submitting oneself to it with the proper dispositions will one advance in depth or clarity. The peculiar quality of this search is that one's own being or self is both the passenger and the ship, both the crafts-person trying to uncover the beautiful form and the tools the craftsperson must use. The Greek genius was to attend to the precisely noetic, intellectual conditions, structures, and aspects of the luminosity, but these pioneer explorers of the human mind never forgot the moral and mystical sides. The person disturbed by passion would never integrate the intellectual light properly with the rest of the personality, nor with the social life of the community at large. The person unaware of how the logical dimension of the light related to the more comprehensive mystical dimension similarly would miss the point of balance. Plato later would describe the whole rich, complicated field of human consciousness that was trying to move toward greater clarity as a *metaxy* (an in-between). Principally, human awareness is that we exist between physical nature and the divine, between the many of the cosmos and the one of the First Principle or Ground. We are both finite and infinite, both flawed and good, both mortal and immortal, both darkness and light. We exist between time and eternity, between earth and heaven.

PLATO

The genius in whom the Greek search for the nature of mind came to successful fruition was Plato. He is Voegelin's greatest hero, the man who both explored the height and depth of consciousness and kept proper balance between myth and logic. With his forerunner Socrates and his successor Aristotle, Plato forms the apex of classical Greek philosophy. After this trio, the noetic differentiation, the leap in being that showed the structure of precisely human life to be a movement toward and a drawing by the divine ground of reality, was well secured.

As with Homer, Plato's main interest was political order. The *Republic* and the *Laws* are by far his longest and fullest works. Yet Plato realized that the love of wisdom knows no artificial boundaries. To delineate the requirements of good social life he had to deal with questions of nature, knowledge, the gods, and much more. Above all, he had to deal with the human psyche or soul, the structures of human awareness, understanding, wanting, love, and happiness. The form Plato chose for his explorations of these matters was the dialogue, or conversation. Regularly his artistic style is to place Socrates or some other representative of the genuine love of

Herakles. Greek, 480–459 B.C.E. The classical Greek philosophers both feared and admired the power myths about heroes like Herakles had in popular consciousness. *(The Nelson-Atkins Museum of Art, Kansas City, Missouri [Nelson Fund])*

wisdom in conversation with people who think they know a great deal but actually have little solid understanding. Socrates, in contrast, is mainly aware of how little he knows. His great distinction, in fact, is to know that he does not know and to realize that the direction of his desire to know holds the key to his human condition. For if we can know that we don't know something, and then know when we have come to the insight that does give us knowledge, we must have in us the criteria of truth, some inbuilt system that is self-correcting and self-validating.

This was a decisive advance over the poets and Pre-Socratics, because Plato and Aristotle more clearly focused on the structures of the human soul, as the movement of consciousness through questioning after the divine ground of being revealed those structures. As Voegelin has put it,

> The more compact symbols of the myth or of the pre-Socratics cannot remain unchallenged once the empirical source from which the symbols derived their validity is recognized to be the experiential processes of the psyche. The man who asks questions, and the divine ground about which the questions are asked, will merge in the experience of questioning as a divine-human encounter and reemerge as the participants in the encounter that has the luminosity and structure of consciousness. In the Platonic-Aristotelian experience, the questioning unrest carries the assuaging answer within itself inasmuch as man is moved to his search of the ground by the divine ground of which he is in search.[4]

This is not easy language, and the experiences to which it refers, like the yogic experiences we noted earlier, tend to fall outside the attention of most modern Westerners. First, there is a historical observation. Voegelin interpreted Plato and Aristotle as self-consciously distancing themselves from their predecessors, the poets and the Pre-Socratics. They knew that their approach to reality was different and the reason was their focus on the processes of their own souls, which they had not only experienced but taken in hand. For Plato and Aristotle, it was clear that the myths, symbols, and pictures of reality that prior thinkers, or even Greek culture as a whole, had lived by came from the soul. It was to the soul, the vital principle that organized human life and coordinated its vegetative, animal, and intellectual dimensions, that one therefore should attend if one wanted to grasp the structure and range of reality.

Second, the key feature of the psychic processes was questioning, the purposeful wonder that both Plato and Aristotle diagnosed as the dynamic source of the love of wisdom. The goal of human questioning, if one burrows into it deeply enough, is the divine ground, the first cause or reason that might "explain" reality as a whole. Nothing less than this will satisfy the profound human inquirer, will quiet the restlessness of the authentic questioner. But, curiously enough, close examination of the questioning pursuit of the divine ground shows that it is not a one-way street. True enough, the human inquirer is active, restless, searching. But we are also drawn, lured, guided. Reality, as it were, sends out beeps or latches onto us with grappling hooks. Blaise Pascal would say almost two thousand years after Plato that we would not seek God had God not already found us. Thus any thorough description of human questioning, human searching for meaning and order, makes it plain that reality takes on the character of a deepening mystery, a partner or even a lover who beguiles us more and more. Mystery, it soon becomes clear, is the best name for "reality," and mystery does not mean the absence of light or intelligibility but the surplus or excess. The reason our intellectual quest is ongoing is that, for every insight we gain, every problem we solve, a dozen more questions and problems arise. It is wheels within wheels, boxes within boxes. But we are more encouraged than discouraged by this ongoing revelation, because the advance of the light is intrinsically satisfying. Somehow we know that we have been made precisely to sail on this voyage. We are doing exactly that for which we have been fashioned. (This is so true that the Christian theologians who developed this classical philosophical tradition would later define heaven as the ever ongoing "beatific vision" of God. Even in heaven God would remain a mystery, overspilling the limited human capacity yet filling the saints with delight.)

Plato analyzed and described the different movements of the human soul with masterly finesse. The basic structure that he discerned was the metaxy or in-between that we mentioned earlier. The range of human knowledge is from the material basis of creation below to the unity of the divine source above. Human intelligence cannot go beyond this range. Moreover, human knowing always takes place as a process that deals with other realities—nature, society, the divine—to which the knower is bound relationally. There is no way to jump outside of this situation, no way, for example, to deal with nature as though we were not immersed in it or to deal with other people as though we did not have an impact on them and they on us. If we try to prescind from our relationality—a somewhat barbaric but presently necessary word—we falsify the actual situation. Then, dealing with that to which we are related as though either it or we existed independently, we misconceive it and go on to act erroneously. For example, when we detach divinity from the relationship we have to it in the movement of our questioning and its drawing, we start to discourse on "God" as though God were a thing or person unconnected to us. At the worst extreme, we treat God like a product in a market, thinking we can turn over the divine attributes, examine the divine commands, measure divinity and decide to buy or pass on.

The truth, of course, is both humbler and much more encouraging. As the classical Greek philosophers made obvious, the divine is present to our spiritual light, giving our deepest selves their most satisfying orientation. Far more real and more significant than any propositions about God, whether in support or denial, are the experiences of following the light, opening out to the transcendent realm, that constitute the human spirit in its uniqueness and best explain its ever-expanding universe. It is this light that keeps scientists pushing back the frontiers of knowledge, keeps artists trying to express beauty in material forms, keeps saints pursuing greater purity and love. It is this light that can, as the political poets sometimes avow, keep people free even when they are in chains and can cow mighty dictatorships. One word of truth, the Russian dissident Aleksandr Solzhenitsyn said in his Nobel Laureate address, can conquer tyranny. In Platonic terms, back at the beginning of the cultural revolution that spotlighted the paramount importance and central structure of the human spirit, the light that lures us is our crux.

ARISTOTLE AND PHILOSOPHY

Aristotle accepted most of the Platonic program but contributed a more empirical bent. Whereas Plato was the genius who discerned the movement of the human soul toward the divine ground or "idea" of the Good, and who fashioned brilliant myths in which to express the complexity and wholeness of human existence in the metaxy, Aristotle was the genius who stayed closer to earth, insisted on the intrinsic contribution of sense data, and focused more clearly on the structures of the soul. Plato, we might say, was the philosopher-poet. Aristotle was the philosopher-scientist. Each had his distinctive assets and liabilities.

Aristotle's assets included his movement away from the basic analogy of seeing, in which understanding was like physically taking a look, to the precisely spiritual processes of grasping intelligibility in matter and expressing it in an inner word. This word was either a concept or a judgment, depending on whether the understanding was direct or reflective, was concerned with *what* something was or with *whether* what one had said of something was true. Aristotle also made a fuller provision for induction, deduction, and logic generally, and his expositions were more precise because of their abstraction and clearer definition of terms. Although Aristotelian natural science was considerably different from natural science as carried out since modernity, the modern scientific method is historically inconceivable without Aristotelian rationalism.

Aristotle's liabilities included the same abstraction that could be an asset and his lesser sensitivity to the divine mystery that finally grounded all the dynamics of human knowing. By focusing so closely on the forms of things, the intelligible structures of individual entities, Aristotle somewhat neglected the luminosity of knowing as a whole and the mystery of being. Aristotle, we might say, was more concerned with what things are than with the primordial fact that things are. He did not deny this primordial fact, but his wonder about it was less than Plato's. In popular contrast, Aristotle sometimes is said to have taken the Platonic "ideas" or "forms" and brought them down to earth, inserting them in material beings as the souls or **entelechies** ("first, formative acts") that give things their actual designs. This is an acceptable description, so long as it admits that Aristotle, like Plato, knew very well the dynamic thrusts of the human mind toward a realm of intelligibility (a "heaven" where the ideas or intelligible aspects of even material things might be pictured as existing), and that Plato was well aware that the ideas he was stressing gave shape and meaning to the ordinary world that sense-bound human beings dwell in.

At any rate, Aristotle was as interested as Plato and Homer in the problems of political science (the problems of how to govern people or order social life). Voegelin saw his great contribution in terms of practical wisdom, **phronesis**. Aristotle realized very well that politics is a prudential science, a matter of knowing what to do in concrete circumstances that are always varying and can never be completely adequately subsumed under general principles. To fashion a contemporary example: For all the benefit one might get from studying the history and nature of dictatorship, in the actual order of world affairs one has to interpret Latin American regimes as distinct from African or Middle Eastern regimes. Indeed, one has to deal with Country A as it is today, which may be quite different from what it was as recently as three months ago. Politicians therefore especially need the sense of prudence or practical intelligence that bridges the gap between general knowledge about human nature, economic laws, past historical patterns and the rest, and what is occurring here and now, the decisions that have to be made today.

The master of political science, Aristotle finally realized, is the mature person, the **spoudaios**, who has experience, understanding, and virtue. Clearly enough, such a mature person can be little different from the philosopher, the lover of wisdom whose soul is attuned to the divine measure. From such an attunement the philosopher can discern the reasonableness, or logos, of reality, articulating it sufficiently to provide policies for government.

Voegelin has summarized this Aristotelian contribution to political science as follows:

The reality of habituation and conduct in a society [how people tend to act] has prudential structure, and a prudential science can be developed as the articulation of the logos in reality. From this fundamental insight, then, follow the corollaries. The analysis of excellences [the virtues to which human beings should aspire and on which good social, common life depends] can be conducted only by men who know the material which they analyze; and a man can know the excellences only if he possesses them. Moreover, its results can be understood as true only by men who can verify them by the excellences which they possess, that is, by mature men—or at least by men who are sufficiently advanced in formation of character themselves to understand the problem. As a consequence, if we may adapt a famous formula, ethics is a science of mature people, by mature people, for mature people. It can arise only in a highly civilized society as its self-interpretation; or, more precisely, in that stratum of a civilized society in which the excellences are cultivated and debated. From such a social environment the analytical consciousness of the virtues can flower; and this consciousness, in its turn, may become an important factor in the education of the young.[5]

We see in this quotation, which is certainly an agreement with the Aristotelian analysis as well as an exposition of it, both the power of the classical achievement and its limitations. We might have taken another realm, such as natural science, but certainly the political realm is appropriate, for Plato and Aristotle rank among the most influential political philosophers who ever lived. The power of their achievement is its profound realization that what human beings are, both in the sense of their given material-spiritual structures and in the sense of their current state of virtue or maturity, is absolutely crucial to the determination of what they can accomplish or be together politically. Bad people cannot fashion a good state; ignorant people cannot make wise decisions. Because the classical Greek philosophers backed these perhaps commonplace observations with full, rich, detailed analyses of what *bad* and *ignorant, good* and *wise* mean, both in terms of their psychological origins and in terms of the constitution of reality as a whole, they left a lasting legacy. Since them it has not been possible to think of good government, of a flourishing common life, without placing among its most significant conditions wise and good leaders, people who know what is important and are virtuous enough to spend themselves trying to attain it.

The limits of the classical achievement include its relative neglect of economic factors and its elitism. Because of their limited political unit, the city-state, the classical thinkers had nothing like the complexity of modern nation states or contemporary global systems facing them. Moreover, they were willing to write off, in effect, huge parts of the population: women, slaves, people for whatever reason incapable of the "excellences" so central to Voegelin's analysis. Their creation of philosophy, a love of wisdom that would form human personalities by reference to the divine ground that lures us, was an achievement of truly awesome and historic proportions. It changed humanity's self-conception in the West and now is part of the heritage of the entire globe. But their analysis was partial, and their solution to the problem of how to make both leaders and ordinary citizens

virtuous enough to allow for a good social life seems in retrospect inadequate. Both of these factors will occupy us considerably in the last five
chapters of this book.

THEOLOGY, SCIENCE, AND POLITICS

The Greeks virtually created the major categories in which the later Western world did its theological, scientific, and political thinking. To be sure,
biblical revelation furnished much of the content of later Western theology, but the speculative forms were mainly Greek. After modernity, science was more empirical and statistical, leaving behind the Greek ideal of
necessity, but the quest for rational grounds, testable arguments, and the
rest that remained central to modern scientific method came from the
Greeks. Politics, and social thought generally, later became more historical,
abandoning the classical notion of a uniform set of cultural ideals that
would apply at all times and places, but much in the Greek notions of
maturity, the virtues, the types of personalities, and the like continued to be
valuable. Modernity, then, meant closer concern with empirical detail and
temporal change, as well as a fuller realization, through global exploration,
that human cultures have been very diverse. Despite these differences
from the classical cultural ideals developed by the Greeks, modernity did
not mean abandoning the Greek conviction that rationality—nous, logos,
and the rest—were crucial.
    Theology, as the Greek noetic differentiation displayed it, was vir-
tually identical with metaphysics. For Aristotle, divinity appeared as the
first cause in the chain of being, in the set of explanations for why the world
is as it is. Divinity also appeared as the final cause, the good that is luring
the whole train of explanations forward. But this divinity was impersonal, a
"mover" that was itself unmoved and in need of nothing else to explain it.
The contemplative life that Aristotle set at the summit of Greek culture
consisted of considering the structures of the world, above all the metaphysical structures of matter, form, and being. Thus the contemplative life
frequently led one to focus on divinity, which one was to regard as the
dispassionate, necessary, constant reality upon which the world depends.
Lacking a modern sense of history, in which a linear movement forward
predominates, the Greeks thought of time as circular, endlessly recurring.
They speculated that the circle was indeed the most perfect of forms, and
they conceived of the physical world as a series of spheres, the planets and
stars moving in orbits superior to the earth in dignity. Theology therefore
also had a cosmological orientation. The noetic differentiation that clarified the metaxic, or in-between, structure of human consciousness did not
mean abandoning the appreciations of the older cosmological myths. The
world remained quite alive and venerable, as Plato's famous dialogue the
Timaeus shows (this dialogue was very influential even in the Christian
patristic age).
    Greek theology was also influenced by the mystery religions and cults
that greatly preoccupied many of the intellectuals. In later Hellenistic

times, after the conquests of Alexander had brought greater contact with Egyptian and Near Eastern religions, Greek theology was rather **syncretistic**. At the time of Plato and Aristotle the mysteries of Orpheus, Dionysius, and Eleusis (the first two are personalities, the third is a place) placed immortality, "enthusiasm" (being filled with divinity), and visionary experiences in the forefront. Overall, they helped to make philosophy a way of life, and they balanced the somewhat abstract theology founded in metaphysics with a need to take spiritual raptures and experiences of the gods quite seriously.

The common people in Greece were like the common people in most other places. Their religion was close to the earth and myth. Greece never developed a national priesthood, so ritualism and priestly theology never played the imperial role they did in Egypt or the Near East. For the people most responsible for the noetic differentiation, theology and science remained quite closely connected. Indeed, it was modernity, once again, that brought a new set of differentiations that more clearly distinguished science, theology, and philosophy. Because the Greek rationalist ideal was explanation through necessary cause, the study of physics, or the material world, was little different from the study of metaphysics, the world of ultimate causes or being. Thus Plato was greatly interested in mathematics (which he probably considered closer to metaphysics than physics), and Aristotle wrote treatises on the movements of the planets and the generation of animals. "Science" in the classical period was any knowledge that got to the invariant causes of things. This was true, reliable knowledge (**episteme**), in contrast with mere opinion (**doxa**).

In retrospect, we might say that the Greek noetic differentiation stressed, perhaps even overstressed, the contribution that the mind makes to knowledge. It did not deny the contribution of experience generated by the world (some schools actually emphasized this), but the discovery of the movement of the rational spirit toward the ground of being, and of the structure of consciousness revealed by attention to this movement, was such an epochal breakthrough that it got most of the attention. In contrast with other **idealistic** philosophies, such as Indian Vedanta, the Greek superiority lay in its articulation of the limits or borders of human light (the in-between definition). For Plato, for example, the divine ground became technically the transcosmic and transmental "beyond" that gave the human realm its boundary. No other culture's exploration of human mentality achieved the balance and precision of this classical Greek exploration of the mind. The pneumatic differentiation that we shall study in the next section complemented the Greek noetic discoveries, but in contrast with Greek rational control, the biblical revelations seem confused and somewhat unstable. Such phenomena as **apocalyptic**, in which one risks losing solid hold on the metaxy, could easily result.

Last, the political wisdom associated with the Greek noetic breakthrough seems similarly balanced. Granted the qualifications we placed above, the psychological approach, in which the polis is taken as the human psyche writ large, has much to commend it. Virtue alone, to be sure, is no formula for good government. It was not adequate even in the time of

Plato and Aristotle, and since then politics has grown immensely more complicated. But many political problems do turn out not to admit of technological solutions, and virtue or ethics then steps forth to remind us of a deeper bottom line. A people cannot flourish by bread alone, to put it in biblical language. Whereas the biblical prophets cry out for justice, for conversion of heart that stops profiteering and oppression, the classical Greeks cry out for education. The prophets think in terms of sin: aversion of the will from the commands of the holy God. The philosophers think in terms of ignorance: the darkness of mind and soul that is human beings' peculiar and somewhat culpable ruin.

Education, it therefore turns out, is quite political. In the Platonic scheme of things, the deepest warfare is between the sophists and the genuine philosophers. True enough, there are movements afoot today to rehabilitate the sophists, and no doubt they have much merit. But the positions depicted in the Platonic dialogues, even if they present straw men, represent an omnipresent danger. Whereas the genuine lovers of wisdom seek the divine measure revealed in the movement of the human spirit toward the divine ground, the sophists of the Platonic dialogues make human beings the crucial measure. Of course, the formula "man is the measure" admits of an acceptable meaning. The Christian father Irenaeus, for example, shouted that "God's glory is human beings fully alive," and Confucian humanism was both sober and virtuous. But the sophistry that makes either current public opinion, or the language that flatters and persuades, the centerpiece of education disserves all the parties involved. Only when the next generation is offered solid schooling in the metaxic structure of human consciousness and the virtuous requirements of politics that accords with how things really are can individuals be brought to full mental health and societies gain the most crucial goods of peace and cultural prosperity.

COUNTERVIEWS

Many interpreters of Plato or of classical Greek culture in general will not be happy with all or even most of Voegelin's analyses, because they will not have followed or agreed with his judgment that the crux or great achievement was the delineation of human consciousness as a metaxic in-between. The only way finally to settle such a dispute is to point to the texts of Plato and Aristotle that Voegelin depended upon and let the disputants argue out their different intepretations.

We have indicated some of the liabilities or deficiencies in the Greek cultural achievement, and a second group of interpreters, leaning more heavily on these than Voegelin, would conclude that we today are fortunate indeed to have the classical Greek era two thousand years behind us. For example, interpreters who would make the subjugation of women or slaves so central an evil that it would completely discredit a culture or thinker would have little use for classical Greece or Plato. Scientists who would think that the classical ideals of knowledge stood in the way of modern progress in physics, astronomy, biology, mathematics, and chemistry could weigh in with similarly negative judgments. Finally, monotheists who would find offensive either the mythological portions of Greek religion or the abstraction of the Aristotelian deity might well write off Voegelin's enthusiasm as misguided: Why spend such praise on paganism?

Any of these counterviews, if properly developed, would demand of Voegelin a considered response. In most cases he in fact sowed at least the seeds of an acknowledgment of the justice there could be in such objections. What he would ask of those who disagree with his high evaluation of Plato, though, is a reconsideration of the Platonic balance and politics. In a time when the disorder of the world shouts that most of the world's leaders and people alike have disordered souls, the love of wisdom that Plato and Aristotle so wonderfully illuminated should not be discarded without a long and sympathetic study.

SUMMARY

Greece represents the epochal noetic achievement. The Homeric world, as Voegelin interpreted it, made the first moves away from a mythic mentality. Concentrating on ethics and the problems of social order, Homer diagnosed the paramount problems as conflicts between the human passions and reason. The Pre-Socratics focused on cosmology, searching after the mind or reason that gives nature its intelligibility. So doing, they furthered the Homeric exploration of the human psyche, shifting the spotlight onto the precisely noetic component.

In Plato the metaxic structure of human consciousness was fully clarified. Human beings stand in between the divine One above and the material many below. The movements of the human mind in the metaxy, moreover, display a direction. The quest for the divine ground is met by a divine luring. Politically, this means that right order will only come when rule flows from the openness of the rulers' souls to the transcendent divinity. Philosophically, it means that all judgments are falsified if one snatches them out of the metaxy and starts to deal with divinity or humanity, with the self or nature, as though it were not a relational reality.

Aristotle gave philosophy a more empirical and form-focused direction, but he disagreed little with most of Plato's program. Aristotelian politics and ethics virtually coincided, insofar as civic order was seen to depend on the excellences of the mature personality. The Aristotelian description of politics as a prudential science has seldom been surpassed, and the relevance of ethical maturity to social order is as obvious today as it was twenty-five hundred years ago.

Theology, science, and politics, as the Greeks conceived them, all became functions of reason, the faculty differentiated in the classical philosophers' epochal work. Theology virtually coincided with parts of metaphysics, while science pursued an ideal of knowledge through certain and unvarying causes. However much modernity found reason to challenge these views, as well as to challenge the rather static cultural ideals that shaped Greek politics, it preserved much of the Greek admiration for rationality. The Platonic metaxy therefore stands as both a formative factor in modern culture and a challenge to the modern conceptions of politics and education (insofar as these latter neglect the movement toward the transcendent ground of being and the ethical virtues).

In considering interpretations of the Greek achievement that would disagree with our Voegelinian interpretation, we mentioned the centrality of the interpretation of key texts, the problems that the classical institution of slavery and subordination of women do indeed present, and the questions that modern scientists or monotheists might validly raise. Our response indicated that we think the Voegelinian framework able to accommodate most of the points that a balanced presentation of such difficulties or counterinsights would bring forward. It also indicated the continuing relevance that we found in the classical stress on the relation between personal and political order.

STUDY QUESTIONS

1. Why was Homer so insistent that human beings, not the gods, are responsible for evil?
2. How does Gadamer understand myth and what bearing does this understanding have on the achievement of the Pre-Socratics?
3. What is the "luminosity" of human consciousness that Plato emphasizes?
4. Describe the Aristotelian spoudaios.
5. How did modernity alter the classical Greek notions of science and culture?

NOTES

1. Eric Voegelin, *Order and History, Vol. 2* (Baton Rouge: Louisiana State University Press, 1957), pp. 107–8.
2. Ibid., pp. 108–9.
3. Hans-Georg Gadamer, "Articulating Transcendence," in *The Beginning and the Beyond*, ed. Fred Lawrence (Chico, Calif.: Scholars Press, 1984), p. 1.
4. Eric Voegelin, *Anamnesis* (Notre Dame, Ind.: University of Notre Dame Press, 1978), p. 95.
5. Eric Voegelin, *Order and History, Vol. 3* (Baton Rouge: Louisiana State University Press, 1957), p. 301.

CHAPTER SEVEN

Judaism

ORIENTATION

Our argument thus far has been that prehistoric, nonliterate, and early civilizational humanity fundamentally conceived of the world in terms of the cosmological myth, and that philosophy was a leap out of this myth, or a differentiation so extreme that it cracked the myth. To be sure, the cosmological myth varied considerably from culture to culture and epoch to epoch. The Near Eastern form of the cosmic analogue, in which human society was a microcosm and mirrored "below" the organization of the divine realm "above," considerably differentiated the earlier, tighter senses of consubstantiality. But the philosophic ventures that arose in India, China, and above all, Greece went qualitatively beyond the Near Eastern sort of differentiation. India and China both verged on insights—the immateriality of atman and Brahman, the political significance of goodness and ritual—that took people to the verge of challenging the ultimacy of consubstantiality.

In our opinion, neither of these two great cultures went over the edge, leaped out of the cosmological mode of existence. But both made such gains in interiority, in rational analysis of human consciousness, that both reconceived of the self and society. Granting that the most prestigious Indian theories of the self continued to think of a monism that made all reality one, and that the predominant Chinese theories of society continued to set the human collectivity within the cycles of heaven's mandate, the sage that became the most authoritative cultural figure was different from the shaman who had been the archetypal cosmological figure. Whereas the shaman went "out," in ecstatic flight to the gods, the sage went "in," either through Indian yogic techniques or the reflectivity of the Confucian ethicists. When they surveyed the interior problems that they found, whether such problems were the networks of desire that India worried about or the loss of the uncarved block that Lao Tzu lamented, the Eastern sages began building the argument that *reality* is as much mental as physical, that enlightenment and virtue are as crucial to human survival and happiness as are food and shelter. They thereby suggested the previously unthinkable proposition that the cosmos is not all.

The Greeks greatly advanced this proposition. By the time Plato and Aristotle had fully charted the psyche, it was clear, at least in intellectually elitist circles, that our pictures of the cosmos come as much from inside us as from the world without. Further, it was clear that the movements of the human spirit, the searching and being drawn, define the human span of awareness and competence as a metaxy, an in-between between the material matrix of creation and the divine limit that holds out the explanation of creation. Insofar as Plato won the case that this tensional structure is the basic definition of human nature, a divine reality beyond the world became humanity's crux. Plato continued to fashion cosmological myths, and he veiled the implications of a truly world-transcendent deity, but in Voegelin's opinion these were deliberate choices, born of Plato's realization that most of his contemporaries weren't ready for such a radical resettlement. They would have lost balance, Voegelin argued, so Plato kept the traditional figures of the gods, the traditional myths and virtues. It was only a matter of time, however, before the later thinkers who appropriated Plato boldly proclaimed the consequences of the classical Greek intellectual differentiation: creation from nothingness, an absolutely self-sufficient ground of being.

The momentum of the Greek noetic discoveries alone might well have brought later thinkers to creation from nothingness and to further refinements of the metaxic structure of consciousness, but, when the pressures of biblical revelation were added, the results became well-nigh inevitable. For the Hebrew Bible and the Christian New Testament alike spoke of a God utterly free of the world who yet had chosen to establish interpersonal relations with human beings. *Revelation* is the word we shall be using to designate this choice and establishment. The central experience behind both the biblical and the Qur'anic worldviews is the self-disclosure of the world's Creator, the personal expression of the Creator's will.

Several points cry out for immediate treatment, and skimming their surface will complete this orientation to the revelational religious cultures. First, Voegelin called the general form that the revelational differentiations took *pneumatic*. As we have explained, this spotlights the full and deep human spirit, the awareness or luminosity that is loving as much as knowing, volitional as much as intellectual. If the divine ground lured the classical Greek mind, the divine heart or personality lured the decisive biblical thinkers, impressing upon them the sovereignty of the Creator's will and the amazing goodness of the Creator's love.

Second, the archetypal personality within the revelational cultural complexes was the prophet. Whereas the shaman stands at the center of the cosmological cultures (somewhat supplanted by the priest in the cosmological civilizations or empires), and the sage stands at the center of the cultures that turned to human interiority for a directive personal and political philosophy, the prophet stands at the center of the biblical cultures that arose in Israel, within early Christianity, and in Islam. This is not to say that shamanic and sagacious types did not appear in the biblical cultures, any more than it is to say that prophetic types can't be recognized in India, China, and Greece. Later Judaism had the rabbi, later Christianity had the priest, and later Islam had the lawyer or *mullah*, all of whom tended to be less prophetic than philosophic. But, in our opinion, the religious personality or functionary who makes the biblical cultures distinctive from the cosmological and philosophical cultures is the prophet. Seized by "the word of God," impelled to announce the divine judgment on present times and the divine call to repentance, the prophet fashions reality to a different configuration than it has in either the cosmological or the philosophical cultures. In the prophetic cultures the divine is a powerful personality who very willfully calls for ethical performance: justice, mercy, goodness responding to the goodness that divinity itself has shown.

Third, for the prophets, the intent of divinity, and so the import of revelation, is salvation. The breakthrough that comes from receiving the Word of God, from accepting the divine overtures and commands, takes one into a pneumatic zone where profound healing becomes possible. For the individual, this means the chance to overcome evil, guilt, fracturedness. For society it means powers to counter the foundational and structural evils that are responsible for so much poverty, violence, and abuse. The prophets claim that the love of God—the warmth and light divinity extends, and the wholehearted response that believers try to return—is the key to the most painful human problem, the cure to the worst human ill. They call this problem and ill *sin* (Islam perhaps speaks more of *weakness*), and they claim that it is more than intellectual. So, whereas the philosophers propose reeducation in order to let the noetic advances they have achieved take hold, the prophets propose conversion: resetting the personality in the love of God, giving human beings new hearts (centers of desire and affection). The prophets do not propose the ousting of desire. They are ardent personalities themselves, and they want to cast the fire of ardor upon the earth. What they therefore propose is the purification and redirection of desire— love of God with whole mind-heart-soul-strength, love of neighbor as oneself. (Islam speaks more of obedience.)

Our goal in this section must be as modest as it has been in the previous two sections. Judaism, Christianity, and Islam are all rich religiocultural complexes, and our delineations can claim no more than to lay out some stimulating angles of interpretation. Throughout, we shall simply be trying to explain the pneumatic breakthrough of the major figures and to show how the biblical worldview followed.

We conceive of these three chapters on Judaism, Christianity, and Islam as parallel to the chapters on India, China, and Greece. Thus our

Judith with the Head of Holofernes. Simon Vouet. Chapter 13 of the Book of Judith, probably written toward the end of the second century B.C.E., after the successful Maccabean revolt, depicts a valiant daughter of Israel, who personifies the Jewish people, murdering a general of the Assyrian foe that conquered Israel (the Northern Kingdom) and threatened Judah (the Southern Kingdom) toward the end of the eighth century B.C.E.   *(The Nelson-Atkins Museum of Art, Kansas City, Missouri [Nelson Fund])*

task in the present chapter is to present some of the experiences and conceptions that went into the making of revelation, Voegelin's second dramatic "leap in being." Most of our reflections focus on biblical texts, and because biblical interpretation is a very sophisticated business nowadays, it is well for us to say explicitly that we are not pretending that our interpretations of Abraham or Moses or the prophets are obvious from the letter of the relevant texts alone. Only when such texts are approached with a sense of the history of consciousness such as Voegelin's can they at least plausibly express what we are finding in them. We ask you, then, to let the texts and the theory of human awareness that we have been developing play back and forth, illumining one another and suggesting how revelation can be both something that happened uniquely in the past and something that is still happening today.

ABRAHAM

In Voegelin's interpretation, the pneumatic breakthrough that finally displays divinity as the creator of the world and the transcendent source of human order can be glimpsed as early as the covenant struck with Abraham (Abram). To be sure, the stories of Abraham that we find in Genesis have been worked over by many hands. It is much safer to say that the incipient pneumatic breakthrough occurred in the mind of the editor of the traditional tale than to place it in the mind of the historical Abraham. Whatever the creative source, however, later Judaism received the sense that the "father" of its faith, Abraham, had come to a unique relationship with God. Against the background of the cosmological myth that ruled the rest of Canaan, where the gods were naturalistic forces, the story of Abraham's promise from God (Genesis 15) stands out as a new venture.

Of the significance of the experiences behind this story Voegelin has written

> Genesis 14 and 15 together are a precious document. They describe the situation in which the berith [covenant] experience originates in opposition to the cosmological order of Canaanite civilization, as well as the content of the experience itself. . . . The spiritual sensitiveness of the man who opened his soul to the word of Yahweh, the trust and fortitude required to make this word the order of existence in opposition to the world, and the creative imagination used in transforming the symbol of civilizational bondage into the symbol of divine liberation—that combination is one of the great and rare events in the history of mankind. And this event bears the name of Abram.[1]

Voegelin is playing with the theme of liberation that will become dominant in the story of Moses leading the people out of bondage in Egypt. At another level he is saying that life in any cosmological culture is a kind of slavery or imprisonment. In a cosmological culture one is bound to nature, the material extension and rhythms of the physical cosmos. Any spiritual flights are contained by the sense of consubstantiality, by the strong assumption that reality is an organic whole whose parts all share the same stuff. Abraham's experience breaks with this assumption. A God speaks to him from outside the circuit of nature and makes promises that are both personal and historical. They are personal in that it is as though Yahweh, the God of Abraham, speaks in the first person and pledges that Abraham will have a vast progeny. They are historical in that they regard the unfolding of future time as though Abraham's relation with Yahweh has assumed the character of an ongoing story, a drama that will make Abraham's progeny the carriers of special meaning.

The response that Abraham makes to this personal address of Yahweh is equally personal: "And he believed the Lord; and he reckoned it to him as righteousness" (Genesis 15:6). Abraham said, in effect, "So be it. I trust that it will happen as you say." The righteousness mentioned here has a famous later history, because it is taken up by the Christian apostle Paul and made the cornerstone of his theology. Even on its own, however, it is momentous, for it implies that faith in this personal, world-transcending God can make human beings acceptable to divinity. We are used to this notion, for we are the heirs of perhaps three thousand years of "Western" history through which it has sung and danced. Placed in its original context, however, the notion was extraordinary. How could ignorant, mortal, sinful humanity stand before God as acceptable? Who could believe that the power that made the world could look favorably on disfigured human beings simply because they were willing to open their hearts and rely upon it?

The imagery in which the text couches this differentiation of a personal God who pledges the divine word, an act of faith that takes the pledge to heart, and the righteous relationship this establishes between a human being and his or her Creator might disturb the modern reader. The ancients who fashioned the narrative and listened to it accepted visions and divine speech rather matter-of-factly, knowing that they were simply useful fictions, ways of trying to express inner experiences that were finally inexpressible. Some, of course, could have taken the report of the conversation between God and Abraham literally, but the majority would have heard the story with an ear more interested in the essential spiritual import than the particular physical details.

The essential spiritual import was that the father of the people, the first ancestor to whom "Israel" owed its existence, had become personally bonded to a particular God, Yahweh (usually referred to as "the Lord"), who finally was discovered or believed to be the sole God, divinity in its fullness. Moreover, the story of Abraham's becoming bonded to this divinity in what was later considered a covenant (berith) or compact had the motif of wandering out of a prior cultural situation into an unknown, new situation that only future time would make plain. Thus in Genesis 12 the accounts of Abraham begin, "Now the Lord said to Abram, 'Go from your country and your kindred and your father's house to the land that I will show you.'" Abraham and his people were nomadic shepherds, and their faith began to take on the structure of a wandering journey in the company of their strangely pledged God. Indeed, Abraham began the process, later refined by his successors, of defining their existence by reference to their covenantal sharing of time with the Lord. The land mentioned in the call of Abraham, and promised to Moses at the exodus, remains an important motif. But more central is the notion that the people are who they are, live out their real identity as children of this father of faith, in terms of their righteous sharing of time with the sole Lord.

The sole Lord has to endure many backslidings of Abraham's descendents, who are regularly unable to escape the lure of the cosmological gods and mode of existence. The cosmos is so massive a presence to early peoples that they find it almost impossible to live by a transcosmic reference. But the first blows have been struck in the pneumatic fracturing of the cosmological myth, because the Lord to whom Abraham is pledged controls time as much as space and so surely stands beyond all natural processes.

Voegelin was not claiming that Abraham, or the writers of Genesis, or the majority of Israelites fully grasped these implications. One of his principal subthemes in the first volume of *Order and History*, in fact, is the way that Israel constantly fell back into worldly modes of existence. Yet the experiences of Abraham and Moses, as retrieved and perhaps deepened by the great prophets Jeremiah and Second Isaiah (chapters 40–55), stood against this sort of relapse, judging the people who wanted a worldly monarchy or status among the cosmological nations as unworthy of the true God.

The true God was beyond the rhythms of nature, purer and more powerful than the cosmological deities of Israel's neighboring peoples. The proper mode of existence, determined by the initiative of this true God in fashioning a covenant with Abraham and Moses, was not harmony with the cycles of nature but faith in the divine word. The pledge of God, the assurance that the transcosmic mystery would preserve the people for a good future, had to weigh more than the so palpable turn of the seasons, the cycles of life and death, the power of fertility and blood. This was a hard task, of course, as it has been in all historical periods. Flesh and blood do not inherit the kingdom of God; one must learn something about genuine spirituality. Abraham was a religious hero to the later generations of biblical believers because he made a momentous move to the spiritual mode of existence called faith.

MOSES

If the covenant with Abraham is the beginning of the Israelite revelation that introduces the new mode of existence called faith, the covenant with Moses is the full elaboration, indeed the codification. And parallel to the role of Genesis 15 in presenting the experiences underlying the Abrahamic covenant is the role of Exodus 3 in presenting the experiences underlying

The Sacrifice of Abraham. Peter Paul Rubens. The supreme test of Abraham's faith was being commanded by God to sacrifice Isaac, his only son (Genesis 22). *(The Nelson-Atkins Museum of Art, Kansas City, Missouri [Nelson Fund])*

the Mosaic covenant. It could help us to have the relevant verses (13–15) close to hand.

> Then Moses said to God, "If I come to the people of Israel and say to them, 'The God of your fathers has sent me to you,' and they ask me, 'What is his name?' what shall I say to them?" God said to Moses, "I am who I am." And he said, "Say this to the people of Israel, 'I am has sent me to you.'" God also said to Moses, "Say this to the people of Israel, 'The Lord, the God of your fathers, the God of Abraham, the God of Isaac, and the God of Jacob, has sent me to you': This is my name for ever, and thus I am to be remembered throughout all generations."

Just as he praised the writer of the account of Abraham's commitment in faith for depth and spiritual acumen, so Voegelin praised the author of the account of the encounter between Moses and God at the burning bush. The upshot he sees in this Mosaic account is a further development in the notion that revelation—the self-disclosure of the transcosmic God—creates a new mode of existence in time. By orienting themselves to such a God, making their own identity depend on such revelation and faith, the Israelites in a sense create "history." Their self-naming thenceforth comes from what is going on between them and the transcosmic God in time, from the covenant. As the presence of God is only mediated to them moment by moment, generation by generation, whatever happens from moment to moment or generation to generation colors their defining relationship. Thus the innermost strand of their story as a people is the account of how it goes between them and God: whether the covenant matures or decays, whether they advance in faith or slide back.

Another aspect of the genius of the author of Exodus 3, or another aspect of the experience that was expressed as God's self-naming at the burning bush, is the stress on the divine being. Moses gets no ordinary name from God. The Lord's description of himself is quite mysterious. To be sure, the account makes it clear that this divinity is the same as the one who dealt with Abraham, Isaac, and Jacob. But "I am who I am" hardly gives out much information. Thus the later commentators, especially those who came under the influence of Greek metaphysics, often speculated on the existential aspects of this God's nature. Could it be, they asked, that divinity most essentially is pure be-ing, sovereign is-ness? Modern critical historians are naturally reluctant to read this much into a text that purports to present the basic experiences of a man from about 1200 B.C.E. On the other hand, such historians could be crippled by evolutionary assumptions and therefore unable to see that genuine events of revelation can create new categories or insights and so are somewhat independent of prior cultural developments. In other words, they just might fail to see that, if Moses actually encountered the transcosmic divinity, he need not have mastered Greek metaphysics to express the germ of the insight that God simply is, that God can only be named in terms of what it turns out that God has done or shown divinity to be over time. The metaphysics implied in the account therefore need not be static. The nomadic motif can continue (in fact it certainly does continue after the exodus, when the people wander in the desert), and with it, the historicity of revelation, of existence in the modality of faith, only grows. "I am who I am" then becomes "I am what the mystery to which you have bound yourselves turns out to be in our common history, our ongoing covenant." God, we might say, is willing to let those who live bound to God in faith have the main say about what divinity is (whether the mystery is good or evil, creative or destructive, healing love or crippling condemnation, and so on).

Thus, Voegelin saw profound implications in the self-disclosure of God at the burning bush. One could call it the kernel of the new way of standing in the world or thinking about humanity that revelation should connote. Reasonably enough, therefore, he was disappointed with historians who neglected these profound possibilities and critical of their inability to appreciate what he considered one of the decisive moments in the history of human development.

More than twenty-five years after Voegelin's analysis of Exodus 3, interpretations of Moses have not necessarily improved. The historians whom he criticized for not having the philosophical depth to see the most profound possibilities in the Mosaic revelation have only ceded to a generation at least equally superficial. So, for example, one finds interpretations such as the following, in which Moses is reduced to the rank of a magician, and the self-disclosure of God is reduced to a magical tool:

> Amulets found in both Jewish and non-Jewish graves in Egypt dating from the Greco-Roman period bear Moses' name and feature a rod-like symbol; clearly Moses ranked high on any list of well-known Merlins familiar to the credulous of the age—which means to almost everyone. How had Moses acquired the secret and esoteric knowledge which enabled him to be a wizard? He had asked for it and at the Burning Bush God had provided it. Moses says: "When they ask me, 'What is His name,' what shall I say to them?" God answers: **Ehyeh Asher Ehyeh** (Exodus 3:13–14). The passage was read as the gift to Moses of God's name and of the knowledge necessary to use its power. Nearly everyone in that time and place took for granted that the use of a power-laden Name could heal the sick, bring the rain, or strike one dead if used in a curse. Readers of the time would not have thought it curious that Artapanus identifies the weapon Moses had used in the murder of the Egyptian taskmaster as the utterance of God's Name. One who knew The Name had no need of a knife.[2]

It follows that there is a wide range of interpretations of Moses, exodus, the covenant, revelation, and faith, and perhaps the principal reason for scholars' divergencies is the different outlooks they themselves bring. The bias of the author of the statement just given is that Exodus gives little if any of Moses' own personal experience, and he shows little inclination to take on the demanding task of interpreting just what revelation and faith might mean in personal, existential terms. History is reduced to the rather flat proportions of the people's outward changes. How biblical revelation introduced a new thing, in terms of changing the human consciousness that makes all people potentially capable of a covenantal relation with God and consequently of a precisely historical form of existence, falls outside his interest. So there is no appreciation of the pneumatic breakthrough that rivals the Greek noetic breakthrough for the honor of being humanity's most significant leap in being, humanity's most precious advance in understanding reality. The immense significance of appreciating that the transcosmic divine presence, when profoundly accepted as the basis of one's whole self-definition, refashions the meaning of *humanity* goes by the boards. We are in the all-too-familiar predicament where the vision of the interpretation depends on the depth and clarity of the interpreter's wisdom as well as his or her bias.

THE PROPHETS

The peaks of existential faith glimpsed by Abraham and Moses were succeeded by valleys of lesser belief. As Voegelin, echoing many of the prophets, interpreted the period when Israel was a monarchy, the people proved unable or unwilling to live in direct relationship with the transcosmic God. So they insisted, like the other nations, on having a king who could mediate heavenly power to their earthly realm. Certainly the rise of kingship is more complicated than this, but the spiritual issue might finally boil down to these terms.

The *judges*, as they are called, who preceded the kings were **charismatic** figures who depended on the inrush of divine inspiration. The prophets who contended with the kings similarly depended on the Word and Spirit of God, but their understanding of pneumatic revelation was more profound than that of the judges. To the prophet's mind, the twin requirements of covenantal faith were pure cult and social justice. Both stemmed from a consciousness formed by openness or receptivity to the genuinely mysterious, transcosmic divinity. The prophets lamented the lack of such faith, and they tried to call both kings and commoners back to the holiness or authenticity that the disclosures of God made imperative. One could not live righteously with the true God and worship or do business as though the old cosmological style were acceptable. The power politics in which the kings and leading officials were indulging ill fit the people covenanted to the Lord. Similarly, the official cults that many thought satisfied their obligations to God were worthless without clean hearts that took pity on the downtrodden, the widow, and the orphan. Steadily, the prophets advanced toward a morality that spotlighted individual responsibility and renovation from within. By the time of Jeremiah, the prophetic theology was speaking of a new covenant, written not on tablets of stone but on the chambers of the heart.

Jeremiah 31:31–34 is one of the most dazzling texts produced by the deeper prophetic theology. In it the reader can see the penetration of the pneumatic differentiation to the point where the writer knows that knowledge of God sufficient to found a life worthy of covenantal relation with God must be given by God at the centermost portion of the personality. Moreover, the writer glimpses that with this gift of God comes salvation:

forgiveness of sins, restitution to moral wholeness. What the Greek spiritual heroes appreciated in intellectual terms—how the divine forms the human consciousness to right order—the prophets had come to appreciate in pneumatic terms. Unless the Spirit of God recreated the "heart" of human beings—the integral personality—by taking it into the divine power and creativity, there could be no fully right order, and so no full prosperity. Just as the Greeks came to think of the polis as the psyche writ large, so the prophets came to realize that the basic site of faith is the center of the individual personality. Voegelin has been criticized for overlooking the social motif that runs through Jeremiah 31:31–34 (note the recurrent phrase "the house of Israel"),[3] but there is no denying his main point: Jeremiah has focused on the heart of the individual believer as the crux of the differentiated appreciation of the covenant that the prophets had achieved.

> Behold, the days are coming, says the Lord, when I will make a new covenant with the house of Israel and the house of Judah, not like the covenant which I made with their fathers when I took them by the hand to bring them out of the land of Egypt, my covenant which they broke, though I was their husband, says the Lord. But this is the covenant which I will make with the house of Israel after those days, says the Lord: I will put my law within them, and I will write it upon their hearts; and I will be their God, and they will be my people. And no longer shall each man teach his neighbor and each his brother, saying, "Know the Lord," for they shall all know me, from the least of them to the greatest, says the Lord; for I will forgive their iniquity, and I will remember their sin no more.

The older view of the covenant, in which the commandments given to Moses had become the basis of **Torah**, divine guidance or law, had proven inadequate. Although the people were bonded to God like a bride to her husband, a motif that Hosea especially developed, they had fallen into infidelity, sullying both their cult and their social ethics. So Jeremiah ponders what sort of remedy or renovation might save the situation, and as he moves deeper and deeper into the problem, he has visions of taking *covenant* to a new level. Without abandoning the social context, in which Israel as a people or community were together in their bondedness to God, he goes below mores, customs, legal constraints and the like to rivet upon the real crux. Unless people know divinity from the center of themselves, in their midmost hearts, their covenantal fidelity, and so their authentic historical existence, will always be shaky. The only way to obtain the genuine worship and kindly social dealings that the revealed God requires is to have people who are formed by the divine goodness from within. The revealed God does not "require" pure worship and kindly social dealings by whim or extrinsic decision. Praising God and treating one's neighbors justly is not something that the Lord decided upon one day when business was slow. It flows from the nature or reality of God to be light and truth, beauty and love. Thus any profound relation with God requires attitudes toward ultimate reality and one's fellow human beings that are compatible with truth and justice, beauty and goodness.

Once again, however, the people as a whole prove unequal to the task of living with this degree of pneumatic purity, so Jeremiah's successor as dean of Israel's prophets, the author of Isaiah 40—55, has to take the drama to its last stages. First Isaiah (for example, 1:9; 17:5–6) had spoken of a remnant, a small portion of the people, who might prove faithful once history had moved beyond the current disaster of threat by Assyria. Trying to make sense out of the people's later sufferings in Babylon, Second Isaiah discerns how God might bring good out of the present evil. Thereby, he brings into full relief the salvational or **soteriological** aspects of pneumatic differentiation. The experience of God at the midmost point of the personality is more than exhilarating or enlightening. It seems to hold the possibility of confronting the worst human evils and somewhat drawing off their poisons, making them submit to a purity or goodness that proves much stronger.

In the figure of the Suffering Servant, Second Isaiah ruminates about how the people might emerge the better for their sufferings, purified of their sins. Christians have from the beginning considered the Suffering Servant to be a prefigurement of Jesus Christ. Probably the prophet himself had Israel (the people personified) in mind or some representative figure. Either way, the point is the transformation that deep faith had by this time worked in the notion of "divinity." No longer are power and dignity to the fore. Not even holiness predominates now. In the poems about the Suffering Servant, the ways of God become as lowly and self-sacrificing as a victim who suffers simply because of his or her innocence and goodness. As the poem in Isaiah 53 in part says:

> He was despised and rejected by men; a man of sorrows, and acquainted with grief; and as one from whom men hide their faces he was despised, and we esteemed him not. Surely he has borne our griefs and carried our sorrows; yet we esteemed him stricken, smitten by God, and afflicted. But he was wounded for our transgressions, he was bruised for our iniquities; upon him was the chastisement that made us whole, and with his stripes we were healed. All we like sheep have gone astray; we have turned every one to his own way; and the Lord has laid on him the iniquity of us all. . . . Therefore I will divide him a portion with the great, and he shall divide the spoil with the strong; because he poured out his soul to death, and was numbered with the transgressors; yet he bore the sin of many, and made intercession for the transgressors (Isaiah 53:3–6, 12).

With Second Isaiah, innocent suffering becomes integral to the divine way of freeing sinful humanity from the chaos it makes, becomes a way of triumphing over evil and reintroducing order.

REVELATION AND CREATION

The prophetic mode of experience clarified the divine demand for mercy rather than sacrifice, for fidelity to God rather than power politics. The patriarchs, Abraham, Isaac, and Jacob, and the great covenant maker

Moses all strove to set Israelite existence under God, to make time the medium of an ongoing intimacy. Kingship brought other features of covenant to the fore, for the Davidic covenant was supposed to be less conditional than the Mosaic. Whereas the Mosaic covenant, especially as interpreted by Deuteronomy, made God's favor depend on the people's good ethical performance, the Davidic covenant sought a continuity of relationship with God under a permanent royal house and due finally to the graciousness of the divine nature. In other words, the covenant prevailed because of God's goodness, not humans' good ethical performance. Nonetheless, the cosmological motifs that surrounded kingship in the ancient Near East entered into the Israelite monarchical theology. Thus the priestly theology that coexisted alongside the prophetic shows signs of the cosmic analogue, in which the state becomes a miniature of the heavenly realm. This does make the divine rhythmic and near, but it also tends to obscure the transcendence that is at the heart of the pneumatic breakthrough.

The Wisdom Literature that followed after the prophetic literature also speculated in a somewhat cosmic vein, with the result that Creation became a more important theme. By and large this Creation was a molding or fashioning rather than a drawing from nothingness, but it did buttress the idea that the divine is the sole source of the reality we have, natural and cultural alike. In the Psalms one sees the twin motifs of God's redemptive activity on behalf of the people and God's sovereign kingship over the world. The authors of Genesis pictured the divine creativity more dramatically, giving God only a watery chaos with which to work and stressing the primacy of the divine Word: "Let there be."

Overall, the heritage left by the Hebrew Bible therefore represents a considerable achievement. If the pneumatic differentiation was not brought to ultimate clarity, it nonetheless was sufficiently advanced to make history different ever after. The core of the biblical conviction was that the divine is free of the world, able and willing to make overtures apart from the intimations given by the cycles of nature. The ultimately inexpressible experiences of the great figures who punctuate the story of revelation all point in the direction of the divine freedom and personality.

In contrast with the impersonality of the Eastern ultimate and the rather small-scale personalism of the natural divinities that were given definite names and stories, the sole God of the Israelite fathers is both intensely personal and transpersonally mysterious. If *personal* connotes a center of intelligence and will, then certainly the biblical deity is personal. The basic structure of the revelational exchanges is conversational or dialogical. Abraham makes his act of faith in response to God's personal pledge. Moses becomes the friend of God, the one who can speak with God directly. The prophets receive a call from God that they protest and struggle with, as though it were a choice that God might change or at least be held responsible for. On the other hand, if *personal* connotes a limited center of intelligence and will, an identity unique because it is an unrepeatable slice or facet of intelligence and will at large, then the biblical deity is not personal. None of the great interlocutors of God, of the archetypal figures who wrestle with the Divinity, conveys the sense that God can be put into focus the way a human person might be. Always the sense comes through that the Other with whom they wrestle is free, unpredictable, much more than they can control.

Revelation therefore does not destroy the mystery of God, and the Creation that the theologians of faith work out brims with something awesome. The figures from Near Eastern mythology that have the Divine wrestling with the forces of chaos, the beast Leviathan for instance, reflect a raw core of respect for the one who works through the storm and the earthquake, who is finally responsible for the lion and the whale. The Book of Job, a wonderful achievement of Israelite Wisdom Literature, uses the awesomeness of Creation to place the problem of evil in context. Job has been accusing God of injustice, because he has been suffering innocently and God is the one ultimately responsible for the way things run in the world. When God finally answers Job, significantly enough, it is from out of a whirlwind. Symbolically, the Divine is like a force that would blow human beings away, were they to presume to stand on its level. The first question that the Lord puts to Job establishes that Job hasn't the stature to attempt to pass judgment about the final justice or injustice of history.

> Where were you when I laid the foundation of the earth? Tell me, if you have understanding. Who determined its measurements—surely you know! Or who stretched the line upon it? On what were its bases sunk, or who laid its

Adam. Auguste Rodin. Rodin captures both the nobility and the fallenness or shame of this first parent and image of God.   *(The Nelson-Atkins Museum of Art, Kansas City, Missouri [Nelson Fund])*

cornerstone, when the morning stars sang together, and all the sons of God shouted for joy? (Job 38:4–7)

Although the imagery does not suggest creation from nothingness so much as a craftsmanlike construction, it nevertheless establishes that the Divine is the only one who knows how the world has been measured out. And although the symbolism is physical, much more impressive in a time when nature greatly overpowered humanity than it is today, the suggestion could be extended into the moral order. Who is any human being to pretend to know or be able to judge the niceties, or even the gross features, of ultimate evil and good, ultimate outrage and justice? This point of view is liable to abuse, of course, and human beings have to struggle along, making moral decisions as best they can. The whole weight of the prophetic call to justice makes it plain that one cannot abandon ethics because of the mysteriousness of God's final ordinances. But the sapiential aspects of biblical revelation, the perspective that the pneumatic breakthrough lays before the mind of the person of faith, is a salutary corrective to any presumption to know the divine will in detail or be able to call the divine plan to account.

In Voegelin's view, the immersion of Israel in the cosmological symbolism of the ancient Near East, and the inability of most of the Israelite theologians to separate the transcendence of God from the ethnic overtones of the covenant, somewhat frustrated the outreach of the pneumatic breakthrough. In contrast with the noetic breakthrough of Greece, the Israelite revelational breakthrough always struggled to balance the this-worldly and the other-worldly (its sense of in-between was not so precise as the Platonic), and in contrast with the Christian pneumatic sense of definitive salvation, the Israelite sense remained bound to the particular history of the one people descended from Abraham. These are Voegelin's own interpretations, of course, and many Jews, Greeks, Christians, and scholars would refuse to second them. One does not have to agree fully, however, to see the important issues they raise, issues left us by the pneumatic breakthrough itself.

First, what is the proper affective or ethical balance between now and then, between the realm of humanity mired in nature and the realm of God that lures the human spirit upward? What, in other words, is the pneumatic equivalent of the noetic metaxy that the Greek experience of seeking and being drawn disclosed? Over-immersion in the cosmological style erred on the side of "now" and "below," whereas some of the prophetic visions of a transfigured earth erred on the side of "then" and "above." This problem remained in Christianity.

Second, how should the pneumatic breakthrough be extended beyond the ethnic confines of Israel, under the conviction that one God dealing with a somewhat uniform human nature probably offers saving love everywhere? This is the question that challenges the notion of a chosen people, and we shall see it in different form when dealing with both Christianity and Islam. To Voegelin's mind, any breakthrough is bound to occur only in given minds, times, and cultures, but once the breakthrough has occurred, it is at least the potential property of all humankind. Thus to refer covenant or grace or revelation only to Jews, Christians, or Muslims would be to whittle down the full import of what happened in the Bible, the Gospel, or the Qur'an. Similarly, to refer the noetic differentiation only to the Greeks or Westerners who followed in the train of the classical philosophers would be to whittle down the luring of God and obscure the tensional structure of all human consciousness. For Voegelin, history shows humankind to be an ecumenic or universal entity, with all people equally invited to progress toward the order disclosed by the noetic and pneumatic breakthroughs.

REDEMPTIVE HISTORY AND RABBINIC JUDAISM

The overall experience of the Israelite spiritual giants convinced them that the God who had addessed their people was surpassingly good. Although history might be a mixed bag, full of suffering as well as joy, the Lord of history had to be consistently and reliably good. Like Homer, the typical Israelite person of insight referred evil to human beings. Divinity was not responsible for warfare, injustice, mayhem on the left or robbery on the right. It was the fault of disordered, sinful humanity. Thus, a Psalm such as 136 could enter, as a steady refrain or **cantus firmus** on which faith might rely, the phrase, "for his steadfast love endures forever." One was to give thanks to the Lord, open up one's mind and heart in praise, because in creating, the Lord had poured forth the divine goodness. Similarly, in leading Israel out of Egypt and establishing the people in their own promised land, the Lord had but manifested the steadfast character of the divine interest, concern, mercy, love—the whole collection of attributes or qualities that a faithful covenant partner might display.

With the prophets, however, the appreciation went even deeper. The mystery of iniquity, the opaqueness of the human depravity and will to do evil, boggled the minds of the biblical seers. It made no sense that people created for intimacy with God, given all the splendors of creation, should turn away from the Lord of mercy, should slash their brothers and sisters for puny profit. What the Greek poets such as Aeschylus had called **nosos**, madness bent on destruction, the Israelite prophets and sages called sin: evil freely, culpably chosen.

The message of Second Isaiah was that God had even done something about sin. Using the figure of *redeemer*, one who buys back people sold into slavery, God was at work to repair the ravages of human depravity and sin. The Servant of the Lord who would take upon himself the sins of the people was the foremost symbol of the divine will to restore what human evil had wrecked. But the whole traditional belief that God was active in history not simply to keep the course of nature going but also to guide Israel to full human prosperity finally begot the notion that God would actually transform history, would actually redo the sinful world that had wobbled so far off course.

The visions of the apocalyptic writers, such as the authors of Daniel and the **extracanonical** books of Enoch, laid out this later Israelite notion in wild imagery. (The Christian Book of Revelation stands in this tradition, and most of its imagery comes from the Old Testament.) The "Son of Man," as Daniel called the heavenly figure who would come on the clouds to transform the earth, sits awkwardly alongside the Servant of the Lord whose redemptive manner was innocent suffering, but together they expressed the Israelite conviction, born of more than fifteen hundred years of covenant experience, that God was both able and willing to transform the human portion of creation, the history that had gone astray.

Jesus and the New Testament patch of Jewish history, as we shall note in the next chapter, take much of their context from this apocalyptic intensity. The Maccabean revolt against Rome in 168 B.C.E. gave Israel a short-lived independence, but the final Roman response to this revolutionary temper in 70 C.E. devastated Jerusalem (the spiritual center of the promised land), destroyed the Temple (the center within the center), and cast much of Judaism out into a **diaspora** from which it has yet to recover (although the establishment of the modern state of Israel in 1948 was a major restoration).

During the Babylonian captivity (sixth century B.C.E.), when the Southern Kingdom was largely ripped away from Jerusalem, Jews had had to live without the Temple on which to center their ritual life. Scholars debate whether we ought to locate the origin of the synagogue and rabbinic Judaism in this experience, but certainly it was at least a preparation for the shift toward studying Torah and exalting the rabbi that dominated Judaism in the Common Era. For our purposes, the question is, What happened to the pneumatic breakthrough after prophecy ceased to be the compelling mode of religious experience (the last centuries before the Common Era)?

For Voegelin, the general fate of the epochal breakthroughs, pneumatic and noetic both, was unfortunate. In Greece the thinkers who succeeded the classical philosophers were not of their stature, so the sense of reality that obtained in Hellenistic times, and that then shaped the Christian patristic and medieval eras, was not so profoundly or clearly differentiated as it might have been. Analogously, the pneumatic breakthrough that occurred with the Israelite prophets and their successors Jesus and Paul derailed in both Judaism and Christianity. To speak now only of the Jewish derailment, the rabbis certainly filled out many of the details of the Mosaic covenant law, but it seems necessary to say that they lost the depth and power of the original experiences of revelation.

One can debate, of course, what has been necessary for Jews to survive all the catastrophes, from expulsion from Jerusalem to desecration in Nazi concentration camps, that have written their history in lines of blood through the Common Era. The argument that the rabbis gave their people a solid psychic defense against the evils and absurdities they had to endure is quite compelling. This does not mean, however, that one cannot lament the loss of spiritual depth one senses when comparing some of the talmudic commentaries with the prophetic originals. Whereas the prophetic originals brim with direct encounters with the divine mystery, with elevations of spirit personally felt, the talmudic commentaries deal at second hand. Even the great interpretations of Moses, such as those of the medieval Jewish genius Maimonides, suffer the limitations of the noetic and pneumatic constrictions that had occurred in both the classical and the biblical streams of the Western spiritual heritage.

The result for Voegelin was a general derailment or blockage that played a major part in the spiritual aberrations of modernity. Probably it is the Christian failures that we should especially spotlight when we make this charge, because Western culture at the time of modernity was supposed to be Christian rather than Jewish. We shall turn over the Christian patterns quite fully, both in the next chapter and in the last section of the book. But the phenomenon of rabbinic Judaism, in both its assets and its liabilities, could serve almost equally well as a test case with which to ponder the vast problem of how to institutionalize or democratize the leaps in being that point humanity toward its best order and destiny.

These leaps disclose a realm in which human consciousness or reflectivity is the basis of human dignity. Thus, they dissolve all ethnic or narrowly religious claims to special status. In the light of the great noetic and pneumatic clarifications, the divinity that made the world is available everywhere. To be sure, there is the mystery that these clarifications only occur in specific times and places, and so there is the honor of being the particular people, Greek or Israelite, who bore them forth. But this honor, as the greatest prophets and rabbis realized full well, is more a call to service than a basis of self-satisfaction. Everywhere human beings seem crippled and almost self-ruined for lack of the light of philosophy and the love of revelation. So everywhere those privileged to partake of the traditions of genuine philosophy and revelation have the responsibility to exemplify, share, and advance the human prosperity, the spiritual flourishing that Plato and Jeremiah, Aristotle and Jesus, saw was possible. Because Judaism has been a major source of humanity's awareness of this responsibility, it has been a great benefactor of humanity at large.

COUNTERVIEWS

The opposition to Voegelin's reading of Israelite pneumatic experience comes from several quarters, but perhaps the strongest opposition comes from more historicist critics who fail to distinguish as he does between rather literal accounts of the past and *paradigmatic* or ideal accounts. Voegelin's primary interest was the human or divine-human potential that the great moments in cultural history reveal. In fact, as we have made plain, he would periodize *history* itself in terms of these great moments. Scholars more interested in the transmission of a text such as Exodus 3 or Genesis 14–15 than in its exemplification of new ways of conceiving human existence understandably think that Voegelin's views are very speculative.

Another group of critics would contest Voegelin's evaluation of rabbinic (or later Christian) doctrinalization of the original prophetic experiences. In Voegelin's view, things later flattened out or lost much of their profundity. In the view of other interpreters, what the rabbis and the Christian leaders did in routinizing the covenant relationship with God was right and necessary, because human beings cannot live on the heights regularly. One could say, then, that we are back at Dostoevski's story of Christ and the Grand Inquisitor. Voegelin was more interested in the freedom that biblical revelation and Greek philosophy hold out than in how to constrain the masses into sufficient ethical uprightness to keep society limping along.

SUMMARY

Our first pneumatic religion has been Judaism, and we followed Voegelin in tracing the beginnings of the distinctive mode of existence called faith back to Abraham, the father of the Jews. In accepting the promise of a transcosmic God and in effect making a covenant that laid time out as a straight path into the future, to be walked in company with this God, Abraham at least potentially broke with the cosmological myth. Moses, as interpreted by the author of the account of God's self-naming at the burning bush, worked further clarifications on the nature of the transcosmic deity of the fathers. The "I am who I am" that Moses received accents both the mystery of the divine interlocutor and the be-ing or is-ness that time will show this God to have. As with Abraham, then, sharing time with God became characteristic of Mosaic faith. Thus history, as an inner form of existence, a new way of standing in the world, was further clarified by God's self-naming.

The prophets plumbed the depths of covenantal faith and historical existence, focusing on the disorders of the human heart that mottled Israel's existence. Jeremiah came to speak of a new, interior covenant, and Second Isaiah spoke of a Suffering Servant who would carry the people's sins. Both brought into focus the moral reformations that pneumatic revelation demanded. This revelation almost completely transcended the cosmological style regnant in the Ancient Near East. However, the Israelite monarchy somewhat resembled the kingdoms of Israel's neighbors, and the Israelite penetration of Creation remained less than complete. Nonetheless, the creativity of Israel's divine Lord was impressive, as a great text such as Job 38 makes clear.

Our last topics were redemptive history and rabbinic Judaism, the former taking us into apocalyptic literature and the latter raising the question of how to translate the pneumatic breakthrough into popular religious forms and prevent its derailment. Rabbinic Judaism got some demerits for stifling the prophetic spirit but received commendations for helping Jews survive their very troubled history throughout the Common Era.

Last, we indicated two sorts of criticism that Voegelin's reading of Israelite revelation would tend to provoke. The first demands more attention to the actual historicity of the texts in question and has little interest in their more paradigmatic or ideal significance. The second contests Voegelin's preference for prophets over rabbis or priests, believing that what Voegelin called a derailment was in fact a necessary adaptation.

STUDY QUESTIONS

1. How might Abraham's faith represent a freeing from "civilizational bondage"?
2. What was the value of the mysterious divine name given to Moses at the burning bush?
3. What sort of knowledge of God did Jeremiah foresee and what new sort of covenant?
4. Explain the logic of God's response to Job from out of the whirlwind.
5. What are the gains possible from trying to codify the implications of the pneumatic breakthrough and what are the losses likely to occur?

NOTES

1. Eric Voegelin, *Order and History, Vol. 1* (Baton Rouge: Louisiana State University Press, 1956), p. 195.
2. Daniel Jeremy Silver, *Images of Moses* (New York: Basic Books, 1982), pp. 71–72.
3. See Bernhard W. Anderson, "Politics and the Transcendent: Voegelin's Philosophical and Theological Exposition of the Old Testament in the Context of the Ancient Near East," in *Eric Voegelin's Search for Order and History*, ed. Stephen A. McKnight (Baton Rouge: Louisiana State University Press, 1978), pp. 62–100; also Lynn Clapham, "Voegelin and Hebrew Scripture: *Israel and Revelation* in Retrospect," in *Voegelin and the Theologian*, eds. John Kirby and William Thompson (Toronto: Edwin Mellen, 1983), pp.104–37.

Christianity

ORIENTATION

In this chapter we continue to deal with prophetic themes, although now we meet them in the perhaps more familiar garb of Christian doctrine. Our point here, as throughout, is the mutual illumination that a given tradition and our interpretational scheme cast on one another. That is, we claim that Christianity comes into more interesting focus when one deals with it in the context of the cosmological myth, noetic differentiation, and pneumatic differentiation than it does without such theoretical perspectives. And, correlatively, we claim that these analyses of key moments in the history of human consciousness (indeed, in history, pure and simple) also become more focused or more concretely persuasive through their engagement with Christianity.

Partly to parallel previous chapters, in which we have dealt with historicoparadigmatic figures such as Confucius and Lao Tzu or Abraham and Moses, we begin with Jesus and Paul. Then, as has also been our custom, we deal with some of the capital issues and realities that the influence of the central figures has recolored. As has been true now for several chapters, these issues and realities are fairly demanding. One has to pay attention and even reflect and go back over the line of argument again, if their Voegelinian significance is to become clear. But we feel that such reflective effort will pay rich dividends, because in the final analysis a liberal education (especially one well versed in the roots of the traditional world cultures) depends as much on developing an active appreciation of one's own mind as it does on accumulating a rich data bank.

JESUS

Many of the people who encountered Jesus of Nazareth probably thought of him as a prophet. Others probably accounted him a **hasid** or holy man. The writers of the New Testament used such titles as Son of Man (partly due to the influence of Daniel), Son of God, and Christ (or Messiah). All of these titles, however, stemmed from the Judaism contemporary with Jesus. Jesus greatly developed some of the intuitions of Israelite theology, especially in his speaking of God as an intimate parent ("Abba" or "Daddy"), but his general thought and speech alike were fully indebted to his Jewish heritage. The notion that dominates the Jesus we see in the **synoptic** gospels, the Reign of God, comes from Israel's monarchical experience and originally had a foothold in the cosmological myth. As David and Solomon were kings on earth, so was the Lord King of heaven and earth. But Jesus spiritualized this notion, making it bear more on God's reign in people's hearts and daily lives. For him it meant the transformation of human affairs, because people had opened themselves to God's Word and Spirit.

Thus the preaching of Jesus of Nazareth stood in the tradition of both the prophets and the writers of apocalyptic literature. Jesus seems to have expected the end of present, disordered history to occur rather soon. Then God's order would dominate, and present injustices would be swept away. Most of the ethical teaching one finds in the New Testament has been shaped by this conviction or hope. So, for example, the **beatitudes** listed in the Sermon on the Mount (Matthew 5—7) are probably best interpreted as an expression of the revolution implicit in the Kingdom of God. When God comes to reign in human affairs, the poor, the meek, and the peacemakers will have it better than the wealthy, the proud, and the violent. The teachings of Paul also reflect the early Christian conviction (which continued for several generations after Jesus' death) that the end of history as presently known was close at hand.

It follows, therefore, that both Jesus and early Christianity present us with the problem of pneumatic balance that we saw above in the case of Israelite revelation. To be sure, the later Paul, the Johannine writings, and parts of the pastoral literature balance the expectation of the end of history with affirmations that the essential transformation of which Jesus spoke had already occurred in his mission, death, and resurrection. Thus what theologians sometimes call **realized eschatology**, the sense that the final things (*eschata*) have already come to pass, calls the reader back to present, worldly life. The accent shifts to the life of God or life of Christ available to the believer "right now," and the consummation of history or the "heaven" that will fulfill the individual believer "then" is conceived of as the full flowering of something already germinating.

The Kingdom of God, as Jesus put it, or the life of Christ, as Paul put it, that faith made available to those who accepted Jesus had a markedly salvational character. The early Christians were convinced that God had drawn near, and openness to God—the Christian version of the sort of existential trust begun by Abraham—could heal people of their deepest ills. Thus the gospels portray Jesus as curing lepers, the blind, and the mute. The fuller sense conveyed, however, is that these physical cures, for all their value, but symbolized the renovation of humanity's depths that strong faith could accomplish. We shall see more of this in the next section, when we take up the Pauline notion of justification by faith. It is clear even in our records of Jesus, however, that the first Christians thought that the new covenant foreseen by Jeremiah had become possible through the Spirit of God that came in Jesus of Nazareth.

Thus far, we have presented a thumbnail sketch of the New Testament Jesus that most interpreters probably would credit. For Voegelin, however, the analytical framework in which to place such a sketch is the pneumatic breakthrough that Jesus inherited from his Israelite forebears. The center of Jesus' spirit opened to the God of the fathers, and the result was a self-definition more radical than any previously known. It is hard to know precisely what parts of the New Testament's **Christology** come from Jesus himself and what parts come from the communities that stand behind the different New Testament writings, but both in Jesus' speech about his

Byzantine Book Cover. Syrian, sixth-seventh century C.E. Christian revelation often became equated with the Bible, and the Bible often became epitomized in Christ's cross. *(The Nelson-Atkins Museum of Art, Kansas City, Missouri [Nelson Fund])*

relation to God as to an Abba and in the New Testament speculations about Jesus' divinity we find an identification of Jesus' inmost reality with the divine. In other words, the reference to the ground of reality that the noetic differentiation made plain is necessary for an ordered human personality became so intense in Jesus' case that the "*I*" of Jesus was a projection into God, or an expression of God in human terms.

Voegelin tended to deal with matters such as these symbolically, so his Christology does not match at all points the **dogmatic** Christology developed by the Christian Church.[1] Nonetheless, we can see the historic proportions of what happened with Jesus—the advances in human awareness of the structures and possibilities of reality—from a Voegelinian pneumatic analysis. Whereas the Greek giants clarified the structures of intellectual awareness, Jesus advanced the prophetic sense that the divine could encounter the human psyche at its ground or basic center, and this encounter or call would become the undeniable crux of the personality ever after. So the biblical language of the will of God becoming Jesus' "meat and drink" expresses something more holistic than the noetic clarifications. If Jesus and Paul do not show the analytic precision about searching and drawing that one can develop from Plato's writing, they more powerfully express what happens when the divine rushes into the human spirit and reforms it from within.

Language is clumsy at this point, and we are at the verge of mysticism. The experience of the divine Spirit (the root metaphor is the divine life breath) animating the human personality is so primordial that all subsequent analyses are bound to falter. From Jesus and other prophetic figures, one gets the sense that reality is completely transformed, so that wherever one goes the ultimate source of reality is like a buoyant support. Thus Jesus displays a remarkable trust that his Father will care for him and his cause. Even when he seems depressed, for example, in the gospel scenes of his prayer in the Garden of Gethsemane prior to his crucifixion (see Mark 14, Matthew 26, Luke 22), he is able to trust that God will see him through. The accounts of the resurrected Christ suggest that after his death it was possible for his intimate bonds with God finally to be displayed in all their splendor. Jesus is transfigured, able to move through the physical world as though master of even its natural laws.

Where others would probably go beyond Voegelin's symbolic reading of such a Christology is in bringing out its soteriological dimensions. Voegelin is skeptical of any claims to transform human nature, for some good reasons that we shall fully discuss in the last chapters. The New Testament and Christian tradition alike sometimes speak of faith and grace as though they could make possible a new, divinized human nature. We see this in the Pauline discussions of a new creation, of Jesus as the Second Adam (a new beginning for humanity), and of the justifications worked by faith and grace. We see it in the figures of Revelation that speak of a new heaven and a new earth. For his followers, the pneumatic intensity of Jesus' experience burst the bonds of human sinfulness. The Suffering Servant, one of their major traditional categories for understanding Jesus, had not only borne humanity's sins, but had also washed humanity clean with his blood. Thus the cross the Servant mounted became finally less significant than his resurrection from the grave. In his resurrection, sin, death, and all the other disfiguring powers had in principle been routed. The possibilities disclosed in the pneumatic differentiation, we might say, had become constitutive: substantial bases for reconceiving of *humanity* and *divinity*.

PAUL

The New Testament writers who most deeply pondered the structural issues that Voegelin considered crucial were John and Paul. John spoke of a "drawing" by divinity quite like the Platonic drawing, and his realized eschatology offered Christians an alternative to apocalyptic expectations that would in effect have dissolved the present world. But Paul is the writer on whom Voegelin concentrated more, probably because Paul played the greater role in Christianity's expansion into a worldwide religious possibility.

Paul himself never knew the historical Jesus. His conversion to Christianity, if we can believe the three versions in Acts, was due to a dramatic encounter with the risen Christ. So there is virtually nothing in the Pauline corpus that deals with the gospel materials about Jesus' preaching, healing, miracles, or personality. This does not mean that Paul was unfamiliar with these materials. As a well-instructed convert he probably knew the traditions about Jesus' historical life rather well. But his interest lay elsewhere. For Paul the death and resurrection of Jesus represented a new historical

Wood Figure of Christ. Spanish, second half of thirteenth century. This crucifix conveys not only the suffering of Christ but also his composure and regal victory.   *(The Nelson-Atkins Museum of Art, Kansas City, Missouri [Nelson Fund])*

axis. Pneumatically (and perhaps, by inference, noetically as well), Jesus' "passover" had inaugurated a new creation. Principally the reign of sin, as Paul conceived it, symbolized by the fall of Adam, the beginnings of humanity, had been crushed. Satan, whom late Israelite religion and early Christianity sometimes personified as the strongest agent of radical evil, had met his match. The resurrection of Jesus therefore was more than God's ratification of Jesus' person and message. It was the dawning of a new historical era, a new set of pneumatic possibilities. The Spirit poured forth by the resurrected Messiah could renovate human beings from within as in Jeremiah's anticipatory vision.

To Paul's mind, one could gain access to the Spirit and the new set of pneumatic possibilities by faith in the paramount significance of Jesus the Christ. The path begun by Abraham could, in the aftermath of Jesus, take one into God's own forgiveness and sanctification. Compared to this path, the way of following the Torah, conceived as a set of ethical prescriptions, paled to insignificance. Scholars presently debate the extent to which Paul intended to deprecate Jewish religious law, in general tending to find Paul more appreciative of Judaism than past generations of New Testament analysts had been, but it remains clear that Paul thought that Jesus meant a new thing in history, something that prior Judaism had been unable to accomplish.

The great Pauline writing that displays the mature vision Paul had of these matters is the Epistle to the Romans. In chapter one Paul treats of the depravity of humankind apart from faith, setting the stage for the utter necessity of the salvation available in Christ. In chapter five he makes the extended comparison between Adam and Christ, the era of sin and the new era of grace, that in effect divides history into a before and after. In chapter eight he writes movingly of the Spirit made available by Christ's victorious resurrection, reaching a high point of Christian pneumatic vision. The passage we quote at one and the same time suggests the cosmic import of Christ's work of redemption, the tension between its beginnings in the present and its outreach to a final consummation in the future, and the basis for the believer's inner confidence in divine grace.

> I consider that the sufferings of this present time are not worth comparing with the glory that is to be revealed to us. For the creation waits with eager longing for the revealing of the sons of God; for the creation was subjected to futility, not of its own will but by the will of him who subjected it in hope; because the creation itself will be set free from its bondage to decay and obtain the glorious liberty of the children of God. We know that the whole creation has been groaning in travail together until now; and not only the creation, but we ourselves, who have the first fruits of the Spirit, groan inwardly as we wait for our adoption as sons, the redemption of our bodies. For in this hope we were saved. Now hope that is seen is not hope. For who hopes for what he sees? But if we hope for what we do not see, we wait for it with patience. Likewise the Spirit helps us in our weakness; for we do not know how to pray as we ought, but the Spirit himself intercedes for us with sighs too deep for words. And he who searches the hearts of men knows what

is the mind of the Spirit, because the Spirit intercedes for the saints according to the will of God. [Romans 8:18–27]

First, despite the exclusively masculine pronouns, it is clear that Paul is speaking of all believers, women as much as men. Second, the imagery retains much of the urgency, even the anguish, of apocalyptic versions of faith, and it makes this cosmic: All creation is groaning with the need to give birth to what has grown within it (its great passion for salvation and fulfillment). Third, the discussion of hope, especially when placed in concert with Pauline discussions of faith and charity in other places, recalls the probings of Heraclitus and might be generalized in the direction of the noetic realization that if one is to understand or come to the light one has to be oriented positively, able to hold oneself open. Fourth, the gift of the Spirit as the first fruits is the most acute point, for it brings to mind the experiences, such as deep prayer, that make it credible that salvation has occurred, that grace is now available as an existential force, that human beings can think of themselves as children of God.

Voegelin has great admiration for the intensity of the Pauline pneumatic experiences and the depth of the Pauline articulation. But he finds lacking some of the metaxic balance that Plato had achieved. Especially from our vantage point almost 1950 years after Paul, the expectation of creation's soon being delivered, of the first fruits of the Spirit soon ceding to the full adoption of God's children, seems, if not naive, at least strongly in need of nuance. Analytically, in terms of what one can say apart from privileged commitments stemming from a more than rational faith, the Pauline rendition seems often to have been read without doing justice to the symbolic character of all speech about the divine mystery and about what happens when the Spirit gives human beings intimations of radical healing. Thus Paul's vision holds within it the strong danger of leading people to take literally what can only be metaphoric language. For example, although it is powerful poetry to speak of creation in labor to give birth, it is a dangerous misreading to take this literally and start planning a new ecological community or a new politics in which human beings are thought innocent of temptations to injustice or wrongdoing.

In a word, Voegelin's analysis of Christian pneumaticism, that of Paul and that of other early Christian writers alike, places them in the context of utopian creations, downplaying their literal value without denying their powerful symbolic truth.[2] This, to Voegelin's mind, would better preserve the force of the gospel than the doctrinalization that occurred in later Christianity. As we noted previously, Voegelin thought that any tearing of the contents of consciousness away from the relationalism of primordial spiritual experiences, any **reification** in which these contents are taken as independent entities, distorts reality and prepares great michief. The Pauline symbols of a new creation and a heavenly fulfillment express profound experiences of what human life ought to be. Those experiences are crucial to the Christian appreciation of the salvation accomplished in Christ, who died a witness to the fuller life that right relation to God could accomplish, and they offered all subsequent Western history a richly differentiated appreciation of the divine interactions with the human spirit. Voegelin did not at all want to minimize or contract the truth of this. But he saw the need for a more careful exegesis of spiritual experience, if we are to work out the political consequences of the Christian sense of a germinating salvation struggling to reach full flower. Too much chaos has come from Christian efforts to leap out of the present human condition into a heavenly communion of saints for the sober student of history not to stress the dangers, as well as the treasures, latent in the Pauline pneumaticism. One Oliver Cromwell calls seriously into question the Christian claims to perfectionism and a mandate to bring all the earth to holiness.[3]

THE WORLD AND THE SPIRIT

The Christian pneumatic differentiations, particularly as they were expressed in the person of Jesus, who became an icon or living symbol of what God could do with human flesh, both completed the Israelite breakthrough and clarified the agenda that remained. As we shall see in the next section, the Christian notion of a trinitarian God went considerably beyond Jewish monotheism, and the principal reason for this development was the Christian conclusion that what had happened in Jesus in the last analysis could only be understood by accepting his true divinity. The dogmatic expression of this conviction at the great Christian councils of Nicaea (325) and Chalcedon (451) was more literal-minded than Voegelin and other symbolists would have preferred, but it did safeguard the conviction that Jesus was the uniquely privileged place from which one was to derive one's interpretation of reality. As the incarnation of divine truth, Jesus became the nodal point or **hermeneutical** center.

The consequences for Christian cosmology did not take long to unfold. If Jesus were the Logos or divine Word, the enfleshment of the self-expression of God spotlighted by the Israelite patriarchs and prophets, then he must have had an important role in Creation. Genesis portrays God creating through verbal commands, and such early Christian hymns as Colossians 1:15–20 placed Jesus the Word at the foundations of creation.

> He is the image of the invisible God, the first-born of all creation; for in him all things were created, in heaven and on earth, visible and invisible, whether thrones or dominions or principalities or authorities—all things were created through him and for him. He is before all things, and in him all things hold together. He is the head of the body, the church; he is the beginning, the firstborn from the dead, that in everything he might be preeminent. For in him all the fulness of God was pleased to dwell, and through him to reconcile to himself all things, whether on earth or in heaven, making peace by the blood of his cross.

This hymn takes us quite a distance from the simple carpenter from Nazareth. Yet it was written and sung within a generation of Jesus' death and resurrection. One sees, therefore, the spark that Jesus was for the ready tinder of Jewish speculations about wisdom. The Logos of Hellenistic philosophy had been taken over by Jewish writers for their speculations about God's construction of the world. Easily enough, the early Christians, many of whom were Greek-speaking Jews, applied this speculation to Jesus. By virtue of his resurrection, he could be considered the cornerstone and the pattern of creation. God had made him the firstborn and archetype of the new creation. He had been the principal agent of both the reconciliation between God and creation and the reconciliation among the different creatures that his passover from death to resurrection made credible. So it was but a further step, back to the origins of God's creational plan, to see him as the expression of God in whom creation itself had occurred. The first chapter of the Gospel of John speaks similarly: "He was in the beginning with God; all things were made through him, and without him was not anything made that was made" (1:2).

The legacy to later Christian faith was a sense that the world and humanity had become congenial to one another. The world, matter, the flesh—these were all amenable to being divinized, being taken up into the divine love that was life. What had happened in Jesus was the crucial first step. Later progress would develop the incarnational process, and eventually God would be all in all. This sort of language, once again, outstrips common sense and daily experience. It is brilliant at disclosing the possibilities that both human nature and simple matter enclose, but it is no basis for calculating a realistic technology or politics. These latter enterprises, without which social life cannot proceed, must factor in the recalcitrance of matter or nature and the waywardness of human beings as well. The notions of finitude, sin, and (later) systemic injustices all have a part to play. As a result, the mature Christian vision of the world became quite complicated or sophisticated. Again and again, the best theologians spoke of both/and. The world is both a sacrament and a realm apart from God. The Creator both is and is not present to creation. Human beings have the potential to be both saints and sinners. What happens in time both is and is not decisive for our estimates of God and humanity.

The advantages of the Christian creeds and doctrines that expressed this complicated view of reality were their ability to keep the general Christian populace fairly well attuned to the balance that a mature following of Christ entailed. The disadvantages were their distance from the pneumatic experiences that alone make sacramentality and the vision of what human beings might accomplish together (were they to be fully converted to God) persuasive from within. The Spirit was necessary for these pneumatic experiences to keep a steady flame, but the letter of the Christian doctrinal law, no less than the letter of the Jewish rabbinic law, tended to kill the life of the Spirit.

Overall, the Christian sense of the world was more praising of matter than the Indian or even the Greek sense had been. If the Word of God had taken flesh, the cosmos and human affairs both had an intrinsic dignity. From time to time Christians disparaged temporal life, sexuality, eating and drinking, but the mainstream of their religious faith strove for a restrained love of this created order. The world was not heaven, and attempts to transform the world into heaven missed the mark, but the world could be made better if people would shift their sight to the values witnessed by Christ.

So, paradoxically enough, the Spirit believed to be poured out by Christ's resurrection pointed in the direction of improving the human condition by prying people's hands from worldly treasures. The preaching of Jesus about love of neighbor, especially as it was developed in such texts as Matthew 25, where how one has treated one's neighbors becomes the crux of one's judgment by God, inclined the Christian heroes to spend themselves serving the poor and the sick, the ignorant and the miserable. Thousands of charitable institutions—soup kitchens, hospitals, schools, counseling centers—owe their origin to this impulse. Insofar as Voegelin sometimes seemed to downplay what human beings can do to transform their condition, so impressed was he by the ultimate mystery of God and the dangers of apocalyptic fervor, he was out of phase with the example of the Christian saints. However, insofar as the Christian saints, too, have

St. John the Evangelist on Patmos. Erhard Altdorfer. The artist accepted the traditional view (now disputed) that the Gospel of John and the Book of Revelation had the same author. Both books do stress the divinity of Christ as the incarnate Word (note the Madonna and child in the picture). *(The Nelson-Atkins Museum of Art, Kansas City, Missouri [Nelson Fund])*

spoken of leaving everything to God, of attributing all salvation or human improvement to the Spirit, the tradition has honored Voegelin's concerns.

There is room for debate, therefore, about the sort of worldliness or secular commitment implied in the Christian pneumatic differentiation. By giving the world the most concrete locus of divinity, the flesh of an actual historical figure, Christianity said that heaven had come to earth, the divine had assumed the human condition. Despite all the changes wrought by modernity, this saying continues to exert great influence. The very modern sense that most evils should not be, that most sufferings should not occur, is grounded in the iconic figure of Jesus, the one who suffered to defeat evil and suffering.

GOD

The God that the modern West deals with, even when the dealing is only by way of rejection, also has been shaped decisively by the iconic figure of Jesus. For although it is inaccurate to depict the God of the Hebrew Bible as an angry judge superseded by the Christian notion of God's parenthood, it is true that Jesus' dealings with God introduced an amazing intimacy. Similarly, even though the Israelite theologians had spoken of God's Word and Spirit, the Christian trinitarian God made these notions more intimate to the divine essence. In fact, a major controversy between early Christians and their Jewish confrères stemmed from the Christian claim that Jesus was more than the Messiah (most Jews would not even have granted Jesus' messiahship), that indeed he was the privileged locus of the divine upon earth. To the Jewish mind this ran afoul of monotheism, the utter uniqueness and transcendence of the God of the fathers, the Lord of Creation. Christians claimed they were not compromising this monotheism, but most Jews and Muslims have not accepted the Christian claim. Nonetheless, the growth of the Christian religion meant the promulgation of a divine imagery in which God was one "nature" but three different "persons" (unlimited centers of knowing and loving).

The personalism of the Christian God, some historians of science have claimed, played an important role in the development of Western science. Because they believed that God had made the world analogous to human craftsmanship, the early Christian investigators of nature could be confident that an intelligent probing would yield up nature's laws. That belief has proven more complicated in recent times, as science has moved out of its mechanistic views of nature and come to appreciate the wonderful, perhaps even mysterious depths, interconnections, and relations to reason that nature displays. Still, guiding even the contemporary scientist in his or her research is the conviction that whatever first made or now grounds the natural world bears affinities to human intelligence. Our scientific and technological success is eloquent grounds for this conviction, just as our confusion about how to use the power this success has brought testifies that future science cannot be divorced from profound questions of ethics (nature's rights, our responsibilities to the future, the rightfulness of attaining powers one may never use, and so forth).

The personalism of the Western God, sharpened in the Christian image of the divine as a community of Father-Son-Spirit, no doubt has consoled the average believer with the sense that God knows the depths of human pain and confusion, loves even the slightest human effort to do good. On the other hand, it has been part of an **anthropocentrism** that the ecological crisis now suggests has become vicious. If God were personal, to the degree of having the divine Word take human flesh, then human beings must be the center of creation—so did the Christian instinct run. In the background lay the depictions of creation in Genesis, according to which Adam and Eve had been placed over the rest of creation. The idea of Genesis 1:28 that human beings were to fill the earth and subdue it gave the literally minded or fundamentalist reader the sense that the earth existed mainly for human benefit, even for human exploitation. No doubt biblical scholars are right to argue that the Bible probably wanted a stewardship over creation, rather than an exploitation in the pejorative sense, but the message conveyed to the average Christian through the ages, peasant and lord alike, was that human beings could use the land as they saw fit. As technology improved, humanity seemed to relish its increased control over nature, as though it could now make up for the tens of thousands of years during which nature had terrorized it. Only in the past few decades, as the implications of unbridled technological incursions into nature have become clearer, could ecologists or theologians see the full extent of the dangers latent in the biblical anthropocentrism.

Returning from these dangers to the mainstream of the historical Christian tradition, one finds other paths that might have been taken. For example, the Christian reflection on the nature of God that came from the schooling of the fathers and the medievals in the Greek noetic tradition had a strong place for God's *impersonal* character. A line of "negative" theology that ran from Neoplatonic thinkers such as Plotinus to Christians such as Denys the Areopagite and Scotus Erigena stressed the mystery of the divine nature, the way it overspills all human categories. One can see in this negative theology the imprint of Plato's conviction that the divine is always "beyond," ever on the far side of the upper limit of the human metaxy. This means that God can never be personal in the way that human beings are. Despite the full presence of divinity that orthodox Christian faith saw in Jesus, the divine Word incarnate, the Godhead itself could never be captured by human formulas. Indeed, divinity had to be present quite fully to any being for that being even to exist. Thus one could speak of the divine dignity of subhuman creation, insofar as animals, trees, and stones, too, were expressions of the ultimate source of being and creativity. Had it taken this profound metaphysical instinct to heart, the Western tradition might have balanced its technological developments with a reverence for nature like that of nonliterate peoples.

At any rate, the Christian Godhead came to be pictured as a fullness of light and life, love and power. The Johannine conviction that God is light in whom there is no darkness at all (1 John 1:5) took to its final conclusion the biblical instinct that evil reposes outside the divinity, whereas the Johannine reflections on the interrelations among Jesus, the Father, and the Spirit prepared the way for later speculation, such as that of Augustine and Aquinas, on the intellectual and volitional modalities of the interactions among the divine persons. Briefly, the Father was conceived of as the font of light, creativity, and love; the Son was conceived of as the expression of the Father, the perfect image; and the Spirit was conceived of as either the breathing forth of the Father's love for the Son (the conception of Eastern Christian theologians) or the mutual love of Father and Son (the Western Christian conception). The general result, at least among the better theologians, was a theology that made God constant knowing and loving, eternal light and warmth. In fact, heaven would be the small human person's endless enjoyment of the dazzling light and warmth of the infinite divinity who had invited humanity into the Godhead's bliss.

Practically, this was too rarefied for the average Christian, so devotion to Jesus, his mother Mary, and the saints dominated the popular devotional theology. The Church came to be thought of as the community representing God on earth, and the leaders of the Church had great psychological power. Because they could cast one out of good standing in the community of those who would be saved, the simple people feared them greatly. This meant that long periods of Western history—certainly the medieval and reformation eras—flowed along in an atmosphere of uneasiness, doubt, and guilt. With hellfire licking at their heels, the ordinary people looked to the sacraments and the Bible almost superstitiously or magically as their means of escape into heaven. Once again, the experiences that lay beneath the gospels' claims to joy, peace, salvation, divinization, and the rest were essentially forgotten. Insofar as this brought such experiences into contempt (however ignorant), the history of medieval and reformation Christianity paved the way for the modern ambiguities about religion. The God too often presented was not the God of Abraham, Isaac, Jacob, Jesus, and Paul but the God of incompetent philosophers and credulous clerics or commoners.

GNOSTICISM, FAITH, AND REASON

Early in the Common Era a movement called *Gnosticism* arose, and Voegelin took it as the stimulus to name a whole class of losses of metaxic balance.[4] Essentially, his Gnosticism is a sense of spiritual power, of intellectual and imaginative creativity, run riot. In the early movement that Christianity branded heretical, strong thinkers speculated on the process by which a world shining with luminous possibilities had fallen into its present disorder. Confusing such speculation with solid, empirically grounded truth (or deliberately distorting what they were up to, for the sake of gaining power), these thinkers came to speak of a privileged knowledge (**gnosis**), access to which could give one salvation from the evil or disordered present age. They tended to link this knowledge with spiritual regimes that deprecated the material world and to declare those who possessed such knowledge free of the constraints of ordinary morality. The Christian mainstream responded by upholding the rights of matter, which the Logos had sanctified in taking flesh, and by declaring the way of salvation both to be open to all who would believe, hope, and love and to require a straight path of high ethical performance. In a word, the Christian authorities branded the Gnostics' claims bogus, warning that they represented a pernicious turning away from the solid truths of the gospel.

We have seen that metaxic balance is never an easy matter, and Voegelin said straight out that no society has ever been founded on a noetic differentiation of any significant degree. Always the power of the cosmological myth, and the strength of pneumatic movements, make the delicate midpoint of the noetic golden mean very difficult to achieve. In this case, however, the truth of the cosmological myth would have been salutary, for the Gnostics were precisely in danger of trying to leap out of the material world, to ignore the hard realities of human embodiment and limitation. Equally, they were in danger of missing the truth that all genuine mysticism trumpets: the unknowability of the divine, the primacy of the Platonic "beyond."

Thus Gnosticism became for Voegelin a species of aberration in which a sort of intoxication with mental powers turns peoples' heads and leads them to ignore realities both commonsensical and mystical. The heresy that the Christian fathers fought was relatively harmless, however, compared with the modern versions that have bloodied the world map. For Voegelin, Hegel, Marx, some of the thinkers of the French Revolution, and others whose theories led to slaughter and totalitarianism all suffered from a Gnostic intoxication. Missing the metaxic mark, they developed a "secondary" reality that they could manipulate by imaginative power, while their followers rode out to crush the infidels who resisted life in such a distorted realm. Stalin, Hitler, and Mao are recent examples.

The question therefore becomes, What is the proper relation between an enthusiastic, Spirit-filled faith and a calm, Spirit-given reason? Throughout Christian history, theologians have wrestled with this question, and their wrestling continues today. Voegelin's preferences in this matter align with the Eastern Orthodox and Roman Catholic tendencies and against the Protestant tendency (although he himself was raised a Lutheran). By this we mean that he tended to seek a correlation of faith and reason, out of a conviction that they should complement one another, and to avoid the clash that much Protestant theology has thought necessary. However, this is not to say that Voegelin fully approved of what happened in patristic and medieval theology or that he fully disapproved of what happened in the Protestant Reformation. He thought that all the Christian schools have done the Greek experience an injustice, insofar as they have fashioned a distinction between the *natural* origin of philosophy and the *supernatural* origin of biblical revelation. Moreover, he thought that this false distinction had played into the **doctrinalization** that Christian faith suffered and that such doctrinalization played a pernicious role in both the Reformation and the disorders of modernity that crystalized in the Enlightenment.

The grounds for denying any hard and fast distinction between the divine origin of philosophy and the divine origin of revelation are experiential, as are the grounds of most of Voegelin's key arguments. Plato certainly conceived of philosophy as a pursuit of the divine ground that was initiated and drawn forward by that ground itself. Moreover, he spoke of the illuminations that moved the pursuit forward in terms that most prophets and mystics could have used. In no way, therefore, can one properly speak of genuine philosophy as something that humanity attempts or accomplishes on its own. Throughout, genuine philosophers are dealing with the mystery of being and luminosity, which they know is holy, and therefore divine. From the other side, we can also see that the experiences of revelation involve the mind and require human effort for their articulation. True enough, the prophet and the mystic feel the divine irrupting into the ground of their human personalities, and so have a more holistic experience than the philosophers. But the ground of their human personalities is not divorced from their minds, so the irruption is lightsome if not precisely intellectual, illuminating if not precisely noetic. Moreover, if they are to express what they have experienced, prophets must do their best to name, configure, and judge their meetings with God. From the lovely figure of the Lord being not in the earthquake or the fire but in a small still voice (1 Kings 19:11–13) to the full descriptions of John of the Cross, the pneumatic experience of God invites the mind to ponder, appropriate, and express. Should one call this activity merely natural? For all that it differs from the prior, often ineffable, time of address or seizure, it too can occur under the guidance of the Spirit and for the Spirit's ends. As Paul made plain in the classical text of 1 Corinthians 14, prophecy (in the sense of articulate religious experience) is preferable to mere enthusiasm or speaking in tongues, which edifies only the recipient and cannot express itself to others.

In addition to this argument from the similarity or at least compatibility of the experiences of noetic and pneumatic differentiation, Voegelin would link faith and reason because of the disasters that follow when they are separated. This is the charge he raised against the Protestant theology that broke the medieval ideal of correlating faith and reason. By despising reason, which Luther called a whore and Calvin named a factory of idols, the Reformers cast away the anchor that enthusiastic faith needs if it is not to be blown hither and yon to shipwreck. They also tempted later thinkers to reject their version of faith as unreasonable and to create a view of reason that had nothing to do with divine mystery or pneumatic experience. The result was the modern schizophrenia in which the union of faith and reason, mysticism and science, absorption in the spirit's defining movement toward the divine ground and critical analysis of all theories of reality became a lost ideal. At the extremes we have the equally despicable options of a faith so unintelligent or uncritical that it seems simple-minded and a reason so spirit-less that it seems mechanical, inhuman. The scriptural fundamentalists (whatever their religious tradition) who simply thump their holy books to justify their denials of scientific findings, or even their bloody purges of "infidels," are proof positive of the perils in a faith that has thrown aside reason and thinks that pneumatic inspiration alone can suffice. The **positivistic** philosophers, scientists, and politicians who find no mystery in nature, no directional search drawing the human spirit, no sacrality in either the cosmos or the polis show but the reverse of the fundamentalist abuse. In their case human potential is perverted by an overconcentration on reason or a denaturing of reason to a purely technical faculty. Either way, faith and reason have separated, reality has come unglued, and the result has been much suffering.

COUNTERVIEWS

As we indicated, orthodox Christian theologians would tend to want a more explicit acceptance of Jesus' divinity and of the literal truthfulness of Christian doctrinal claims than Voegelin provided. Apologists for Protestant theology no doubt would dispute Voegelin's reading of the slippage of faith and reason in their tradition, whereas Catholic apologists would contest the low marks that Voegelin gave doctrinalization.

From the secular or atheistic side, critics no doubt would deplore Voegelin's acceptance of Christian religious and theological claims, tending to dismiss the speech of Jesus and Paul as at best pious poetry. Thus Marxist critics would want to rewrite the gospels and subsequent Christian history in terms of economic contests, and empiricists would greatly limit any talk about divine transcendence and religious mystery. Moreover, these and other modernists would be unhappy with the normative character that Voegelin gave the noetic and pneumatic differentiations of consciousness that were available by the Christian Middle Ages. We shall see that Voegelin accepted at least as much from modernity as he rejected, but it is true that he found the Enlightenment an inadequate spiritual movement and that Hegelian dialectics (another characteristically modern achievment) draws some of his harshest criticism (because he thought that it tries to divinize human reason).

SUMMARY

Christianity is the second religious tradition that we are considering from the viewpoint of pneumatic differentiation, and Jesus appears in the lineage of the Israelite prophets. The rich materials relevant to Jesus' own preaching of the Kingdom of God, to say nothing of the traditions about Jesus' messiahship, resurrection, and divinity, suggest the significant degree to which Christians restructured the Israelite sense of God's presence in the world. The Pauline doctrines of justification by faith, Christ as the Second Adam, and the redemption of creation that the Spirit given to believers assures only further underscore this suggestion.

The Christian repositioning of the ingredients of the sense of the world and the Spirit that was available from Israel continued in such visions as that of Colossians, in which Jesus became the cornerstone of creation, and that of the prologue of John's gospel, in which the Word was the medium of creation. These visions came from Spirit-given faith, and the question for the interpreter of history (as demarcated by leaps in being) is how to evaluate them. For Voegelin, they were best read as symbols rather than as literal affirmations; so too with the Christian developments in the doctrine of God. The symbol of the trinity discloses riches of the Godhead previously unappreciated, but neither it nor the personalist view of the Creator should be snatched out of the metaxic consciousness in which the experiences that generated them occurred. When they are, such disorders as an anthropocentrism that finally has come to imperil nature can occur.

Under the name *Gnosticism,* Voegelin lumped together several other ways that, historically, groups within Christian history have lost balance and taken their imaginative or spiritual forays for literal reality. To counter this he proposed dropping the traditional Christian separations between nature and the supernatural, between philosophy and revelation. He also proposed revisiting actual noetic and pneumatic experience, whether historical or contemporary, to restore the complementarity of faith and reason and counter modernity's schizophrenia.

Last, we noted the counterviews that orthodox Christian thinkers, both Protestant and Catholic, would probably have of Jesus and the Christian worldview, and we also noted the problems that modernists, whether Marxist or empiricist, would probably find with Voegelin's positive views of Christian faith.

STUDY QUESTIONS

1. What sort of experience probably underlay Jesus' use of the beatitudes in the Sermon on the Mount?
2. What is the truth in the vision that Paul lays out in Romans 8?
3. How did the Christian notion of Jesus as the Logos enfleshed reconfigure the biblical picture of creation?
4. Explain the "impersonalism" of the Christian God that might have alleviated the ecological crisis.
5. Describe the ideal relation of faith and reason that both fundamentalism and positivism deny.

NOTES

1. See Bruce Douglas, "A Diminished Gospel: A Critique of Voegelin's Interpretation of Christianity," in *Eric Voegelin's Search for Order in History,* ed. Stephen A. McKnight (Baton Rouge: Louisiana State University Press, 1978), pp. 139–54; William Thompson, "Voegelin on Jesus Christ," in *Voegelin and the Theologian,* eds. John Kirby and William Thompson (Toronto: Edwin Mellen Press, 1983), pp. 178–221.
2. See Eric Voegelin, "Immortality: Experience and Symbol," *Harvard Theological Review* LX (1967), pp. 235–79.
3. See Eric Voegelin, *The New Science of Politics* (Chicago: University of Chicago Press, 1966), pp. 133–61; also Igor Shafarevich, *The Socialist Phenomenon* (New York: Harper & Row, Pub., 1980).
4. See Eric Voegelin, *Science, Politics and Gnosticism* (Chicago: Henry Regnery, 1968); also Pheme Perkins, "Gnosis and the Life of the Spirit: The Price of Pneumatic Order," in *Voegelin and the Theologian,* pp. 222–52.

CHAPTER NINE

Islam

ORIENTATION

In this chapter we focus on what is perhaps the acme of prophetic consciousness. After Muhammad one can speak of *prophecy* in an accommodated sense (for example, as a way of characterizing the passionate quest for justice that drives a Karl Marx or as a way of underscoring the prescient quality of the ethical views of an Albert Einstein), but the word no longer carries the full overtones that it has in Islam, where it designates serving as the direct mouthpiece of God.

It is difficult for Westerners to handle Islam fairly, of course, because Islam usually has stood over against us as a threat or a foe. And whereas the religions of India and China have often seemed the more alluring for their foreignness, Islam has labored under the burden of being quite like Judaism and Semitic Christianity. Finally, the atmosphere of the middle 1980s, when Islam was being claimed by psychopaths and killers as their strongest motivation, has triply burdened reflections on this religion.

Muslims have traditionally felt that they could not get a fair hearing in the West, and many of them certainly have good grounds for continuing to think this today. On the other hand, many Muslims seem not to understand the rules of scholarship in matters of religion and so take offense with little justification. These include most prominently the Muslims who insist that the Qur'an be made the criterion of all truth and wisdom. We are bound to disappoint them, just as we are bound to disappoint Jews who think that Torah should never be subjected to criticism or Christians who think that the New Testament must be swallowed whole. Our criterion, we must repeat, is the one handed down by Plato: Something is not good because someone claims that it is godly or "revealed"; something is godly or revealed because it is remarkably good. Muslims, in fact, should have less difficulty with this criterion than many Asians or shamanistic peoples, because in many Asian or shamanistic schemes divinity is not bound to be moral, even in a supereminent or merely analogous way. If they are willing to drop their demands for a privileged revelational status (admittedly, a big requirement), Muslims can contend quite well in the arena where divinity and goodness coincide, because their God is repeatedly, thematically, said to be compassionate and merciful.

MUHAMMAD

Muhammad (570–632 c.e.) is probably *the* great rival to Jesus for prophetic preeminence. Islam is now second only to Christianity in terms of world population, and his followers make more of Muhammad's prophecy than Christians make of the prophetship of Jesus. (Islam denies that Muhammad was divine, while the Christian divinization of Jesus shifted attention away from his prophetship.) Indeed, Muslims believe that Muhammad came as the seal or final chapter in the story of revelation that began with Abraham. They revere Abraham, Moses, and Jesus as spokesmen of God, but the prophecy of Muhammad makes Abraham, Moses, Jesus, and other spokemen but forerunners, precursors of the *rasul* through whom the Lord of the Worlds gave the definitive divine Word.

One of the most striking features of Muhammad's prophecy was its poetic grandeur. The Qur'an preserves this feature, being considered by students of Arabic the purest and most elevated specimen of that language. This fact can occasion the reflection that prophecy, and pneumatic inspiration generally, seem related to the wellsprings of eloquence. Certainly the Hebrew prophets gained renown for their poetry as well as for the challenges of their message. Jesus displayed lively and memorable speech, especially in the parables (which some scholars nominate as the most reliable indications of how Jesus preached and taught). Muhammad, then, is of a piece with his predecessors in bringing forth dazzling language, figures of speech and rhythmic utterances that burned into his hearers' memories and hearts.

Muhammad was also like his predecessors in feeling that his call had come from without, through no focused effort or desire of his own. He was about forty when he started receiving the visions recorded in the Qur'an, and a psychologist might say that they were the answer to a deep quest for life's meaning. As with the other prophets who made a profound impact, however, Muhammad did not receive visions that concerned only himself. The "recital" that God imposed upon him was a message for his times. Like the times of other religious founders, Muhammad's were out of joint. The tribal or clan system of Arabia was breaking down, so that widows, orphans, and other unfortunates were falling through the cracks. The answer

Muhammad received included the demand that the Arabs reconstitute themselves on a broader basis. By accepting the revelations granted to Muhammad and arranging themselves under his leadership, they could forge a pan-Arab unity. It took Muhammad some time to win acceptance of this, but when he did the Arab tribes united into a military and cultural force of which history has seldom seen the like.

We shall deal more fully with the conceptual content of Muhammad's recital in the next sections. Here let us concentrate on a **surah** of the Qur'an that suggests what his original pneumatic experience might have been. Surah 97, known as **Qadr** or "Glory," gives us a glimpse of the impression that his seizure left on the Prophet.

> We revealed the Koran on the Night of Qadr. Would that you knew what the Night of Qadr is like! Better is the Night of Qadr than a thousand months. On that night the angels and the Spirit by their Lord's leave come down with His decrees. That night is peace, til break of day.[1]

The Qur'an is full of angels (Gabriel has a special function) and full of the Divine Spirit. Islam does not make the latter a "person" of the deity, as in the Christian trinity, but it conceives of God as spiritual, both beyond matter and tending to come with a rush, like a breath. Whatever happened to Muhammad was by divine choice, and the burden of the Qur'an that Muhammad received to recite was the divine decrees, God's will for Muhammad's people. We are therefore at the delicate and difficult point where a human being feels compelled to announce a Word from beyond, a command and revelation brimming with divine authority.

This is close to the heart of the prophetic experience, and it explains much of how Muhammad became a figure of historic importance. He was utterly convinced that God had chosen him to bear forth a message and execute a program. When he brought the Arabian people around to this conviction, both he and they could ride forth with no hesitations, in total confidence that their cause was God's own. From a perspective such as Voegelin's, this degree of absorption by a pneumatic experience offers us a fine opportunity to assess the gains and dangers of revelation.

The gains certainly include the overwhelming conviction of God's sovereign reality. As no other religion, Islam makes God the willful ruler of heaven and earth, the absolute monarch. The only fitting response that human beings can make is submission (the root meaning of *Islam*). When Muslims bow low in prayer, they act out or dramatize in gesture their sense that Allah alone is in charge. Muhammad launched this rigorous monotheism not as an intellectual conviction but because of his personal experience. He had met the Lord of the Worlds and when that Lord spoke he had no choice but to obey and promulgate the message.

Analytically, of course, one can, and probably should, distinguish between the time of pneumatic seizure and the later formation of the message received. What form the divine communication originally took is hard to determine. One can say with certainty that Muhammad, like other prophets, felt moved or grasped at the base of his reality. Any verbal expression of this movement, however, any specific set of commands or requisite responses, would seem both secondary and less central. The confession of God that has become an epitome of Muslim faith probably is our best hint of the innermost portion of Muhammad's experience: "There is no God but God." The rest of Muslim theology and ethics, that of Muhammad as well as that of his followers, involves more inference. Because of his experience of God's absolute existence, Muhammad merited the status given him in the second part of the Muslim confession: "And Muhammad is His prophet." No one in Arab history had been addressed by God so powerfully, and from this address Muhammad gained his right, indeed his responsibility, to leadership. But how the sovereign God and the prophetic leader conspired to develop the message of impending judgment, to say nothing of the rather complicated interpretation of the Prophet's movement as the successor and purifier of Jewish and Christian revelation, is a more complicated question. Still, the cogency of the program that Muhammad developed and the effectiveness of the Qur'anic revelation speak for themselves. To this day they represent "the path that is straight" for hundreds of millions of people.

The dangers in pneumatic experience of this intensity, of revelations that claim to come directly from the sole God, range from megalomania to holocaust. Muhammad seems to have avoided megalomania. He always insisted that he was not divine, and among the submitters to Allah he was the foremost. In the beginning he doubted his own sanity, wondering whether the revelations were the product of a diseased mind. By the end he seems to have become relatively tranquil, able to lead his troops in battle and legislate for the practical affairs of the community with a humble, almost shy personal style that yet never compromised his decisiveness. The danger of holocaust, slaughter, great excess in the prosecution of evildoers who resist the divine message haunts Islam to this day. We shall have to consider this issue quite fully, for it most disfigures the whole notion of prophecy.

THE QUR'AN

When Voegelin studied the history of differentiation, of what happened to the epochal noetic and pneumatic breakthroughs, he found a pattern of doctrinalization and reification. The original experiences get reduced to the part that can be taught ("doctrine"), and the ingredients of the original experiences get torn from the metaxy and treated as independent things (**res**). One of the ways this happens is through the formation of *scripture*.[2] The experiences of revelation are written down, and the writings come to be taken as sacred utterances. This happened with Jewish revelation, Torah in some historical periods being thought to have coexisted with God from eternity. It happened with Christian revelation, the Bible frequently being taken literally as dictation from heaven. To a lesser extent or analogously, it happened with the Hindu, Buddhist, and Chinese holy books.

For example, the Buddhist holy text called The Lotus Sutra has been for some sects *the* path to salvation.

Probably no religion has absolutized its scripture as greatly as Islam, however. Because Muhammad was always denied divine status, and the accent always fell on what Allah had given Muhammad to recite, the record of the recital came to take center stage. For many Muslims, probably the majority throughout history, the Qur'an has literally represented the Word of God. God dictated it (for some commentators this took place in time, for others the earthly Qur'an was but a temporal replica of an eternal heavenly archetype), and Muhammad was merely the receptacle or conduit by which it entered human history. No translation from the Arabic in which it was received could ever do the Qur'an justice. No agency of Muhammad, let alone of the followers who pieced the text together after Muhammad's death, was of any significance. What one had in the Arabic text was the definitive Word of God on which human success depended. Anything commanded in the Qur'an was absolutely required. Anything forbidden was absolutely vetoed. The basic pattern of Muslim devotion has always revolved around the Qur'an—study, recital, sermonizing on its basis. Whereas other religions have developed pictorial art, music, sacramental ceremonies, and the like, Muslims have been content with this Word of God. Islam therefore offers a wonderful case in which to study the processes and implications of scripturalization.

It is not hard to determine why people would scripturalize the experiences that generated their religious tradition. When a religious tradition is vital, alive, and genuinely formative of a people's worldview, it is the most precious part of a cultural heritage. Thus people easily strive to fix it in forms that will not change or be ambiguous or require considerable interpretation. On the one hand, they want to safeguard the precious revelations or insights that set them on their way as a people. So, for example, the Jewish rabbis spoke of the Talmud as a *fence* for Torah. Torah already was a fixed form, designed to preserve and codify the revelation that had come down from the fathers and prophets, but the rabbis wanted a further safeguard or fixing. To be sure, they built in safeguards against utter rigidity—principles of interpretation and development—but they were happiest with the notion that the revelations of their Lord were well protected. In fact, they tended to make Torah, rather than unmediated experience of this Lord, the centerpiece of their faith, as Christians sometimes tended to do with the Bible. Similar things happened in Islam, as though to make it plain that referring to texts, scriptures, and traditions is a nearly universal religious phenomenon.

On the other hand, this phenomenon can clearly be a way of excusing oneself from the awesome experience of meeting the divine directly. To be sure, reading a scriptural text, just as participating in a liturgical ceremony, is supposed to take one to the God about whom the text reports. And, in fact, believers from all traditions report that this frequently has been the case. It can happen, however, that the scripture or liturgical ceremony becomes for many believers an end in itself, as close to the divine source as they ever get. The irony is that the more fixedly or literally such represen-

The Meeting of the Theologians. 'Abd Allah Musawwir. Muslim theology traditionally has been based on memorizing and discussing the meaning of the Qur'an. *(The Nelson-Atkins Museum of Art, Kansas City, Missouri [Nelson Fund])*

tations of the divine are dealt with, the more likely they are to become ends in themselves rather than transparent means to God.

In Judaism, the phenomenon called **Hasidism** can be interpreted as a response to the overdoctrinalization or scripturalization of revelation through focus on Torah and Talmud. The history of Christianity has been punctuated by similarly charismatic movements. Whenever the official religion got too burdened with law and ceremony, some group would cry out for a return to the basics of religious experience. Indeed, one can read the Protestant Reformation as in good measure such a cry, although the spotlight it turned on the Bible could frequently have stopped the return halfway. In Islam the charismatic movement that arose when religious experience seemed frozen into legal or doctrinal forms was **Sufism**. Like their counterparts in other religious reform movements, the Sufis claimed to be *more* committed to the scriptures (here, the Qur'an) than the lawyers and theologians, not less. But they developed meditative techniques that went considerably afield from the explicit teachings of the Qur'an, which both made the establishment leery of their movement and suggested some limitations to the Muslim scriptures.

The Armenian Clergy. Persian, about 1425. Persia (Iran) has been the stronghold of Shiite Islam. Many Armenian clergy have been Christian. Note how the hands of the clergy suggest a discussion going in all directions, while the space between the two on the left and the three on the right implies disagreement. *(The Nelson-Atkins Museum of Art, Kansas City, Missouri [Nelson Fund])*

The Sufis notwithstanding, traditional Islam, both **Sunni** and **Shia**, treated the Qur'an as the nearest presence of God. And what was the basic message of the Qur'an? That the single Lord of the Worlds was calling human beings to leave off their idolatries and immoralities, accept the prophecy granted to Muhammad, and prepare themselves for the Judgment Day that would come very swiftly. The greatest sin in the Muslim catalogue, as we shall show in the next section, is idolatry, putting anything in place of the sole Lord. The straight path that nonidolatrous, correct religion walks has traditionally been laid out in "five pillars" that all claim a Qur'anic basis. First, one has to profess the simple Muslim Creed: There is no God but God, and Muhammad is God's Prophet. Second, one has to pray five times each day. Third, one has to fast during the lunar month of Ramadan. Fourth, one has to give alms to the unfortunate. And fifth, one has, if possible, to make the pilgrimage to Mecca at least once during one's lifetime. It is a program of genius, simple, practical, and utterly demanding. Execute it and you can be an exemplary Muslim, well-prepared for Judgment Day. Fail to execute it and you have no defense against the divine decree that you should go into the Fire, because it is so simple and practicable that you can have no excuse.

Beyond the rudiments of Muslim faith couched in the five pillars lay plenty of room for saintly generosity. Once again, the Qur'an was the principal resource, if one wanted to do more than the basic requirements, although the **hadith** (traditions about Muhammad), the devotions to the many saints that Islam begot, the techniques of the Sufis, and the like offered a rich repertoire of further possibilities. The Qur'an suggested how Muhammad himself had interacted with God, because many of the surahs showed the effects of the divine address in the Prophet's human spirit. It warned believers against the varieties of false belief, including the Jewish and Christian forms of prophecy and interpretations of God. (So, for example, the Qur'an is adamant that God can have no Son or partaker with God of the divine nature.) The alternatives of the Fire and the Garden set the parameters of the reader's fate, much as Hell and Heaven mapped out the Christian's final alternatives. Property rights, marriage rights, warfare, divorce, and many other practical matters came in for at least passing commentary. But the great message, repeated a thousand ways, was the sovereignty of Allah. That each surah traditionally has been prefaced by the phrase, "In the name of Allah, the Compassionate, the Merciful," shows the softening that experience of Allah introduced into the divine sovereignty. The Lord of the Worlds was not so judgmental or threatening that believers could not rush to the Qur'an with high hopes.

ALLAH

In principle, the Lord of the Hebrew bible and the Father of Jesus Christ are both the sole deity, transcendent of the world, who created everything finite. It took some time for the notion of creation from nothingness (rather than formation of a vague preexisting matter) to differentiate, but the seeds of this notion are available in both the Old and New Testaments. Islam appears even more radically monotheistic than either Judaism or Christianity, however, because it has given less play to a Word and Spirit that either have coexisted with God from the beginning or are in fact fully divine "persons." The angels that Islam, along with Judaism and Christianity, has included in Creation mediated some of the power of the divine to the human realm, just as the **jinn** (devils) suggested spiritual powers bent on human beings' harm, but on the whole, the Muslim concept of God has stressed the divine transcendence. The Creator might be as close as the pulse at the believer's throat, and always compassionate and merciful, but the gap between Creator and creature yawned cavernously. No Incarnation of the divine into human flesh or covenant of the divine with a particular people threw a bridge across. Muhammad was a faithful spokesman, and Allah had plans for the House of Islam, as the community of believers was called, but always Allah was the Lord of the Worlds.

Thus Muslim theology shows some of the ultimate reaches of the pneumatic differentiation. Where Voegelin's Plato glimpsed how the divine lies beyond the upper limit of the metaxy, and can properly be expressed only in symbol or myth, Islam drew out the implications of experiencing the seizure of this transcendent divine realm, in the process both doctrinalizing what can never be captured in objective propositions and developing a powerful appreciation of the Creator's dominion.

One important result of this appreciation was the Muslim warfare against idolatry. Because Allah was the sole God, any attempt to center life on something other than Allah was a serious perversion. In the beginning Muhammad focused his opposition to idolatry on the polytheism of the Arab tribes. For although there was a tradition of monotheism in one strain of his Arab heritage, the popular religion honored many naturalistic and spiritual forces. The Qur'an blasts such popular religion with both barrels, warning that the idolaters will go straight to the Fire and making it plain that only worship of the sole God can fulfil the human heart.

Later Islamic theology has developed the notion of **shirk** ("idolatry"), so that an ideology such as Marxism, a fixation on wealth, or even (in some extreme cases) the affirmation of human freedom can emerge as a challenge to the sovereignty of Allah. The mainstream has wanted to preserve some sense of human freedom, in good measure because the Qur'an clearly makes human beings responsible for their acts, but often popular Muslim piety has come close to **fatalism**, thinking that whatever happened was the will of God.

The Islamic strictures against religious art stem from this same fear of idolatry. Judaism, too, has had periods in which it prohibited representations of God, and the controversies among Eastern Christians about icons probably owed much of their intensity to Jewish and Muslim influence. But Christianity has taken its doctrine of the Incarnation of the Word in Jesus of Nazareth as a solid foundation for a sacramental view of God's creation, with the result that Christian religious art has been well sponsored. Muslim religious art has gone in the direction of splendid architecture, calligraphy, and skill in chanting verses of the Qur'an, but its painting, sculpture, and ritualistic embellishments have been restrained. The Qur'anic Word has seemed the safer and surer presence of God.

One exception to this Muslim instinct might be the many saints venerated by popular tradition. Clifford Geertz, in his intriguing studies of Moroccan and Indonesian Islam, shows from an anthropological perspective the charismatic power that the Muslim saints have exerted.[3] Certainly the analyst of religious experience can see in this power a mediation of the divine quite like that exerted by the Jewish hasidim, the Christian saints, the Hindu **sadhus**, and the Buddhist arhats. The common people, it seems, will have their humanized presences of divinity, whether the official doctrines of their religion approve of such presences or not.

What are the lessons or suggestions latent in the Muslim version of the prophetic theology developed from pneumatic experience? Once again, they boil down to the necessity and difficulty of achieving a metaxic balance. On the one hand, the official position of the Muslim orthodoxy, especially as represented by the several different recognized schools of Islamic law (**Shariah**), can seem too stark or distant from religious experience, from the inner light and warmth necessary for a religion to be fully alive. So, for example, the rigorism of the Wahabis, the sect that has dominated Saudi Arabia, and therefore Mecca and Medina (the prime Muslim holy cities) in recent decades seems harsh and severe. When representatives of this school, such as Ismail al Faruqi, try to explain its theology to modern Westerners, it can come out as a rationalism that seems excessive in its protestations that Islam, finding nothing sacred in nature, conceives of physical creation as quite profane.[4] This is being presented as an ideal or a proud achievement, but the student of religious history doubts it could ever be achieved on the popular level, and the person whose own religious (or even ecological) sensibilities are alert doubts that it ever should be.

On the other hand, there is much to be said for the sovereignty of the divine and the deep appreciation of its transcosmic status, especially when this is present as the main formative power in human consciousness. Islam, as with all other traditions, shows the problems that arise when this appreciation is not strong. Much of the criticism leveled against the Sufis, for example, comes from the perception of the Muslim orthodoxy that they were responsible for rampant superstition, ignorance, and even idolatry among the masses. The cult of the saints ran the same danger. When people are not sufficiently mature, both pneumatically and noetically, to focus most of their attention on the quest of the divine and the luring by the divine that give right order from within, they can fall into various species of **fideism**, enthusiasm, ecstatic fervor, and fundamentalism that quickly throw their culture off balance. The divine must be near enough to animate a lively faith and to order people in actual fact, rather than simply in external cultural ideal. Yet the divine must be far enough to relativize all human undertakings, including quite definitely human religious undertakings, and keep them in proper perspective. In the past few centuries Islam has been enduring a very painful struggle with modernity, trying to work out which Western advances (scientific, technological, political, cultural) it should accept and which it should reject as incompatible with its deep religious traditions. The horrible mess in Iran is but one of several Islamic examples of the great difficulty of working out such development or accommodation.[5]

The Muslim divinity therefore is no easier to estimate than any other prophetic or noetic divinity. How to orient one's individual personality, let alone an entire culture, by a transcosmic reference and yet not lose a proper respect for the world, a proper responsibility for history and culture, is among the most demanding of human problems. The number of leaders, religious or political, who have a sure hold on the issues involved is slim indeed, and the general masses struggle along barely aware there is a problem. (However, the masses might in fact solve the problem better than the leaders, because a good percentage of most religious populations achieves both a reference to heaven and a sense of responsibility for the earth [their families and work.]) But any time a political crisis occurs or a technological innovation calls for deep cultural reconsideration, the lack of a firm understanding of the structures of consciousness, of the factors vital to achieving historical order, produces large-scale dysfunction and suffering. Allah or God is a difficult crux, at least as demanding as consoling.

REASON AND MYSTICISM

The Muslim lawyers present a quite rational face, as do the Jewish talmudists and the Christian **canonists**. The Sufis and other Muslim mystics, like the Jewish Hasidim and Kabbalists or the Christian contemplatives and ecstatics, show that Islam was not satisfied with such rationality. The mystics have sought a deeper and more experiential knowledge of God. At the extreme, a Muslim mystic such as Al Hallaj spoke of being identified with divinity, and so was put to death by the orthodox as a pantheistic idolater. In the middle, a religious genius such as Al Ghazali balanced learning and more-than-rational prayer, fidelity to the Qur'anic tradition and an experiential awareness that no words can capture the divinity that manifests itself directly to the soul. Overall, Islam has had a rich cultural development, nurturing philosophers and poets, warriors and solitaries. The ingredients are there for a full-bodied appreciation of what reference to the transcendent God can do to ground a culture in deep sanity. As in all other traditions, however, the historical actuality has failed to accomplish what the ingredients promised.

So, for example, there has been a Muslim Puritanism that both missed the midpoint between reason and mysticism and did not know how to integrate strong yet guilt-free affections. Value judgments enter in at this point, but an analytical position such as Voegelin's, which takes only the noetic and pneumatic geniuses as the masters to whom it owes loyalty (and which, in addition, pledges to serve the full vision implied in the geniuses' beginnings, looking to what might have only been implicit in their own accomplishment), finds the Muslim law, like the Jewish and Christian laws, too constrained.

The "reason" with which the noetic and pneumatic breakthroughs are pregnant is considerably richer than the rationalism displayed in the law codes of any of the prophetic traditions. One can see the function of the Muslim prohibitions against eating pork or drinking alcohol, just as one can see the function of the Jewish **kosher** and Sabbath laws or the Christian requirements that priests be male or celibate, but this does not necessarily justify these laws before the bar of noetic and pneumatic differentiation. Overall, the prophetic traditions have legislated less than profoundly. Had their lawyers been wiser, they might have brought more people to freedom and maturity.

The examples suggested above imply that the God whom the prophets glimpsed did not make the prophets' peoples fully at home in the world. To be sure, some measure of asceticism, denial, segregation, and the like seems necessary if people are to be happy and whole. The world does not seem rich with possibilities, aglow with a third dimension of spiritual presence, if one is overly immersed in sensual matters. So restraint in diet, sexuality, public affairs, and the like can be helpful. Often, however, the legislation that aims at providing such help takes on a life of its own, becoming opaque rather than transparent, with the result that animals such as the pig are considered "unclean," liquids such as whiskey are considered perverse, and sexuality is kept in the psychological closet, where it tends to fester.

A case in point is all the prophetic religions' treatment of women. To be sure, women were (at least by today's egalitarian standards) also badly treated in traditional India and East Asia. The personalism of the prophetic deity, however, led to no great improvement in women's personal status. Thus traditional Judaism and Christianity have kept women from the priesthood, while many rabbis and monks in effect have seen women as a threat to their spiritual goals. Islam, like Judaism, never approved celibacy or a monastic way of life, but it also never gave women access to religious authority or dignity equal to men's. In the early years of Islam, Muhammad improved women's lot considerably, compared with what it had been in pre-Muslim Arabia, but the Prophet was not long dead before women were a distinctly second-class sex. The parallels in Judaism, Christianity, Hinduism, and Buddhism would not be hard to make. Yet the Muslim institutions of **purdah** and the harem (to say nothing of clitoridectomy), along with the virtual abandonment of women's education (either secular or religious) and the sanctioning of child marriage, meant that Muslim females often have had a very hard lot.

There is a traditional religious defense of these practices, of course, and one has to try to give it a fair hearing. The main line of such a traditional defense is that women received a religious dignity or basis for respect quite superior to that which they find in the modern West. On occasion this argument rings true. For example, the Muslim doctor, who is probably the most arresting figure in the film on Islam in the series *The Long Search*, is a woman of great dignity. If she is what the tradition sought to produce, the tradition indeed has a great deal to commend it. Unfortunately, however, there is much evidence that she is the exception rather than the rule and that in most traditional Muslim villages women have lived in poverty and ignorance, if not abuse.[6]

The "reason" that has produced the laws leading to such results, like the "reason" behind the laws that has led to comparable phenomena in traditional Christianity (for example, witchburning) and Judaism (for example, liability to divorce at the husband's whim), falls far short of the noetic goals disclosed by a Plato or an Aristotle. And the mysticism of the traditions involved must equally have failed the pneumatic goals disclosed by a Jeremiah, a Jesus, or a Muhammad, because the tradition did not come up with the love and appreciation necessary to overthrow the laws that such a devalued or debased reason concocted. In other words, one can judge a tradition by its fruits, and just as the good fruits spotlight the heroic achievements, so the rotten fruits spotlight the grievous deficiencies.

Reason and mysticism (love that goes to the heart of reality) ideally balance and encourage one another. In fact, in the most outstanding religious figures they are both strong and seem both to flow from the "heart," the center where the person is perfected by a warm reason, an enlightened love. Still, it makes sense to consider both aspects of a personality and a tradition, because either can initiate religious reforms. If a potential reformer is seized by the love of God, and that love flowers in compassion for the poor and suffering, then practices or institutions that discriminate against classes of people—women, children, the aged, people of color, or whatever—provoke strong protest, cries for their overthrow that will not be hushed easily. Similarly, if an honest and penetrating mind takes a careful look at how the wealth of a given society is being distributed, or the power, or the religious opportunities, and finds patterns of systematic discrimination or injustice, that mind is bound, by its own inner principles, to label such a society irrational, unworthy of the divine light, in need of strong criticism and reform.

The fact that reformers moved by love and insight have regularly arisen in Islam, in the other prophetic traditions, and in religious cultures generally shows the basis for the Johannine conviction that "the light shines in the darkness and the darkness has never overcome it" (John 1:5). The fact that traditional Islam, the other traditional prophetic societies, the other traditional religious societies, and the majority if not the totality of modern and contemporary societies have systematically discriminated against classes of people or systematically devalued parts of creation presents the sober countertruth that the darkness has always been terribly strong. None of the prophets, therefore, can be wholly satisfied. All of the sages must be saddened.

THE WORLD AND FUNDAMENTALISM

When consciousness is rightly ordered, the world is as finely balanced as the metaxy. People know that the world is their home, is the material fundament without which they cannot stand straight and tall. So they love the world, and they tell stories or enact rituals that keep this love warm and lively. The anthropologist Colin Turnbull's depiction of the Pygmies of the Congo singing to their beloved forest shows this ancient wisdom unforgettably.[7] Neither the Pygmies nor any other healthy people confuse the world with the limits of human potential or reality. In the metaxy, the world cannot contain the utopian thrusts of the human spirit after truth and justice, holiness and healing love. So the world is bounded by "heaven" and "God." Thereby, it cannot be an idol or deflect people from the crucial movement of their spirits toward the divine ground. But it can be a sacrament, a lovely series of signs pointing to a Lord who is compassionate and merciful, long-suffering and abounding in creative love.

Both secularism and puritanism miss this mextaxic right order, the one by overvaluing the world and the other by undervaluing it. When a culture overvalues the world, it tends to cut off the topmost layer of consciousness or to deny the quest of the human spirit for the divine ground, and so to flatten or truncate reality. But spirits imprisoned in such a shrunken room, unable to fly toward the realm of inexhaustible light that gives them their best hopes, easily turn twisted and malformed. Neurosis, cruelty, boredom, despair, and a dozen other pathological symptoms can result.

Alternatively, the undervaluation of the world (history, nature, human affairs) leads to an equally pernicious series of neuroses. When people are so absorbed with what they take to be divine matters that they neglect politics, economics, health care, education, and the like, they lose the foundation of their mental health. In mild cases or with people of low energy, this merely means squalor, untidiness, weeds, and jungles. In serious cases, it leads to heinous crimes: murders, exterminations, genocides. Because they have lost the balance that a love of the earth might give, so-called spiritual leaders can rouse their thoughtless followers to holy wars, pogroms, crimes against whole classes of people. Voegelin lived in a century distinctive for such massacre. He was forced to leave his native land because of Hitler and Nazism. So he saw the modern thinkers responsible for this century's bloodlust as great villains and enemies. Hegel and Marx, Hitler and Stalin, showed him in gigantic, grotesque form what happens when transcendence is not properly directed, when people miss the real God and take the exaltation of their spirits as a commission to rule as though they had inherited God's mantle.

The prophetic religions all house this latter danger. Israelite biblical theology contains the doctrine of holy war, as though the Lord would commission the slaughter of its enemies. Christianity sent out crusaders to ravage and pillage, and then the infra-Christian strifes gave birth to the Inquisition and the modern religious wars. Islam has developed the doctrine of **jihad** or holy war, and this continues to explain much of the apparent craziness in Iran, Iraq, Lebanon, Libya and other violent Muslim lands.

The connection of fundamentalism to such phenomena is the use that fanatics, fervent spiritualists who have lost the balance or humility that proper rootage in the earth (a proper appreciation of their own creaturehood, finitude, sinfulness, and mortality) might give, can make of the literalism of fundamentalists. Thinking that a scriptural text, read with virtually no sense of its symbolism or of the original experiences behind it and with virtually no noetic or pneumatic differentiation to offer control, can launch a direct plunge into action, fundamentalist fanatics can convince themselves that even systematic murder is a holy deed, is obedience to the will of the Lord of the Worlds.

Consider the following description of the plight of the Bahais of Iran as the year 1985 dawned. The Bahais are an offshoot of Shiite Islam (the version that dominates Iran), and they work for a sort of ecumenic peace among all the world religions, which they feel at bottom are quite alike. This was anathema to the regime of the Ayatollah Khomeini, and the response of that regime was an all-too-powerful example of the mental disease that can occur when people lose the world and metaxic balance.

> With a design not seen in four decades [since the Nazis], the Iranian government has set about erasing the Bahais and their culture from the land. Recently, wholesale arrests and imprisonments of Bahais have led to torture and to execution by firing squad and hanging. The torture, under the guise of interrogation to uncover anti-Iranian activities and the names of other Bahais, involves such devices as the bastinado [a cudgel for beating the soles of the feet], the rack, the rubber hose, and psychological torment. In the case of female prisoners, the Shiite guards carefully cover the victim's body with a **chador** [a black cloak] as they whip her, so that they will not have to view a woman's bare flesh—a sight that is anathema to a good Shiite man. The only aspect of this eradication of a people which remains to be carried out is a more efficient, mechanized method of extermination.[8]

The report goes on to compare this evil with the previous genocides of this century: the slaughter of Armenians by Turks and the holocaust of the Jews. It might have cited African tribal massacres or switched grounds slightly and shown the parallels in the systematic murders by Latin American dictatorships. One would have to analyze each of these depravities individually, but a hypothesis bound to leap to mind early on is that a psychological inflation regularly occurs. Somehow people lose all ordinary sense of restraint, all common decency. They start to think that their cause, or even their own dignity, can justify eliminating all who oppose them, can even justify torturing other human beings with unspeakable cruelty. The fact that this inflation, or actual madness, often claims a religious justification has been a major factor in the modern rejection of traditional religion.

Thus the noetic and pneumatic breakthroughs call for nuance in one's estimates of "religion." Insofar as the traditions preserve balance and wisdom about the need of the human personality to stand in the middle, with feet on the earth and spirit opening to a heaven that makes the human personality both ardent and humble, they are a treasury that humanity desperately needs to employ. Insofar as their bastardized forms can lead to an ignorance justified in the name of revelation, or to a fundamentalism that can turn savage, or to an ecstasy of killing, they show some of the worst human perversions. The Platonic verdict again comes to mind. Something is not good because someone says it comes from "God." Something comes from God if it is good. To abandon personal responsibility and balance, personal judgment about what is good, for the sake of what some "scripture" or "holy tradition," let alone what some current religious leader, preaches is to default on one's own most serious responsibilities as a human being.

That is the direction in which Voegelin's reflections on the historical record would run. The traditions, or course, house much that is holy and wise. We should go to the scriptures and classics with a humble willingness to learn. And the scriptures, if read with any common sense and good health, hardly counsel crimes and slaughterings. Their main message, overwhelmingly, is justice and mercy. But they have their problematic passages, and when an unbalanced personality feels itself under the influence of the "Spirit" or can cite a puritanical law code, the scriptures can become props for high crimes and atrocities. To be sure, many of the modern regimes that have wreaked the worst evils have been militantly anti-religious. The Nazis and Communists stand out. But in their psychological profiles, these butchers are so like the fanatical fundamentalist murderers that *religion, party*, or *movement* become indistinguishable. Whatever, people can lose the world and spill rivers of blood in the name of their ideals or their cause.

COUNTERVIEWS

Critics of our somewhat complicated evaluation of Islamic prophecy certainly would cluster at both of the poles that we have tried to avoid. From the fundamentalist and scripturalist side, those who hold either that the Qur'an is privileged truth pure and simple or that divine revelation in a fairly straightforward, not-to-be-criticized sense should dictate the play, have great problems with our effort to honor both the wisdom or depth in Qur'anic revelation and the judgments of modernized humanists that Islam, like Christianity, has frequently been a source of abominations. From the more secularized or critical side, readers who have no sympathy with prophetic experience or no mystical appreciation of how a Word from beyond might rush into a soul formed by desert solitudes will be equally put off. The fact is that Islam centers in a marvelous appreciation of the primacy of the divine mystery. Not to appreciate this and the holiness that it has often begotten is to expose oneself to the charge of being crippled, lacking a faculty or capacity that full humanity always requires.

More telling criticisms, no doubt, will come from scholars sufficiently versed in Islamic literature to show where an Al Ghazali or an Avicenna in fact has anticipated the problems of imbalance to which Islam has been subject, and so has given this tradition the cure for its biggest problems. By emphasizing these cures one could, as with Christianity, claim that the problem is not the tradition as such but the poor understanding and living of the tradition that the mass of its adherents have almost inevitably manifested. We would be quite willing to entertain this argument, for it would only make more prominent the Islamic sources of the health whose promotion has been Voegelin's and our major reason for writing.

SUMMARY

Our topic has been Islam, taken as the third and perhaps most fully prophetic of the religious traditions launched by pneumatic differentiation. The experiences of Muhammad that generated both the Qur'an and the Islamic movement are a fine specimen of prophetic seizure, and the eloquence of Muhammad's message shows the poetry that the divine Spirit can inspire. The Qur'an both gave the revelation that Muhammad received a permanent housing and became subject to the dangers of scripturalization. The program of the five pillars, founded in the Qur'an, was a work of practical genius, and the sovereignty of Allah with which the Qur'an brims is perhaps the distinctive mark of Muslim theology.

This theology shows the full sense of the gap between the transcosmic Creator and creation with which the pneumatic differentiation is pregnant. As a result, Islam has made idolatry the central religious failing. Allah is Lord of the Worlds, and human disorders come from putting lesser things in His place. Despite this clear theology, however, Islam, like the other prophetic traditions, has struggled to keep reason and mysticism properly coordinated. Its law has often manifested a reason more technical than profound, and its Sufi forms of mysticism have been liable to the charge of underplaying tradition or fostering superstition. The treatment of women offers a good case with which to study how Muslim reason and mystical love both failed to attain healthy fruits, as has been true in most other religious traditions.

Any of the traditions can be usefully analyzed in terms of its view of the world, and here too Islam shows us the difficulty of working out the pneumatic ideal. Muslim fundamentalism, finally, suggests the kinship between religious and atheistic forms of mental imbalance so serious that they result in wholesale murdering. Like its parallels in too many other lands, the Iranian savagery toward the Bahais shows how critical we must be of "religious" claims to inspiration, revelation, or the power to interpret the patterns of history. Noetic and pneumatic balance alike say that things are not good because some authority says they are, but that all things genuinely good can pass the tests of right reason and compassionate love.

As counterviews we considered the likely objections of critics from the right, who would insist that the Qur'an be given the power to determine what is wise or good, as well as the likely objections of critics from the left, who would have no sympathy for the Islamic centering in the divine sovereignty. We also indicated a more centrist view, which would be better able than we to draw from Islamic tradition many solutions to the basic human problems that Muslims' aberrations have spotlighted.

STUDY QUESTIONS

1. What in Muhammad's experience on the Night of Qadr explains the roots of Islam in "submission"?
2. What are the benefits of scripturalization?
3. Describe how the divine must balance between nearness and farness.
4. What is some of the evidence that the "reason" of the prophetic religions, as it has taken form in religious law, has been inadequate?
5. Compose a brief warning, based on the recent plight of the Bahais in Iran, about the murderous potential in prophetic religious experience and its kinship with other deadly pathologies.

NOTES

1. N.J. Dawood, trans., *The Koran* (Baltimore: Penguin, 1981), p. 27.
2. See Eric Voegelin, *Order and History, Vol. 4* (Baton Rouge: Louisiana State University Press, 1974), pp. 48–57.
3. See Clifford Geertz, *Islam Observed* (Chicago: University of Chicago Press, 1968).
4. See Ismail al Faruqi, "Islam," in *Great Asian Religions*, ed. W.T. Chan, et al. (New York: Macmillan, 1969), pp. 308–10.
5. See V.S. Naipaul, *Among the Believers* (New York: Random House, Vintage Books, 1982).

6. See Erika Friedl, "Islam and Tribal Women in a Village in Iran," in *Unspoken Worlds: Women's Religious Lives in Non-Western Cultures,* eds. N.A. Falk and R.M. Gross (San Francisco: Harper & Row, Pub., 1980).

7. See Colin Turnbull, *The Forest People* (New York: Simon & Schuster, 1962).

8. "Notes and Comment," *The New Yorker*, February 4, 1985, p. 31.

CHAPTER TEN

After Philosophy and Revelation

ORIENTATION

We have now dealt with three of the four analyses that make up our sketch of the history of world religion. The cosmological myth was our candidate for the analytical tool necessary to clarify humanity's compact experience of nature, society, divinity, and the self through most of its millennia. We dealt with the noetic differentiation, the clarification of the structure of human reason, that represents the great leap in being, the advance in existential awareness, after which the philosophical cultures strove, finding the fullest noetic achievement to be the classical philosophy of Plato and Aristotle, in which human reason realized its metaxic and tensional structure. Third, we dealt with the pneumatic differentiation that the great prophetic figures of Judaism, Christianity, and Islam made possible. By realizing the implications of their seizure by the transcosmic divinity, such prophets as Jeremiah, Jesus, and Muhammad made possible the realization, complementary to the noetic differentiation, that love must primarily be directed toward the divine ground.

In this last section we are concerned with the aftermath of the noetic and pneumatic breakthroughs, especially as they have become problematic in modernity. *Modernity* clearly is not a fully precise term or notion, but it will suffice for our purposes to consider it as the movement, begun in Europe in the sixteenth and seventeenth centuries and since spread throughout the world, away from traditional, religious cultures into a new, more critical and anthropocentric sense of reality. Modernity could not

158

have occurred without the noetic and pneumatic breakthroughs from Greece and Israel, but at the same time it has taken serious issue with them. We shall consider such examples of the modern move away from the classical and biblical cultures as modern science, modern history, and modern philosophy. These considerations will lay out much of the case that modernity can make against traditional philosophy and prophecy, as those differentiations were claiming authority in sixteenth-century Europe. Then, turning to the Enlightenment, Marxism, Voegelin's *The New Science of Politics*, and Modern Gnosticism, we shall consider the counterattack that the noetic and pneumatic differentiations should muster, their proper charges that modernity has lost right order, if not reality.

Today we are in what many commentators describe as a *postmodern* situation in which the main doctrines and confidences of the modern thinkers no longer pass muster. The wars, ecological pollution, mental distress, and now nuclear threats of the twentieth century can make the assurances of the Enlightenment thinkers seem terribly naive. The blood spilt in this century by socialist dictatorships has discredited Marx and Lenin, and the widening gap between rich nations and poor nations has discredited the capitalist regimes that modernity nourished. For people schooled in the assets and liabilities of the cosmological myth, in the gains and dangers of the noetic differentiation, and in the visions and problems latent in prophecy, modernity is but another phenomenon crying out for balanced analysis. The ideal, certainly, would be a study sufficiently sympathetic to appropriate the advances of modernity over the classical and biblical achievements, yet sufficiently critical to note carefully the losses to be laid at modernity's door.

To finish our analysis of modernity and summarize the argument we have made, our final chapter will redescribe the great leaps in being, stressing how they show divinity to be the crux of a proper understanding of both humanity and reality. This in turn will allow us to suggest the proper view of the cosmos that mental health demands and the ways that the wisdoms of the cosmological peoples are now ripe for reconsideration. Psychologically, as well as ecologically, we have much to learn from the peoples who dealt with the rest of creation in a consubstantial partnership. In the same way, our reconsideration of the design of a properly ordered human consciousness will suggest the crux of the social theory that contemporary politics should be seeking. After modernity, what are the visions, symbols, and analyses that might take a rapidly swelling global population away from war, toward the justice and mutual respect that its very survival now requires? Relatedly, what is of permanent validity in the achievements of the cosmological, philosophical, prophetic, and modern cultures, and how might these achievements link up with precisely contemporary experiences to at least sketch a new religion or lifeway viable for the future that will confront the year 2000?

Finally, we shall conclude our analysis of the story of world religion and world history with a sober but perhaps consoling reflection on the equivalence of what people have experienced in all places and times. If nature, society, the self, and divinity have interacted always and everywhere, one can speak of a functional equivalence of the symbols and cultural systems of all peoples. This does not mean, of course, that one may make no estimates of progress and regress, may enter no judgments of praise or blame. However, it does mean that in ultimate perspective, when the task is fashioning a worldview sufficiently realistic to assure survival and give human beings hope, much of what we in the modern and contemporary West have come to praise is open to serious criticism. At the least, we should ask for a second opinion that takes into account the humanity achieved by our predecessors through cosmological symbolism, philosophy, and prophecy.

Even better, we should ask ourselves how a full analysis of the past, both premodern and modern, sets up the future of religion—the dealings with divinity and struggles for justice or love that lie before the next generations. What are the main lessons we should take to heart, if we are not to repeat the terrible mistakes of the past? Where ought we to direct our energies, and what sorts of educational and ascetical regimes should we start to develop? The divine mystery is not going to go away. No denials of past generations have removed the haunting silence of the Beginning and the Beyond, just as no presumptions to know the divine nature or will have long been credible. Similarly, human nature is not going to pass outside of the range of possibilities revealed in the metaxy. Within these two most fundamental parameters (divinity and humanity), how ought the shamans, prophets, and sages of the future, the future teachers and students of religion, to conceive of and try to achieve a postmodern sacrality?

In our scheme, after philosophy and revelation comes the next major chapter in the history of human consciousness and religion, the rise of modernity. This was not a leap in being parallel to those of the noetic and the pneumatic differentiations, but it certainly stamped humanity as thoroughly as they did. We try to show the gains and losses that science, history, and philosophy worked in the period from the early sixteenth to the mid-twentieth centuries. We focus especially on the Enlightenment and Marxism, which could stand for the noetic and pneumatic (or political) changes that modernity worked on the heritage it had received from Athens and Jerusalem. Our assumption throughout this chapter is that the "modernity" we are discussing has now become a worldwide phenomenon, transported from the West on the coattails of the traders, missionaries, soldiers, and scientists who spread out from Europe to tramp the globe.

The tenor of this chapter will no doubt complete the characterization of our book as atypical. We criticize modernity more directly and deeply than most products of the modern university system tend to do. Such criticism probably reflects our immersion in the materials of the world religions, for which no human institution is immune from strict criticism. It also reflects our tutoring by Eric Voegelin, who did not have a high opinion of the spiritual maturity of his fellow moderns, including his fellow professors. To his mind, a professor who didn't meditate was dangerous, and the divorce of regular and deep personal meditation from scholarship was the most obvious source of the disorder afflicting the modern intellectual worldview.

Both of the extremes that have mottled modernity—an overconcern with minute facts and an overexaltation of human spirituality—could have been avoided had more of the leading modern artists, scientists, politicians, and churchpeople retrieved the experiences at the core of the classical and biblical wisdoms. The standard by which we are testing modernity throughout this chapter is therefore quite clear. Where modernity lost the lovely balance of the classical and biblical ideals, it proved itself a menace. On the other hand, where it embellished humanity's prior attainments, as it did for instance in the new sciences (as contrasted with the image of human nature that it derived from the new sciences), modernity showed the limitations of the prior attainments and manifested the creative dynamism that always makes it possible for humanity to achieve further and richer differentiations.

MODERN SCIENCE

The cosmological myth encouraged human beings to explore the physical world, as of course did their elementary need to survive. We find, therefore, that archaic peoples and nonliterate peoples of recent times both give evidence of having assembled an impressive empirical knowledge of plants and animals, of the stars and the seasons. Nonetheless, this knowledge was not "scientific" in either of the two principal meanings that that word has gained in Western history. The first meaning was the classical sense of "certain knowledge through causes." As initiated by the Pre-Socratics and consummated by Plato and Aristotle, classical science wished to penetrate to the invariant reasons of things, and so thought of achievements such as Euclidian geometry as its ideal. The *episteme* that Plato sought was scientific in this sense, although certainly Plato was aware that sure knowledge of deeper matters, such as human political arrangements, only springs from the process of searching for the divine ground and being drawn by it.

The second principal meaning of *science* arose in the modern West, and it is tied to the methodology of experimentation. Knowledge is scientific in this context when it stems from incursions into nature, or observations of nature, that are carefully monitored, can be repeated, and are then subjected to rigorous processes of forging hypothetical explanations of the data gained and critically verifying such hypotheses. The shift from the classical ideal was thus largely in the direction of closer and fuller empirical contact with the world. In addition, the classical notions of necessity and causality gained considerable nuance, and new mathematical tools allowed a statistical sort of regularity to qualify as explanatory of natural phenomena.[1]

This history of the rise of modern science out of its medieval forebears is a fascinating story, and its kinship with what we have studied in the previous parts of this book lies in its stress upon the mind of the scientific investigator. For although the empirical accent that modernity developed (it was present in ancient and medieval science, but modernity dealt with it in a more sophisticated way) meant more concern for observation and experimentation, the real power in modern science came from the theoretical genius of the pioneers, such as Galileo and Newton, who were able to generalize to new, often mathematically expressed patterns that cast the richer stores of data into more intelligible form. As we shall see, modern philosophy was sufficiently impressed by this achievement to make epistemology, the study of knowledge, its favorite topic. The point for our purposes, though, is the gains and losses that modern science worked on Western culture's sense of order.

The gains were many. First, a modern scientist such as Newton derived much of his conviction from a solid faith that the world is rational. The ultimate basis for this conviction was his belief that the world came from an intelligent Creator. The facts that Newton himself was quite unorthodox in his Christianity (for example, he did not hold with the doctrine of the Trinity) and that he was absorbed in alchemical studies show that he was still a transitional figure, laboring with a cultural inheritance and a personal sense of reality that in some ways compacted elements of the cosmological myth, of the noetic and pneumatic breakthroughs, and of a new mathematical and empirical awareness or talent.

Still, the confidence displayed by modern scientists has brought an amazing increase in our understanding of nature. Postmodern science could be on the verge of confessing that this knowability occurs in a context of genuine mystery (luminosity beyond what human beings can master), but the affirmation itself of nature's amenability to rational inquiry has literally changed human beings' conception of *reality*. In the ancient past, the vagaries of nature (along with nature's regularities) so daunted human beings that they were liable to all sorts of superstitions. They would strive to placate occult powers, to satisfy spirits and demons, using these entities as symbols of their fear of nature's caprice, indeed of their fear that nature was intrinsically irrational, perhaps even malevolent. No doubt one can find patterns in ancient sorcery, witchcraft, and the like that show the presence of human intelligence in the "systems" they form, but confidence in nature's rationality, in the modern sense, is strikingly lacking.

Second, with this modern confidence, and its buttressing by very impressive achievements, came power to use nature for human beings' benefit. The technology that flowed in the wake of modern science made a better life for millions of people, in that it dramatically improved their health care, diet, housing, burden of labor, and the like. Whatever qualifications one might have to express about modern technology, there is no denying the splendid improvements it made possible. To cite one summary instance: today we have a life expectancy just about twice that of premodern human beings.

Third, there was the gain of increased knowledge itself, the almost pure good of coming to a richer appreciation of the splendor and vastness of the universe. Whatever the traumata of the expansions in consciousness occasioned by the new sciences (astronomy, geology, evolutionary biology, chemistry, physics, and psychology), the advance in truth, the perception of the real proportions of the world, have to be accounted a golden gain. Human beings are made for truth, for correct understanding, and this regards the natural world as much as human nature and divinity. To oppose scientific inquiry is to oppose something at the core of what it means to be human, and so is to blaspheme. Modernity made this less possible.

The losses attendant on modern science came mainly from its abuses or from false inferences transferred from science to metaphysics or ethics. So, for example, many modern intellectuals were so intoxicated with the powers demonstrated in scientific methodology that they canonized this mode of inquiry and came to call religious, mystical, poetic, commonsensical, and other avenues to truth passé, or unreliable, or fit only for the stupid and fearful. The result was a withering of the modern intellectual consciousness, an atrophy, so that science did not contribute as a precious part to a larger whole but was asked to do jobs it couldn't handle (for example, to supply for beauty, holiness, prudence, and other crucially important human gifts).

Second, modern science has tended to obscure or deny the divine transcendence, at least "modern science" as described by scientists and philosophers of science has. (As Albert Einstein said, one must attend to what scientists do more than to what they say.) The processes of science might have been interpreted as another instance of the metaxic quest and drawing, another call to differentiation or noetic refinement, but the majority of scientists were not sufficiently sophisticated philosophically, sufficiently in control of the metaxic structure of their own minds, to integrate their work with the divine One above and the unbounded plurality below. Thus they tended to deny that "God" or religion had more than emotional value, and this encouraged the political philosophers and psychologists to see "divinity" as only a projection of human needs, a fateful move indeed, as we shall see. Overall, then, modern science tended to distort reality by undervaluing the truths of mythology and theology, underappreciating the insights of the compact experience of the world as a consubstantial whole, of the tensional experience of being lured by a transcosmic ultimacy or holiness, and of the experience of wholeness that comes from prophetic seizure and love of a transcosmic ultimacy.

MODERN HISTORY

History, in the sense of a people's story of its origins and developments, was a dominant goal of traditional mythology. In addition to explaining the origin of the cosmos or particular species, traditional mythology usually dealt with where the tribe came from, what the first ancestors or *culture heroes* were like, how the tribe came to its present way of life, why death and suffering afflict all human beings, and so forth. The basic pattern tended to be describing how things were in the beginning, which was often pictured as a golden age, and why they had declined to their present sorry state.

The noetic and pneumatic breakthroughs introduced new bases for periodizing the temporal flow of human experience. Writing provided the possibility of preserving records (although the powers of memory among nonliterate people are prodigious), and when the deeper Indian and Chinese thinkers considered how to organize their data about the past, they tended to search for the most dramatic shifts in cultural meaning. These could stem from changes in imperial rule or from the appearance of sages such as the Buddha and Confucius, who offered new ways of conceiving the world. Plato and Aristotle read their noetic discoveries as a basis for dividing Greek culture into a before and after. In the light of the metaxy they found, the efforts of the poets, dramatists, and Pre-Socratics seemed but preliminary. Socrates functioned as the ideal figure, personifying the love of wisdom that had begotten the new breakthrough, and the fate of Socrates became the prime cautionary tale that classical culture told.

The prophets of Israel offered a similarly paradigmatic way of periodizing history, in that they looked to the covenants with Abraham, Moses, and David, along with such dramatic events as the Exodus from Egypt and the Captivity in Babylon, as the key to unlocking the divine name. It was what had happened in such events that gave content to the mysterious naming at the burning bush, the enigmatic "I am who I am." Christians continued this story through Jesus Christ, making him the basis for dividing human experience into a before, when sin reigned, and an after, when grace more greatly abounded. Islam took the life of the Prophet as the basis for a new calendar and a new understanding of the human story.

Modernity drew from these various starts at understanding human temporality a sense that a linear framework was most appropriate. Premodern history certainly possessed some sense of progress or development, but it was more interested in the paradigms and cautionary tales that told people how to live in any age. Indeed, classical culture quite clearly thought that human nature is essentially the same everywhere and ought everywhere to strive for essentially the same ideals. The modern historians, largely under the influence of the natural scientists (who were perhaps a century ahead of them in developing their disciplines), saw the need for more data and closer control. As they developed their ideal way of dealing with the past, they converged on the goal that Von Ranke made famous: to describe the past "exactly as it was." This in turn meant a critical sifting of sources, testing of witnesses, and the like, so that eventually historians could speak of the *scientific* aspects of their work, the rules or canons against which one could test any historian's achievement.

As they developed their field, modern historians helped the popular conception of culture to become more dynamic. Indeed, one might say that a major difference between modern and premodern culture is the greater appreciation moderns have of historicity itself. Prior to modernity, people certainly knew that they existed in time, developed as individuals and groups, and were always at least somewhat changing. But the ancient ideals of stability, permanence, regularity, universality, and the like blunted this appreciation. By the end of modernity, for many leading thinkers, time had become almost a nightmare, almost the devouring maw that Hindu symbolism had made it.

So, for example, the German thinker Martin Heidegger spoke of human being as moving toward death, its deeply in-given sense of time making it intrinsically anxious. Jean-Paul Sartre thought there was nothing essential or pre-given in human nature: everything could be fashioned as human liberty wished. These were extreme views, but even the average person's sense of reality had changed to something more fluid. History, in the sense of changes from era to era, had speeded up. Evolutionary biology, in the wake of Darwin, led to the notion that the race itself had evolved from very different simian beginnings, and the new geology greatly expanded the time frame of the earth. (Just prior to the impact of this new biology, theologians were speculating that creation occurred in 4004 B.C.E.). The Industrial Revolution provided the means for changing economies and peoples' interactions with nature at a much faster pace, so that alterations that would have taken centuries, if indeed they would have occurred at all, now took place in a decade. The modern wars, leading to the world wars of the twentieth century, meant upheaval generation after generation, and the global explorations that led to colonial empires vastly extended Europeans' sense of the world (they were writing the first universal histories). Thus Voltaire, under the influence of the discoveries of Chinese culture, changed the pattern that had been used since Augustine and no longer made the line of history run through Christian civilization.

Voltaire. Joseph Rosset. Voltaire was a leading figure of the Enlightenment, noted for his biting criticism of traditional religion. *(The Nelson-Atkins Museum of Art, Kansas City, Missouri [Nelson Fund])*

Change was occurring everywhere, and historians began the search for global patterns that later preoccupied such universalists as Spengler, Toynbee, Jaspers, and in his own way, Voegelin.

What has been the upshot of this modern preoccupation with history? In terms of the analysis we have been pursuing, we might call it a further differentiation. Whereas the classical philosophers clarified the metaxic structure of human consciousness, and the prophets showed the place of a love, from the center of the personality, that reached out beyond the world, the modern historians made the case that everything changes, that being human is intrinsically a matter of moving along. Some of this, of course, had been expressed previously, for example in the Buddhist notion of anatman. Because there is no stable self, but only a constantly changing set of relations among the "heaps" that compose the human "person," the best image is learning to move with the flow of reality, to dance to the measure of the dharmic flux. But few of the European historians responsible for the modern sense of historicity were versed in Buddhist metaphysics. Most of their work developed with a sense of newness: they were demarcating a new era, quite different from the classical and medieval eras, in which human affairs would receive the central focus.

To be sure, the Renaissance called for a return to classical humanism, and the Reformation called for a return to biblical sources. But both of these calls sounded with new overtones. Human beings were to be much more active, to take much more responsibility for change, than was true in either the classical or the biblical era. Science was showing the world to be more vast, more evolutionary, and more intelligible than it had been thought to be, and studies of the human past were showing a greater variety or range of possibilities and a greater development than prior historians had acknowledged. So it became increasingly accepted that to be human was to be immersed in temporal flux, perhaps even to be adrift from any eternal moorings. Intellectuals began to ask themselves whether anything human could withstand the corrosive powers of change and why they should think of humanity as destined for more than the grave.

MODERN PHILOSOPHY

The expanded sense of the past that modern history generated did not, therefore, console human beings so much as threaten them. For although they could take pride in the achievements and progress that the past ages of homo sapiens revealed, the very changeableness of the species came home with such force that modern human beings felt deracinated, torn up from their roots. So something poignant comes through in the title of Marshall Berman's study of the experience of modernity, *All That Is Solid Melts Into Air*.[2] Prior epochs of human history might seem benighted or lulled by false securities, but moderns sometimes found themselves looking back upon medievals or people of cosmological civilizations with envy. At least their worlds had structure and regularity. At least they knew who they were and how they ought to live.

Modern philosophy did little to ease this sense of envy. The preoccupation of modern thinkers with epistemology led to less faith in human reason, rather than more, although the Enlightenment thinkers started out with great confidence that the gains in natural science could be matched in philosophy. Kant, probably the greatest philosophical figure of the Enlightenment, accepted the ideal of an autonomous human reason, no longer directed by revelation or tradition uncritically received, but the upshot of Kant's massive studies of speculative reason was agnostic. He concluded that human beings are unable to know things as they are in themselves. The postulates necessary for human action—the existence of God, the immortality of the soul, human freedom, and the like—can be defended through studies of what practical reason must assume, but they cannot be proven positively or negatively by speculative reason (the mind seeking only truth) on its own.

It is incongruous or embarrassing, of course, to launch an ideal of autonomous living in which human beings will rely only upon their own critical faculties and then to find that those critical faculties are seriously limited. Hegel tried another approach, focusing on human spirituality and making the human knower less dependent on (very fallible) sensation than Kant had. But Hegel got so intoxicated with the movements (*dialectics*) of spirituality (or was so dishonest, in Voegelin's view)[3] that he ended up equating the findings of his own mind with the light of the divine Spirit, a pantheism to rival Al Hallaj.

We shall deal more with these negativities later. Positively, the modern philosophers should be credited with displaying more fully the great complexities of human consciousness, its indebtedness to space and time, and the profound sense in which *reality* is a product of human consensus. In political matters, the moderns strove to lay the foundations for a society that would grant more people full citizenship and freedom. Their appreciation of change, in other words, made them dissatisfied with classical models, in which the majority had to be slaves or serfs and only an elite few could lead fully human lives. Scholars debate the extent to which prophetic ideals sponsored by the Bible were responsible for the modern refinements of social conscience. Equally responsible, in all probability, were the technological inventions that were suggesting dozens of ways in which human tedium, suffering, and bondage to nature might be eased.

The positive yield of the Enlightenment push for an autonomous reason was a greater sense of human responsibility for the way the world runs, especially the political world, and so a strong challenge to fatalism and conservatism. If human beings could change things, human beings had the responsibility to change things for the better. In fact, for things to remain in their sorry state or decline to worse conditions was a harsh judgment on human irresponsibility. This attitude had its dangers, of course, from **hubris**, or pride-sure-to-come-to-disaster, to loads of false guilt, but it had the great advantage of helping people mature, of cutting away the props of a false dependency on the divine or past customs. The modern philosophers spawned the critical tools that made fundamentalism untenable, and they paved the way for our recent appreciations of culture

Bust of Benjamin Franklin.
Jean Antoine Houdon.
Franklin and Jefferson led
the effort of the American
founding fathers to
subordinate particular
religious traditions to the
general civility.   *(The Nelson-
Atkins Museum of Art, Kansas City,
Missouri [Nelson Fund])*

and meaning, of the precisely human sort of *reality* that animals never know.

In evolutionary perspective (which most of the modern thinkers favored), these convictions allowed one to see the past as but the childhood of the human species. So Auguste Comte, one of the most influential modern social thinkers, charted the past in terms of a long childhood in which religious mythology held sway, a recent era in which philosophy had developed more critical methods, and a golden future in which *sociology* (knowledge of the human community) would provide a scientific basis for making earthly life a quantum leap better. Comte's views are now discredited, as painful experience has revealed the difficulty of knowing what any society is likely to do, let alone of persuading it to do what is rational and for the global good. But in their day thinkers like him captured the confidence and enthusiasm that the movement toward human autonomy generated.

For Voegelin, the achievements of the moderns were quite problematic. Indeed, by his criteria one can debate whether a Kant or Hegel should be called a "philosopher" at all. Voegelin reserved this name for the venture discovered by Socrates, Plato, and Aristotle. It is a general axiom of his theory of history that the people who experience leaps in being, differentiations great and small, naturally move to express their experiences, and the symbols they use for such expression thereafter have a privileged status. One can only properly understand the symbols or language in reference to the original experiences, and to employ the symbols apart from such reference is to distort the reality that their creators saw. Insofar as a Kant or a Hegel did not recur to the metaxic experience of classical philosophy and was not a lover of wisdom formed by a quest and drawing toward the divine ground, he was not a philosopher in the truest sense. His venture broke with the tradition that might have nourished it, and his work was deprived of what should have been its basis.

Voegelin did not mean, of course, that there can never be progress in the wake of a significant leap in being. He was not saying that Plato or Jesus was the final word about noetic or pneumatic experience. He was saying, however, that genuine lovers of wisdom have the will to try to retrieve the experiences that gave birth to their culture's deepest insights. Indeed, they conceive of their work as forwarding these beginnings: further differentiating aspects hiterto unexplored, studying implications hitherto unappreciated, factoring in data previously unavailable, and so forth. Modernity certainly had new data and new implications with which to wrestle. But Voegelin faulted the modern thinkers for not taking the trouble, or having the good will, to retrieve the epochal breakthroughs of the classical thinkers and biblical prophets. To his mind these represented permanent gains and expressed experiences ever available to human consciousness. Like the physics of Newton, they might have to be taken up into newer contexts ("sublated," a Hegelian might say), but they have a truth that one can discount only at the price of falsifying or trivializing past history.

Indeed, they have a truth that one can ignore only at the price of rendering one's own portraits of reality disordered: truncated or imbalanced. The peril of a new age is the temptation, precisely because of the euphoria that novelty can cause, to ignore the reality gained by past ages. In order to stress one's own identity, one might wrongly depreciate the achievements of one's forebears in the quest for order. The shame of modern philosophy is its self-detachment from the high noetic standards set by the classical lovers of wisdom and so its progressive loss of realism and inability to solve the crucial problems standing in the way of human peace and happiness. For this reason, Voegelin could echo the judgment of Alfred North Whitehead, one of his teachers at Harvard (and himself a leading modern-contemporary philosopher), that "modern philosophy has been ruined."[4]

THE ENLIGHTENMENT AND MARXISM

Whitehead's judgment stemmed from his conviction that modern philosophy never adequately solved the problem of knowledge. Voegelin's judgment focused more on the political effects of what Kant and Hegel launched, especially as these became manifest in Nazism and Communism. For whereas Whitehead saw a "fallacy of misplaced concreteness" in that the moderns failed to appreciate how all of reality is interconnected and **processive**, Voegelin saw a self-deification that led to massive slaughters.

Noetically, the hallmark of the classical philosophical achievement was the metaxic balance. Plato and Aristotle could be faulted for not sufficiently appreciating the extent of change, the centrality of historical development to any proper definition of human nature. But they had a firm hold on the constant features of the human condition, the fourfold disposition of being in terms of nature, society, self, and divinity that is irreducible. Had the Enlightenment motto of autonomy meant the sharpening of this quarternian structure of reality, the finer delineation of how God and nature, individual persons and social groups, interact and shape one another, it would have meant wonderful progress. Indeed, despite the aberrations that the Enlightenment thinkers caused, one has to credit them with making possible our modern and contemporary appreciations of the possibilities within *humanity*. But the price of this achievement was terribly high: the loss of metaxic balance through what Martin Buber has called (and Voegelin has agreed was) "the eclipse of God."

Hegel is the figure in whom the speculative loss of metaxic balance was consummated, so Hegel is the figure on whom Voegelin lavished the fullest noetic analysis. Whereas Kant maintained a general sense of order (although his studies of speculative reason missed the significance of tension toward the divine ground), Hegel in effect divinized human consciousness, making the limits of his own finite awareness the limits of the divine mind. This turning away from common sense (all sane people know they are limited, mortal, and therefore not divine) prompted Kierkegaard, one of Hegel's most biting critics, to remark on the ridiculous conclusion to which the Hegelian "system" led: the divine mind has to pause in its infinite operations while its human vessel turns aside to sneeze.

Still, the figure in whom the modern self-divinization became horrible was Marx, insofar as Marx made possible a loss of reality so pathological that a Lenin, Stalin, or Mao could slaughter millions in the name of his holy cause. To be sure, this sort of imbalance has not been limited to atheistic thinkers and politicians, as we have previously mentioned. When the prophetic sense of seizure by the divine becomes introverted, instead of leading the recipient to an outgoing confession of the divine goodness, it can produce the bloodly megalomania seen in the "Christian" crusaders, inquisitors, and puritan warriors, and in the Muslim fanatics and tyrants. But Marx's theses that Hegel should be turned on his head so that the dialectics of mind become the dialectics of matter, and that religion has been mainly **alienation**, projecting onto "God" energies that should be used for humankind (an idea he got from Feuerbach), set the stage for a hatred of the divine and a slaughter of all who stood against the new movement that claimed to replace the divine, and this had little precedent in history.

Voegelin's work *From Enlightenment to Revolution*[5] documents this interpretation of the pernicious effects of the modern turn to human autonomy. It has the qualifications and nuances one would expect of a first-rate historian and philosopher, so Voegelin did not fail to give Marx his due regarding such matters as the analysis of labor, the importance of which Marx was the first to spotlight. But Voegelin read Marx as a man who was hateful because he found that he was not God. This led to the dishonesty of denying that there is a God and putting a veto against serious discussion of the experiences that show the reality and significance of the human movement toward the divine. In the case of Marx, one might point to a sympathy for working people, who were suffering terribly from the Industrial Revolution, and an accurate instinct that much of bourgeois religion had in fact become a support of the evildoers who were responsible for such suffering. Present-day religious analysts, especially those based in third-world countries and trying to develop a theology that would liberate the suffering masses, tend to take this more sympathetic tack.[6] But no validity in their charges against the American and European capitalists who have played a large part in the economic woes of the third world erases the blood spilt and the spirits crushed by atheistic Marxist regimes.

Voegelin's own biography includes a key transition in 1938 when he had to flee Austria with the Nazi Gestapo at his heels. His crime was opposing the Nazi theories of race, and the wonder to many of his friends was that he would risk so much when he himself was not a Jew or a Catholic or a member of one of the other groups that had come in for automatic suspicion. The Nazis had a different program than the Communists, of course, but Voegelin saw in both groups a similarly mad loss of reality. Both had cast aside the restraints of divinity and proceeded as though human beings were the sole measure. Both subverted the ideals of progress, justice, and human welfare to an **ideological** compulsion that was usually in the service of a base self-interest. The Nazi theories of race and anti-Semitism seem literally crazy to any mind balanced by the noetic and pneumatic gains of classical philosophy and biblical revelation. The Soviet Communist purges, concentration camps, and rewritings of history seem similarly diseased. For both the Nazis and the Communists, slogans and theories came to weigh heavier than real people, who should be the concrete imperatives to justice and mercy. The result has been systematic butchering, lying, and disorder. To Voegelin's mind this was what happened when one tried to deny reality and live in a false world. Reality simply will not oblige. You cannot pretend without horrible consequences that there is no divinity, or that the state precedes individual human beings, or that nature imposes no constraints.

Conservative political and religious thinkers in the West sometimes read these Voegelinian judgments as wholesale support for traditional Christianity, capitalism, or Americanism. That is a serious mistake. Voegelin, and indeed anyone who has interiorized the noetic and pneumatic leaps in being, knew that "God" and "nation" can be abused by any idiot or evildoer, whatever his or her supposed uniform. Voegelin's special interest has been the modern and twentieth-century movements that have denied divine transcendence and subordinated the individual human to the fiction called "the people." But the analogies are all too plain in such supposedly religiously based regimes as the apartheid rule of South Africa, or the dictatorships of some Latin American countries, or the rule of fundamentalist Muslim fanatics.

Whether the analogies in the evils done by the capitalistic regimes are equally plain is a matter for careful analysis and debate, but a cardinal principle in such debate would be that practical atheism or lack of proper metaxic balance and restraining love of God can work through protestations of traditional religion. Equally, one cannot focus only on the virtues of one's own kind and the vices of one's foes. If a movement flying under Marxist colors actually honors truth and wants a peaceful change of social structures currently oppressing or disenfranchising the poor, as would seem to be true of some third-world movements, one cannot write it off simply because it uses the name of a thinker whose defects led to massive sufferings. If a movement flying under the colors of God and a tradition of human liberty in fact is largely just a support for big business, or for national self-interest that disregards the needs of other peoples, one cannot stamp it *approved* simply because it uses the words coined by the leaps in being to designate right order. Right order is present or absent in individual consciousnesses, and through them in social groups, on a case-by-case or existential basis. It is not what people claim but what they actually are and do that shows their order or disorder. If people practically, actually honor the light that finally is divine and the love that makes for real justice, they are in fact rightly ordered. If actually their deeds are unjust and oppressive, their persons more concerned with money and power than with wisdom and service, they are not in fact religious, admirable, or trustworthy.

THE NEW SCIENCE OF POLITICS
AND MODERN GNOSTICISM

Eric Voegelin came to national notice in the United States following his Walgreen Lectures at the University of Chicago in 1951. Published as *The New Science of Politics*, they fashioned a withering attack on modernity and the then current state of political science. Many of their themes anticipate the full developments presented in *Order and History*, but because Voegelin changed the original design for *Order and History*, dropping the plan he first had for volumes 4–6, *The New Science of Politics*, along with *Science, Politics, and Gnosticism* and *From Enlightenment to Revolution*, remains a prime source of his views on modern developments.

The basic thesis of *The New Science of Politics* is that modernity has been powered by a new sort of Gnosticism. For Voegelin, the thinkers most influential and representative in the modern age have all been in flight from right order, especially from the confession that right order makes of a transcendent divinity, and so have bred *pneumo-pathological* results (spiritual illness with profoundly practical effects). *The New Science of Politics*, like *Order and History*, makes it clear that mental health in this context is no mean achievement. For while nonliterate or cosmological cultures might seem healthier than that of the modern West in that they have not tried to canonize the death of God or simply to slaughter those who would dissent against tyranny, they purchased that health (such as it was: the history of cosmological cultures of course shows spasms of cruelty and destruction) at the price of dealing with the fourfold structure of reality only compactly.

As soon as one admits the noetic and pneumatic differentiations, gaining balance becomes a more arduous enterprise. To be sure, the advances in truth are precious, and the overall potential of humanity to deal with reality more effectively is increased. But one also unleashes greater potential for intellectual and emotional misfiring. Unfortunately, modernity has witnessed a large number of such misfirings.

The Gnostic core of modernity that Voegelin found is the intoxication or self-deification we have already treated. In the arch-representative of modern political science, Thomas Hobbes, Voegelin saw both a shrewd appreciation of the Gnostic abuses and the characteristic failing of the modern analyst. Hobbes could see the will to power that corrupted the Puritan revolutionaries (and that dogs all passionate religion convinced that God's cause is its own). However, he had no handle on the drive to a real, transcendent God and so no better definition of human nature than pride, which is actually its supreme danger.

Voegelin's own words are worth quoting:

> In order to maintain his position against the fighting churches and sects, Hobbes had to deny that their zeal was inspired, however misguided, by a search for truth. Their struggle had to be interpreted, in terms of immanent existence, as an unfettered expression of their lust for power; and their professed religious concern had to be revealed as a mask for their existential lust. In carrying out this analysis, Hobbes proved to be one of the greatest psychologists of all times; his achievements in unmasking the **libido dominandi** behind the pretense of religious zeal and reforming idealism are as solid today as they were at the time when he wrote. This magnificent psychological achievement, however, was purchased at a heavy price. Hobbes rightly diagnosed the corruptive element of passion in the religiousness of the Puritan Gnostics. He did not, however, interpret passion as the source of corruption in the life of the spirit [as Homer had], but rather the life of the spirit as the extreme of existential passion. Hence, he could not interpret the nature of man from the vantage point of the maximum of differentiation through the experiences of transcendence so that passion, and especially the fundamental passion, **superbia** [pride], could be discerned as the permanently present danger of the fall from true nature; but he had, on the contrary, to interpret the life of passion as the nature of man so that the phenomena of spiritual life appeared as extremes of superbia.[7]

Another way of saying this is that when people do not have spirits, core personalities, open to the divine and humbled by the light and love that the divine presents, they become liable to all sorts of psychological aberrations and political abuses. The Platonic figure therefore continues to dominate Voegelin's analysis: the polis is the psyche writ large. Have an open soul, rightly ordered by the quest for the divine and the divine drawing, and you will have the paradigm for a society both balanced and stable. Have an open soul, warmed by the love of the divine, and you will want political authority to do more than control the bestial masses. The basic political problem therefore becomes how to fashion a populace mature or virtuous enough to make good social life possible. Voegelin's first answer

Reason's Sleep Gives Birth to Monsters (Los Caprichos). Francisco Goya y Lucientes. Goya's art expressed a prophetic sense that modernity's claims to rational control would turn out specious. *(The Nelson-Atkins Museum of Art, Kansas City, Missouri [Nelson Fund])*

would be that the noetic and pneumatic differentiations are the obvious places to focus.

COUNTERVIEWS

Voegelin's critics, of course, have a lot to say in response. For the positivistic political scientists whom Voegelin castigated as people of truncated spiritual life, Plato and Aristotle represent fascism in ancient garb, and traditional Judaism and Christianity have been passed by because of modern science. Voegelin tended to think there was little one could say to such people. If they cannot retrieve the epochal leaps in being accomplished by the classical philosophers and the biblical prophets, if they will not meditate their way back to the foundations of a rightly ordered self and society, then they cannot participate in any meaningful debate about the diagnosis of modern ills because they lack the elementary competence. In the realm of political science in any profound sense, the disorder of the individual scientist soon disqualifies him or her as unequal to the task at hand. The self is the instrument for curing the polis that is the self written large. A diseased self only furthers the troubles.

To other therapists who have appeared on the scene and focused on the human spirit, but rejected the classical and prophetic differentiations, Voegelin had a similarly negative response. Thus he found Freud, Jung, and Heidegger Gnostics whose knowledge is more symptomatic of the modern problem than likely to provide modernity's cure. In place of the idealistic or Neo-Kantian tradition that has nurtured such Gnosticism in recent generations, Voegelin proposed the Anglo-Saxon tradition of common sense. This viewpoint, which gained rather full elaboration through Scottish thinkers such as Thomas Reid, stays close to experience. It distrusts all flights into the imaginative otherworld, and it is concerned with educating a citizenry to have a sufficient consensus or shared mental health to make possible a realistic social life.

Clearly, Voegelin's "common sense" is no foe of theory or the life of reason and the spirit as the crucial differentiations laid them out. But it marshals a certain primitive resistance to the Gnostics who turn away from the world and blithely justify spilling rivers of blood and calls their flights of fancy a deadly danger. Human beings live within certain unbreachable limits, in the midst of divine mystery. When they disregard this condition, they become diseased, even Satanic. Insofar as modernity appears to have been waylaid by such pride and disease, the therapy is quite obvious. Until divinity and metaxic balance are again made strong and attractive, the world will continue to suffer the writhings of disorder.

SUMMARY

We began our sketch of modernity with a treatment of modern science. The key meaning of *science* in this period has come from the methodology of experimentation and verification. The modern confidence in the intelligibility of the world, the modern technological gains, and the sheer good of increased knowledge show the positive gains that a more empirical approach to nature and stronger theoretical powers could develop. The losses were a tendency to canonize scientific method and to oust traditional approaches that had considerable merit (classical, biblical, and mythical).

Modern history brought human temporality to the fore, making it more intrinsic to human being than it had previously been thought to be. This meant a more dynamic sense of culture but also an erosion of the stability that classical and biblical paradigms had offered. Modern philosophy came to a similar end, increasing our awareness of the complexity of human knowledge but finding little basis for surety about the configuration of the world or the function of the divine.

The Enlightenment program of autonomy summarized much of the modern ideal, and the Marxist interpretation of such autonomy has shown its deadly possibilities. Voegelin saw the ideology that has been so powerful in modernity as a serious default on the classical differentiations, and the worst of the ideological positions has been the eclipse of the divine. His lectures on the new science of politics and modern Gnosticism made his reputation in the United States (and got him classified as a conservative), and they make the case that modernity's prideful sense of having made the divine immanent in the human has been the strongest source of its manifest disorder.

STUDY QUESTIONS

1. What are the reasons for thinking that the modern scientific method alone is not adequate for mapping reality?
2. What is the evidence that human beings are always changing and that human cultures are more diverse than the classical and biblical authors thought?
3. How could a thinker such as Hegel come to identify the movements of the Divine Spirit with his own mind?
4. What validity has the Marxist charge that much religion has supported the status quo and so has been oppressive to the lower classes?
5. How do the noetic and pneumatic differentiations curb pride?

NOTES

1. See Bernard Lonergan, *Insight* (New York: Philosophical Library, 1957).
2. Marshall Berman, *All That Is Solid Melts Into Air* (New York: Simon & Schuster, 1982).
3. See Eric Voegelin, "On Hegel: A Study in Sorcery," *Studium Generale*, 24 (1971), pp. 335–68.
4. See Alfred North Whitehead, *Science and the Modern World* (New York: Free Press, 1967), p. 55; Eric Voegelin, "On Classical Studies," *Modern Age*, XVII (1973), p. 3.
5. Eric Voegelin, *From Enlightenment to Revolution* (Durham, N.C.: Duke University Press, 1975).
6. See, for example, José Miranda, *Marx and the Bible* (Maryknoll, N.Y.: Orbis, 1974).
7. Eric Voegelin, *The New Science of Politics* (Chicago: University of Chicago Press, 1952), pp. 179–80.

CHAPTER ELEVEN

Conclusion

ORIENTATION

Our final chapter combines a review of the main theses we have advanced with a final look at the implications of a Voegelinian reading of world history and world religion. In retrospect the significance of the noetic and pneumatic breakthroughs will stand out most, but perhaps we should again note that these breakthroughs themselves do not decide the issue of how wise a given individual or culture actually is. So although the "Western" aspect of the breakthroughs might be read as a chauvinistic depreciation of the East, in fact it need not be. On a case-by-case basis, India, China, or the ancient Mexican culture might be more admirable than a given period of Greek or Jewish or Christian culture.

The second point to be made is that this final chapter does take a position on the implications of the Voegelinian reading of world history, and so risks prejudice on a second count. One could sketch equal time for atheistic or traditionally biblical or empiricist readings of history that would come up with a quite different prescription for the way back to mental health and world peace. But by now these other points of view should be relatively familiar, so long have we suggested their presence as counter-voices, so we will not try to image the different follow-throughs or prescriptions for the future of religion that they might sketch. Sufficient for this chapter will be the task of summarizing vigorously and concluding with a fairly independent, critical call for an understanding of religion and humanity that honors honesty and love, truth and goodness, wherever found.

THE GREAT LEAPS IN BEING

When we take Eric Voegelin as our tutor, the most decisive events in the history of humankind are the leaps in being achieved by Israelite revelation and Greek philosophy. We shall place due qualifications on this statement throughout the rest of this chapter, but for the moment let its baldness stand. Whereas all prior peoples had experienced reality essentially in the mode of the cosmological myth, and the Indian and Chinese cultures nurtured sages who went to the brink of breaking consubstantiality, the Israelite prophets and the Greek philosophers experienced transcendence sufficiently vividly and profoundly to begin the processes that finally clarified the structures of pneuma and nous as formed by their dynamic relations to divinity. Under the modalities of love and knowledge, warmth and light, the prophetic and philosophic movements established the metaxic structure that is valid for all human beings. The prophets then inveighed against idolatry, to protest all the false depictions of divinity that threatened the realism implicit in their experiences. The classical philosophers set a standard that made clear the advantages and disadvantages of myth and that later became the silent judge of philosophy's derailment.

The crux of both leaps in being was the differentiation of divinity that occurred. However, this divinity stood in defining relation to the physical world, the social group, and the individual human self, so after the leaps in being, all four primary realities stood in clearer relief. The main gain in theology proper, the understanding of God, was encapsuled in Plato's "Beyond." Following the metaxic movements of the noetic spirit, Plato discerned that the divine is the border above which the human cannot go. Just as the human cannot penetrate brute matter below, the "unbounded" potentiality that Anaximander and other Pre-Socratics had explored, so the human cannot penetrate the unknown or hidden God above. This God is the source of the light that illumines the metaxic consciousness, but it recedes out of sight. Voegelin thought that Plato intuited that this God was the **creator ex nihilo**, the God who made the world from nothingness, but that Plato judged such a truth too fragile to be entrusted to the general public. Thus Plato retained a mythic style in dealing with divinity, to communicate indirectly and holistically what literal speech might falsify.

The prophetic or pneumatic differentiation was less lucid, because the prophets were less proficient at precise intellectual analysis than were the classical lovers of wisdom, but more powerful and saving. It amounted to the divine seizure or eruption at the very base of the human personality. One might even call this point of seizure the *dead spot* of the soul, insofar as it passes below what the mind can conceptualize (maybe even below what the mind can notice). Later Christian theologians would say that, generally speaking, love follows upon knowledge (one must appreciate a good before being able to embrace it). But in the case of the divine love, of the pneumatic seizure, love precedes knowledge, because this experience resets the entire personality. After it, the world, the self, and other people are all configured differently. When analysts tried to parcel this out they spoke of faith, hope, and charity, but all three theological virtues or powers stemmed from the **metanoia**, or conversion, that the experience of the divine had produced. The love of God became a new medium of interpretation, another light by which to see. The world took on a quite different glow when one considered it the expression of a pure and loving Creator, as did the self and other people.

Theologians, working in the service of their traditions' formative revelations, have tended to stress the differences between the differentiating experiences of the prophets and those of the classical philosophers. The former were supernatural and yielded saving grace, whereas the latter, the theologians claimed, were merely natural and did little to solve the basic human problems of evil and sin. A fairer analysis narrows the distance between the two experiences and brings out a greater kinship. For the lovers of wisdom became convinced that their progress in the metaxic search was God's doing more than their own (and so, in the theologians' language, it was a matter of grace). And the reality that the philosophers discerned made the divine beyond, or ground, the only proper basis for right order, thereby calling for a considerable conversion. When Plato described the human ideal as becoming as much like God as possible, he was much closer to the saints of the revelational traditions than to the inflated self-divinizers of modernity. He never meant to obscure the metaxic boundary that kept the human seeker on the side of creaturehood, but he did mean to make plain the immortalizing effects of the search and drawing. When people defined themselves by this search, as Socrates had, they passed outside of death, coming to live in a realm where divinity promised a reality that time could never see. This all had to be expressed mythically, for we cannot reify the transcendent, but it squared so well with biblical intuitions that Eastern Christian art often placed Plato among the apostles or Church fathers.

The two leaps in being do differ in their approaches to the core problem that twists human nature, although probably not so dramatically as has usually been claimed. The philosophers think that education, in the sense of getting into the search and drawing that heads for the divine ground, transforms human beings as much as possible. The prophets are more troubled by the perversions of the will or the heart, worrying that people seem able to know what is right and choose not to do it. In actual fact, evildoing is usually a combination of ignorance and bad will, of foolishness and knavery. The stupid who are such because they will not exert their reason, will not put up with the sacrifices or asceticisms necessary (as Plato puts it in the *Republic*) to get out of the cave of sensuality, are brutish in will as well. The passionate who love carnal goods, money, or power more than the divine mystery are ignorant and closed in soul. One might miss the mark, the noetic balance and full love of God, by failing to exert oneself, sinning through sloth. Or one might miss the mark by blocking off the divine (or the neighbor or the physical world) and inflating love of self. An open soul, on the other hand, prepares the way for a disciplined intellectualism that shows the ascent of the mind toward God, just as a disciplined mind that senses the lure of the Beyond is two-thirds of the way toward a mystical confession.

The God glimpsed in other historic experiences, from the regular ecstatic testimony of shamans to the impressive advances of an Akhenaton and the sages of the Indian and Chinese cultures, only gains from this canonization of the prophetic and noetic differentiations. We shall speak soon of the functional equivalence of all peoples' experiences of reality, but here we can explicitly state that a Buddha or a Lao Tzu well deserves comparison with a Plato or a Jesus. They might not have discerned with Plato's noetic clarity or reached the intensity of Jesus' salvific love, but their followers will not be wrong in thinking that some parts of their visions are superior to the Western heroes'. Equally, their followers might want to debate the correctness of Voegelin's judgment that they remained overly indebted to the cosmological myth. Whatever the upshot of this debate, they will seem closer to the great leaps in being than many moderns.

COSMOLOGY AND ANTHROPOLOGY

The new cosmology and anthropology latent in the leaps in being were certainly advances over humanity's previous achievements, but they were not untaintedly pure progress. Discerning that the world does not contain the divine and suspecting that *divinity* is a creative power so self-sufficient that it produced the world from nothingness greatly clarified the status of all worldly things and simplified the human quest for the ultimate treasure. On the other hand, both the classical and the biblical cultures never fully followed through on their intuitions of such a radical monotheism, and as the doctrine of creation from nothingness slowly clarified, it helped make possible an abuse of nature that we are just recently beginning to appreciate. Were the divine more ingredient in nature (as a sophisticated philosophy of creation could make it: the Creator from nothingness has to grant every creature its being continually), people would have a strong reason to reverence nature and not abuse it. Nature would have some rights, perhaps even some legal entitlements, and posterity would broaden the horizons of developers and entrepreneurs. As it is now, too many developers (of all sorts, military and commercial) put the Archie Bunkerish question, "What has posterity ever done for me?" Had theology done a better job of making the world humanity's home and granting nature and future generations the right to prosperity, this question would be stripped of all legitimacy and stand revealed for the irreligious stupidity it is.[1]

The anthropological gains of the great leaps in being included a better appreciation of what comprises human dignity, human destiny, and human responsibility. The biblical doctrine of *imago Dei*, human beings made in the image of God, stimulated a focus on human conscience, knowing, and loving. The Greek noetic discoveries flowed into this anthropological tendency, because they pursued the intuition that human beings are unique because they are rational, are the animals who have logos. Later definitions of human nature, which focused on such central human capacities as symbol-making, work, and play, were but variations on this main intuition. The later modern descriptions, which downplayed human spirituality and stressed race or sociability, represented a decline. Against the classical and biblical standards, they could only make human beings the most signal sufferers in a godless, and therefore ultimately profane, universe. Indeed, their tendency was to oscillate between foolish exaltation of humanity, as itself the new locus of the divine, and despair in the face of the evolutionary evidence that humanity came from very humble beginnings and had no transcendent future.

The biblical God and the Platonic beyond both offered humanity a happier self-understanding. On the one hand, human beings were but creatures of a day compared with the divine eternity, and as such need not ultimately take themselves seriously. When the Epistle of John says that even when human beings' hearts condemn them, God is greater than their hearts, it means to offer a word of consolation. On the other hand, the message of Jesus was that, if human beings, evil as they are, usually do good to their children and loved ones, how much greater good must not God be wanting to do? The Israelite theme that the Lord is always compassionate and merciful, long-suffering and abounding in steadfast love, consoled many Jewish generations. The Muslim anthropology, with its profound appreciation of human creatureliness, pointed toward the joys of pure worship, of absolute confession of God. The result of these prophetic instincts was an anthropology that made worship the supreme human action. The contemplation, praise, and petition of the divinity that had been clarified became the crux of human achievement, because the divinity that had been clarified obviously was the **realissimum**, the foundation and supreme example of reality.

The Greek experience of the metaxy added balance and precision to this biblical enthusiasm, so that Western culture at its best, when it married the Greek and Israelite geniuses, explored the confines and possiblities of *humanity* with admirable competence. Reason then could run in tandem with faith or revelation, neither depreciating the other. Sin and grace both entered into the accounting, but with the hopeful assertion that where sin had abounded grace had abounded more. Human beings were mortal, and so always knew a taste of dust and ashes. Human beings were also immortal, deathless, because they had been taken over, lured, by a God who was intrinsically deathless, **athanatos**. Greek Christian theology, in which the two principal wellsprings had the most natural combination, was the fullest developer of this theme. Grace was the healing of sin, to be sure, but more essentially it was **theosis**: divinization. The difference between this divinization and the pernicious **apotheosis** of humanity suggested by Hegel and Marx was Greek Christianity's sure sense of the mystery involved. Greek Christianity never tried to remove human createdness or supplant divinity with humanity. Always it realized that its discussion of human beings' becoming partakers of the divine nature (2 Peter 1:4) was an attempt to interpret a symbol that sprang from deep faith. The author of that epistle had drawn from the experience of the Christian cult, from the Christian conviction of resurrection, and from the Christian experience of Christ's Spirit the sense that God had taken human nature up into the divine love and life. None of this, however, suggested that the human being had become exempt from death or been commissioned to lead history toward some certain earthly goal. Just as Jesus had foresworn any military or political interpretation of his messiahship, so did the best of his followers. They had obligations to the present, but all those obligations shifted in light of their heavenly destiny.

Many of the problems in later Western, and then later world, history of course derived from the ease with which Western culture lost such a balance. In the Protestant Reformation the ties between reason and faith came undone. In modernity the static interpretation of the old balance came in for rightful criticism, and the tradition proved unable to accommodate to new scientific, historical, and philosophical findings. Later modernity presented evolution and psychoanalytic advances that begged for incorporation into the traditional synthesis, and once again the clerics and conservatives were not equal to the task. Socialist cries for greater justice, for liberation for the suffering masses, might have been assimilated into the cries of the great prophets, but by that time the churches had become part of the oppressive establishment and had lost their original sympathy for the poor.

The struggle for cosmological and anthropological balance continues today. Women and people of color ask for egalitarian treatment, and the whole world culture, religious and secular, Eastern and Western, drags its feet. Nature pleads through its acid rain and smog, through the diminishment of its marvelous species and the erosion of its lovely land, for better treatment, and only the avant-garde have ears to hear. New technologies such as solar heating slowly come into play, seldom because they are ecologically right, but almost always because they are financially persuasive. Medical personnel try to change their attitudes toward death and dying, as the superiority of older attitudes becomes plain. And everywhere the debate about destructive technology, rampant militarism, and the great dynamos of pride and greed rages.

The constant petition, if people could only think and pray with traditional clarity, is for a comprehensive view of the human situation. The eclipse of God, the lack of a persuasive theology, has meant that the majority of moderns are now wrenched out of shape. They do not know how to meditate. They have little rational, articulate faith, hope, and love with which to ward off either the terrors of death and the future or the whirlpools of their own desires. Political and ecological chaos are thus inevitable. Yet for every mark of sin, every reason to despair, there is a bright child or a good deed. So the ultimate questions remain open, the witnesses to balance and the possibility of holiness can still speak. Thus human "nature" remains fascinating and energizing, especially when one can see it in historical and philosophical perspective. We witness, as ever, a tale of two cities, the best of times and the worst.

SOCIAL THEORY AND MODERNITY

We have briefly reviewed the implications of the great leaps in being for theology, cosmology, and anthropology. Social theory, the fourth field of reflection that any adequate worldview must develop, has to be constantly kept in relation to these foregoing three. The Greek thinkers carefully considered the political forms available in their experience, and the noetic breakthrough spotlighted the need for a citizenry sufficiently mature to act rationally. Implicit in the wisdom of Plato and Aristotle was a sense that the particular governmental forms matter less than having a vision and a social consensus that are solidly realistic. Plato longed for a philosopher-king, a leader who would combine wisdom and power, but he did not long indulge the fantasy of seeing one. The classical philosophers were sufficiently immersed in the experience of noetic differentiation to know that a meta-xic worldview is possible, yet the **hoi polloi** in their day, like the common populace in all other cultures, gave little grounds for thinking that the majority would ever have a critical appreciation of the metaxy, an ability to name the quest for the divine ground and the luring by the divine ground from within. The most they could hope for was a common sense suffi-ciently close to the earth, yet reflective, to make possible a golden mean between mortality and immortality, between cynicism and idealism.

The pneumatic breakthrough developed the symbol of the Kingdom of God, principally as a way of speaking about what life is like when the Spirit holds sway. This symbol, and its cognates, placed a tension in West-ern history between now and then, the secular and the sacred, the State and the Church, time and eternity.

In Voegelin's view the *metastatic* aspects of the prophetic visions (the ways in which prophets such as Second Isaiah and Jeremiah sometimes spoke of a change-of-state or completely transformed human nature) housed an ever-present danger either of forgetting earthly responsibilities in the name of heaven or trying to create heaven on earth. The religious fanatics who confuse their own dignity with God's and the secularist ide-ologists who deny God and divinize history both are indebted to these metastatic possibilities. On the other hand, the pneumatic differentiation itself broke open the tight cosmological outlook of traditional culture, so one might look at the possibility of apocalyptic imbalance as the price necessary for a clearer appreciation of divinity.

On the whole, both Christianity and Islam (the two most effective carriers of the prophetic impulse into political power) tried to give the common people a sense of Godward dignity but did not scruple to subject them to harsh ecclesiastical controls. Islam was less hierarchical than Christianity and stayed a more lay religion. Islam was also less differenti-ated politically, never accepting a balance of powers, secular and sacred, or any legitimate tension between politics and theology. The Muslim ideal was a theocracy or **civil religion** in which one voice spoke in command of both realms. This had the advantage of fostering a unified culture, in which people could experience all facets of their lives as pregnant with religious significance. It had the disadvantage of being able to combine with a conservative mentality to produce cultural stagnation and frightful abuses of power.

The Christian differentiation of crozier and crown, religious and secular realms, eventually led to the modern sense of alienation, when the balance swung to the secular realm, and for the past few centuries Western cultures have been like Humpty Dumpty, trying to get themselves back together again. Thus, when it is honest, Christianity and its secular offspring, modernity, have to look at cosmological cultures and theocracies such as Islam with some envy. The latter can have a holism that few Christians or secularists now know.

On the other hand, of course, the line of differentiation between the secular and the sacred has frequently run parallel with the increase of human freedoms. Ancient history massively preferred the tribe to the individual, the group to the solitary person. The noetic and pneumatic leaps in being showed that the individual human spirit is the basic **sensorium** of transcendence, the basic place where the true God makes itself known and felt. This in turn provided a foundation for individual human rights and dignity, however much such religions as Judaism, Christianity, and Islam continued to conceive of the people as a unified social group. Such figures as the Christian "Body of Christ," the Pauline symbol for the union of believers with Christ, could be converted into "the solidarity of the Nordic race" or other bases for the modern nation-state. But when this sort of conversion subordinated the individual to the nebulous group and then, in fact, let a criminal elite trample on individuals' most elementary rights, it clearly represented the worst kind of regression or primitivism. As always, the Nazi and Soviet horrors prompt such Voegelinian thoughts.

One sees a more edifying example of the conflict between the traditional social instincts and the positive insights of modernity in the turmoils of contemporary Roman Catholicism. As Roman Catholicism is the tradition that we authors call home, it might be legitimate for us to use it to exemplify the unvarnished criticism that a postmodern viewpoint, trying to blend the best of traditionalism and modernism, might produce.[2]

Roman Catholicism only came to grips with modernity at the Second Vatican Council (1962–1965), and by then modernity itself was clearly giving way to postmodernity. Nonetheless, the decrees of Vatican II on the place of the Church in the modern world, religious liberty, and the like were a great leap forward. No longer was defensiveness the watchword. Pope John XXIII had used the word **aggiornamento** (bringing up to date) to summarize his hopes for the Council, and those hopes were substantially fulfilled.

Some twenty years later, however, Roman Catholicism has found itself a house quite divided. Pope John Paul II can speak eloquently of social justice, note the bases for social justice in the biblical and traditional Christian documents (especially the *social encyclicals* of his predecessor popes of the past century), but little acknowledge a debt to the modern socialists who forced the imperatives of social justice upon the Western conscience. As a result, he cannot sponsor full religious liberty within the

Catholic Church itself (for example, women remain ineligible for holy orders and therefore from official Church authority), and his deputies (for example, Cardinal Ratzinger, the man in charge of doctrinal purity) propose the strange notion that one must accept or reject a secular view such as Marxism in toto. This is meant to discredit the Catholic *liberation theologians*, based largely in third-world countries, who want to use the manifest truths in certain Marxist analyses of labor, capitalism, class antagonisms, religion, ideology, and the like without accepting Marxist materialism, atheism, deafness to human rights, or violence.

Thus, a traditionalist Catholic blockage, if not an outright self-service, makes for a veto on critical thinking, on straightforwardly taking what is good and rejecting what is bad, and in our opinion that says bad things about the spiritual health of the Church leadership. One could make similar forays into recent Catholic positions on sexual matters, from celibacy for the clergy to abortion (focusing on the strange matter of prohibiting "artificial" birth control). The result again would be a provocative refusal to work through modern insights, accepting what is good and rejecting what actually threatens a transcendent deity, and so a profound human dignity. Probably the bugbear is *tradition* itself, which has become so dogmatized or detached from the experiences of transcendence it is meant to serve that it functions almost idolatrously. Whatever, the tensions Catholicism presently displays are both a sign of life (it is like an organism valiantly trying to adapt) and a sign of the distance the traditional differentiations still have to travel if they are to render contemporary people full service, truth and consolation up to the current need.

THE EQUIVALENCE OF HUMAN EXPERIENCES

The great current need, as we have suggested, is a worldview both comprehensive and realistic. On the basis of the historical record, Voegelin has sketched such a worldview in terms of the four irreducible dimensions of nature, society, self, and divinity. The great leaps in being clarified this essential structure or metaxic situation. The major theoretical failings and practical horrors of history have come from missing such a fourfold mark. In deference to modernity, one should make plain the historicity of all four relationships. People continually change, progressing or regressing, and their worldviews with them. When change is deepening their penetration of the metaxic possibilities, it is genuine progress. When change is distorting these possibilities, forgetting or misreading the fourfold structure of reality, it is regression or derailment.

Because this reading of history and the human situation stems from the noetic and pneumatic differentiations, both of which occurred in the West, it is open to the charge of misreading non-Western experience, and so not being adequate for a global worldview. The charge is serious and deserves a serious hearing. It is true that the noetic differentiation most fully occurred with the classical Greek philosophers, entered into the substance of subsequent Western culture, and so can be called Western. On the other hand, we have shown (on the basis of hints in Voegelin's own work) parallels in India and China, striving to avoid the false impression that philosophy had no analogues in non-Western cultures. We have also suggested, and now want to make fully clear, the classical philosophers' sense that what they had discovered applied to all human beings. Indeed, the reason Plato and Aristotle demarcated history into a before and after that hinged at their noetic discoveries was their sense that pursuit of the divine ground and luring by the divine ground structured all people's consciousnesses. People's modalities of articulating their awareness of this structure certainly differed, myth and philosophy being the two polar modalities (with many hybrids in between), but they all moved between the unbounded below and the divine One above. The noetic differentiation therefore was universal or transcendental in application (in the sense of going beyond any ethnic or cultural boundaries). It applied to all, and so it carried within it, at least implicitly, a confession that all human beings, any who had reflective awareness, constituted a unified species.

The pneumatic breakthrough held similar potential, insofar as reflection could show that any human being might be seized by divinity and inspired with a holy love. Nonetheless, the intensity of this experience in the Jewish pneumatics, from Abraham to Jesus, produced an understanding of *faith* (as the main modality of living by a trustful memory of the divine seizures or overtures) that often seems limited to a single ethnic group. The data are complex and conflicting on this point, for the Bible (and the Qur'an) provides for Gentiles or people of other cultures, but a strong strain speaks of chosenness in such a way that non-Jews or non-Christians (or non-Muslims) either cannot be saved or have a much poorer chance. Christianity, mainly through the agency of Paul, did break through any ethnic barriers to salvation, opening the covenant to the Gentiles. But frequently Christians have made explicit faith in Jesus Christ necessary for salvation, and so have not been fully universal. (Such Christians have, in other words, said that the historical accident of being born in a non-Christian culture could mean the loss of salvation, even the fate of hellfire.)

This position has not squared with the perhaps equally central or influential Christian notion that the "good pagan," the person who has followed the light of conscience faithfully, reaches God and salvation. So in the Christian case, Westernism has in fact often begotten a theological provincialism and the presumption of narrowing the "success" of the divine salvific will to only a portion of world history. The Jewish and Muslim cases are somewhat different, but they too show an ethnic bias and frequently resist a fully democratic or universal reading of the pneumatic breakthrough.

The implications we see in Voegelin's position, which we now extend to a theological position of our own, run completely in the direction of universalism. Voegelin has spoken of the equivalence of human experiences, meaning by this the ground-level similarity and equality of all human beings' senses of reality.[3] What the immense variety of cultural symbols finally all express is the fourfold structure of reality and the mystery of humanity's beginning and beyond. Some symbolisms are better than others—clearer, more lyric, deeper. Some symbolisms are more compact, others more differentiated. The modern symbolisms have seriously missed the mark in trying to deny or ignore the divine transcendence. Many cultures have nurtured personalities who easily fell out of balance to become religious fanatics, apocalypticists, mythologists opposed to critical reason, fideists opposed to scientific research, or politicians so egomaniacal that they would kill for power. Still, always and everywhere the four constant features have pressed for acknowledgement, raising up witnesses who would dispute the neglect of any one.

So, for example, nature has always had its defenders, from the traditional American Indian who would not cut into the bosom of his mother the earth with a plow to contemporary environmentalists. The divine has always nurtured mystics, philosophers, and prophets who had passionately to defend its reality because they had been formed by this reality at their depths. The individual might have been submerged through much of the human story, but always peculiar gifts and needs differentiated the members of the tribe and the polis, making it plain that the human kind were different from ants and bees, from coconuts and cows. And, last, society has always had its defenders, wise people who could defend tradition and explain the priority of the common good.

Place this most general pattern in time, give it a proper temporal flow and development, and you have a fundamental analysis of the human

Reverie. Paul Gauguin. Modern artists such as Gauguin sometimes idealized simpler cultures like the Polynesian as more whole or healthy than the European. *(The Nelson-Atkins Museum of Art, Kansas City, Missouri [Nelson Fund])*

condition that emphasizes the radical equality of all peoples. All have been mortal, nothing more than human beings, whose lives are short. None of them has ever seen God. Some have had immortalizing experiences, insights or seizures that showed how humanity includes a thrust to transcend the grave. Some have had visionary experiences that they could express as a glimpse of the divine, at least from the back. But the metaxic span has held, always and everywhere. To be human has been not to know the most crucial things about one's own situation: where one has come from, where one is going. One might believe certain things about origin or destiny, might enrich one's life by faith. But no one has ever been with the Creator at the beginning or turned with the Tao at the end. (If Jesus and the Buddha were actual human beings, these judgments wholly apply to them.)

The phases of world history—cosmological, noetic, pneumatic, and modern—show the gross features of the evolution of a species formed by this metaxic structure, but they provide no escape from such a mysterious human condition. One can allot praise or blame, urge emulation or disregard, on the basis of such a delineation (or other distinctions for which one can make the case), but the radical equality remains. Functionally, all human experiences amount to grappling with the same mystery, the identical ultimate constraints. Race and sex, age and culture, religion and status all are secondary. They have immense influence, which one has to calculate case by case. The radical equality is no excuse for not trying to remove the glaring inequalities that virtually all cultures have spawned or tolerated. But the radical equality is a baseline, a foundational perspective always relevant, and it can keep people sane about their situation, less liable to lose balance, justice, and joy.

We are simply people, and our lives are short. None of us has ever seen God. We all struggle and die. Each of our lives has good times and bad. From this we can, probably should, derive a great compassion for one another (the religions are nearly unanimous that we should). In this perspective, we can, probably should, gain the freedom to drop the distinctions, privileges, and posturings that contribute so much to injustice and human pain. These most "impractical" considerations therefore prove radical, revolutionary in their practical implications. Set people firmly in a critical realism, teach them to see the world clear and whole, and you will have a tribe of free spirits, of prophets and sages, well defended against the cant and advantage corrupting so many, the illusion and perversion empowering most wrong. Some people would call these sentences *moralistic*, claiming to hear in them a preacher's tone unsuitable to a textbook. So be it. Most such critics are moderns who have something to gain from continuing the present disorders, who have a mind or a conscience unwilling to be real.

THE FUTURE OF RELIGION

The future of religion will stand or fall on its realism and order. If the traditions move in the direction of retrieving and advancing the great leaps in being, they will be a blessing. If they encourage a false compactness, or a noetic imbalance, or a pneumatic missing of the mark, or a closure to the divine they will be a curse. Another way of saying this is that we should challenge all the traditions to lay aside their dogmatism and ideology, to speak afresh from their generative experiences and set these in dialogue, where they may be criticized and supplemented. The modern antireligious positions should be forced to come clean and explain what in fact they offer to build a life upon. The worldviews that lead to bloodbaths and conflicts must not be excused because they chant consecrated formulas about the dialectics of history or the sovereignty of free enterprise.

From beginning to end the Platonic criterion should rule: things are not good because someone claims they are godly (or privileged by atheistic standards). Things are godly or privileged because they are good. To be sure, we have to criticize our criteria for *goodness*, might even have to debate. But there comes a point at which goodness is a primitive term, an ultimate behind which one cannot go. Massive destruction, suffering, murder, and crime, for instance, so conflict with elemental goodness that it is impossible honestly, rationally, to call these *good*. Truth telling, kindness, healing, educating, forgiving may all be abused, but in the main they will all be good.

The Voegelinian prescription for *religion* (a term Voegelin did not much like) is therefore rather simple. The traditions ought to encourage honesty, insight, depth, the pursuit of truth; they ought to encourage love and knowledge of the real, mysterious Divinity (with us only as it proves to be) and kindly, just treatment of our fellow human beings; they ought to help us love and preserve the earth, knowing it is only given us in trust for posterity.

To this we would add, in slight criticism of Voegelin, a greater stress on soteriology and compassion. These certainly are present in our master's schemata, but at times his opposition to the derailments of modernity, his intense aversion to ideology and gnosticism, seemed to freeze his appreciation of the sufferings of the world's majority. Of course, the socialist prescriptions for alleviating this suffering do show the pattern of pneumatic imbalance and noetic hubris that his analyses of modernity delineate. And the liberal ideologies are indeed weak reeds on which to build a counter position. But the conservative philosophies, as these tend to be deployed, more defend the advantages of the privileged than take aim at alleviating the sufferings of the poor. This seems to us diametrically opposed to the instincts of the Israelite prophets, Jesus, the Christian saints, and the **mahatmas** of most other traditions. If these theologies are rooted in a Hellenic sense of superiority at discovering the metaxic reality, so much the worse for Hellas. Such a sense would be pride going before the fall of closure to the pneumatic revelations that would fulfill the mind, closure to the seizures of love that would give the beyond a human face of crucifixion and resurrection.

We mean these last terms symbolically, neither denying their debt to Christianity, the tradition in which we ourselves have been raised, nor limiting their significance to a Christian theological interpretation. The human face of the divine that the traditions must inculcate or solicit might also be described in terms of enlightenment, freedom, actionless action, or what the Muslims mean by remembrance.

The existential crux of any tradition, religious or irreligious, is the wisdom and helpfulness it nurtures, the light and love. Everywhere, we have to ask what worship of the true God this tradition encourages and what progress toward justice. It will be salvific, soteriological, in the measure that it heals both mind and body, both spirit and flesh. It will be whole in the measure that it brings people to love and care for the earth without failing to stretch beyond the earth toward heaven or nirvana, symbols of the mysterious reality that finally makes us human. One might also say, therefore, that the crux of any tradition is the effectiveness of its **mystagogy**. If it denies the mystery at the beginning and the beyond, it is perverse from the start. If a tradition does little to elucidate this mystery and show how we can live with it and draw nourishment from it, a tradition has little wisdom or saving power. We have to be patient, open, and judicious, of course, not forcing any tradition into our own packages. For instance, we have to learn to discern the wisdom about divinity, as well as about the soul and the tribe, that is compacted in the cosmological myth. We have to try on the diction that would stress the impersonality of God, or the naturalism, or the kinship with animal magnetism.

Equally, God might be telling us something through the protestations of the honest atheist, which might differ little from the negative theology of the high mystic. Or the divine might offer us a transmutation of the prophets' message in the nonviolent, self-spending political, medical, diplomatic, or military work of the "secular" humanist. The names are not so important as the realities, a point we have already made. The future of religion lies with the realities, not the names. It is sharing ultimate peak and valley experiences and collaborating for the removal of those evils we humans can remove that will determine whether the traditions do in fact save our little species. It is whether they help us not only see the way but also muster the will to walk it that will be their judge.

One of the great virtues in Voegelin's work is the clarity with which it shows a spirit willing to change and keep growing. When he found that his plan for a history of political ideas broke down, so that he could no longer justify his theoretical premises, Voegelin abandoned thousands of pages on which he had spent prime years. When he found it necessary to understand classical philosophy, he set himself to learning Greek. When he had to pursue Israelite revelation, he took himself to a rabbi to learn Hebrew. So too with Russian, Chinese, and other linguistic or conceptual tools, other ranges of data, that his work came to demand. The analogy for the religious future we hope for is to press on in confidence that the mystery will sustain and save us. The light of understanding is good in itself, so it must come from the mystery and be worth suffering for. The love of human beings forgiving one another, supporting one another, enjoying one another is good in itself, so it must come from the mystery and deserve center stage in our lives. A tradition, religious or secular, intellectual or pneumatic, that cannot hear these things, or see their crucial significance

Woman IV. Willem de Kooning. Abstract art seems postmodern in its break with autonomous reason and new exploration of imagination. *(The Nelson-Atkins Museum of Art, Kansas City, Missouri [Gift of Mr. William Inge])*

for education and politics, or witness to them publicly, forfeits its claim to our respect. A tradition that nourishes us in these things is at one and the same time a good way to be human and a straight path to salvation.

SUMMARY

To summarize our argument throughout this book and drive home its overall implications, we have reviewed or reexpressed the main points. First, we noted the Voegelinian periodization of history in terms of the great leaps in being and what preceded and followed them. The crux of both the noetic and the pneumatic differentiations is the divinity they clarify, and theologians are wrong to make a great distinction between them. The cosmological gain of the leaps was a stronger sense of nature's createdness, but this could alienate human beings from the world. The anthropological gains were summarized in the metaxic balance and realistic love that the philosophers and prophets foresaw.

The traditional social theory took its balance from its relation to the other three primal realities differentiated by the Greek and Israelite leaps, and its implication was that any social form should be judged by its contributions to right order, especially as the divine transcendence disclosed this. Modernity pressed for a keener sense of historical evolution and human rights. Contemporary Roman Catholicism offers a good example of a tradition struggling to accommodate both traditionalism and modernity.

Our concluding sections dealt with the equivalence of human experience and the future of religion, two considerations meant to suggest a final rounding off of Voegelin's work. The equivalence is one of his basic theses and provides a way of showing the universality latent in the leaps. If the basic fourfold structure is irreducible, it applies everywhere and everywhere offers a fundamental guidance. The best future that we saw for religion lay in its trying to forward the critical realism made possible by the leaps. We added to Voegelin's emphases more compassion or soteriology and suggested that any tradition can be judged by its noetic, pneumatic, and mystagogic fruits.

STUDY QUESTIONS

1. Explain the lower and upper boundaries that define the metaxy.
2. How might the cosmological myth enrich our contemporary views of nature?
3. Explain how modern social theory can pressure the traditional interpretation of the leaps so that they better support human rights.
4. What is the basis for holding that all cultures have had equivalent experiences of reality?
5. What sort of compassion should future religion promote as most realistic?

NOTES

1. See Robert L. Heilbroner, *An Inquiry Into the Human Prospect* (New York: W. W. Norton & Co., Inc., 1980), pp. 179–86.
2. See John T. Carmody and Denise L. Carmody, *Contemporary Catholic Theology*, 2d ed. (San Francisco: Harper & Row, Pub., 1985).
3. See Eric Voegelin, "Equivalences of Experience and Symbolization in History," *Eternita e Storia* (Florence: Valecchi, 1970), pp. 215–34.

Glossary

Aggiornamento   Pope John XXIII's Italian word for bringing Roman Catholicism up to date.

Agnosticism   Not knowing one's position, especially on ultimate matters such as the existence of God.

Alienation   Estrangement, divorce, or distancing.

Amulets   Objects, usually worn, for gaining good fortune and avoiding ill.

Anatman   Buddhist notion that there is no stable, unchanging self.

Androgyny   Male-femaleness; sexual complementarity or wholeness.

Animistic   Pertaining to a world populated with spirits or souls.

Anthropocentrism   Pivoting on humanity, making human beings the center and measure.

Anthropomorphic   In the shape of human beings.

Apocalyptic   A supposed revelation about the end of the world or God's coming to render justice.

Apodeiktikos   Greek term for "having the quality of necessary or certain truth."

Apotheosis   Making divine.

Arhat   Buddhist term for "perfected one," "saint."

Athanatos   Greek term for "deathless."

Atman   Sanskrit term for "soul," "self," "substantial human spirit."

Avatar   Hindu term referring to the (usually personal) form in which a divinity manifests itself, for example, Krishna is an avatar of Vishnu.

Beatitudes The blessings Jesus distributed in the Sermon on the Mount.

Bhakti Indian term meaning religious devotion or love.

Bodhisattvas Mahayana Buddhist perfected ones, Buddhas-to-be, or saints.

Brahman Hindu ultimate reality; Indian priest, of the highest social class.

Canonists Church lawyers.

Cantus Firmus Strong, firm pattern that guides a chant or chorus.

Chador Black wraparound garment worn by Iranian women.

Charismatic Concerning the gifts of the Spirit, or endowed with special powers of personal appeal.

Christology Study or doctrine of Jesus as the Messiah.

Civil religion The religion of the political realm, or the blending of patriotism and faith.

Conditioned coproduction Buddhist term meaning the mutual influence of realities, the relational cast of all entities.

Consubstantial Sharing the same essential substance.

Contingent Dependent, not necessary.

Creator ex Nihilo Source who produces the world from nothingness.

Dharma Indian term for "Teaching," "the Doctrine," or "Law."

Dharmas Individual constituents of reality.

Dialectical Having the character of being talked or thought through; back-and-forth, mutual pushing and pulling.

Diaspora Dispersion, living outside one's homeland.

Diviners Religious functionaries who try to discern the future.

Doctrinalization Reducing an experience to what can be taught.

Dogmatic Having the force of authoritative teaching or a position that cannot be criticized.

Doxa Platonic term meaning opinion, in contrast with solid knowledge.

Dualistic Concerning a doubleness or twofoldness, for example, holding that good and evil are twin forces struggling to determine history.

Eclectic Patchwork, drawing from diverse sources.

Ecstatic Going outside oneself in trance or joy.

Ehyeh Asher Ehyeh Hebrew for "I am who I am."

Enlightenment Eighteenth-century European movement that stressed human autonomy and critical thinking; Buddhist experience of realization or fulfillment.

Entelechies Souls or primary forms that give their entities structure.

Episteme Platonic term meaning scientific knowledge.

Epistemology The study of human knowing.

Eucharist Primary Christian sacrament of the Lord's Supper or Mass.

Extracanonical Falling outside the canon or rule (list) of what is approved.

Fatalism Surrendering one's destiny to outside forces.

Feng-shui Chinese geomancy or study and manipulation of the forces that concern the physical earth.

Fideism Excessive reliance on blind faith.

Geist German term for spirit or Spirit.

Geomancy Study and manipulation of the forces that concern the physical earth.

Gnosis Greek term meaning (especially secret) knowledge.

Habisha Hindu ritual for postmenopausal women.

Hadith Traditions about Muhammad.

Hasid Jewish person reputed to be holy or devout.

Hasidism Jewish devotionalist movement started by the Baal Shem Tov in eighteenth-century eastern Europe.

Hermeneutical Concerning proper interpretation or exegesis.

Heterodox Disagreeing with what is orthodox or deemed right faith or worship.

Hoi polloi The many or the masses.

Homonoia Like-mindedness, common sense, basic agreement.

Homo politicus Humanity as social, condemned to politics.

Homo sapiens Humanity as the animal species having reason.

Hubris Greek term meaning pride that invites a comeuppance.

Humanistic Concerning men and women, sometimes to the exclusion of God or ultimate reality.

Idealistic Thinking that only spiritual or mental phenomena are fully real; having (perhaps unreasonably) high goals.

Ideological Concerning ideas or doctrines that have taken on a life of their own and are often substituted for primary reality.

Immanent Existing or being present within (for example, God is immanent to the world or human experience as well as transcendent).

Jainism Indian religion that, with Buddhism, challenged Brahmanism.

Jen Chinese term for "humanity," "goodness," "love."

Jihad Arabic term for "holy war."

Jinn Arabic term meaning demons or spirits that can do harm.

Kalpa Indian term meaning great cycles of cosmic expansion and contraction.

Kami Shinto term meaning the spirits, forces, or gods.

Karmic Concerning the Indian notion of moral cause and effect.

Kosher Jewish term meaning religiously right, fitting, clean.

Li Chinese term for "ritual," "ceremony," "protocol."

Libido dominandi Latin term meaning the lust or will for power.

Logos Greek term for the reason that makes the cosmos intelligible.

Maat Egyptian term for the ordering force or rule running through the world.

Mahatmas Great souls, saints.

Mahayana Buddhist school dominant in East Asia.

Mahayugas Major subunits of Hindu kalpas or cosmic cycles.

Mandala Visual form, often of wholeness, useful for meditation.

Mantras Vocal repetitive form useful for meditation.

Manvantaras Secondary cycles within Hindu kalpas.

Marga Hindu spiritual path or disciplinary way.

Massa damnata Humanity as headed for hell.

Me Sumerian term for "divine force."

Mediums Religious functionaries who serve as go-betweens linking people on earth with ancestors, spirits of the recently departed, and the like.

Messiah The biblical God's anointed ruler or deliverer.

Metanoia Greek term for "change of mind," "conversion."

Metaphysical Concerning the more-than-physical; being as spiritual as well as material.

Ming Chinese term for the "mandate of heaven."

Moksha Indian (largely Hindu) term for "salvation," "release."

Monism View that reality in the last analysis is one.

Monotheism The view that there is only one God.

Mystagogy Inculcation, exercise, or elucidation of the (divine) mystery.

Mysterious Concerning mystery, surplus of intelligibility.

Mythikos Concerning myth or sacred story.

Mythopoeia Myth making.

Nahual Meso-American term meaning spiritual force (or animal representation) potentially dangerous to human beings.

Nirvana Buddhist term meaning state of unconditionedness, completion.

Noesis Thought, intellectual activity.

Nosos Greek term meaning madness, spiritual disease.

Nous Mind, intellect.

Numinous Concerning the divine or sacred.

Pantheisms Systems holding that everything is divine.

Patristic Concerning the "fathers" or authoritative early teachers, especially those of the first Christian centuries.

Peitho Platonic term for "persuasion," "genuine conviction."

Philia Greek term meaning the love of friendship, between equals.

Phronesis Practical wisdom, prudence.

Pilgrim A spiritual wanderer or seeker.

Pneuma Spirit, soul, or life force.

Polytheistic Having to do with many divinities.

Positivistic Holding that only what is empirical or supported by data of the senses is significant.

Processive Ongoing, moving, dynamic.

Psyche The soul as source of feelings as well as of thoughts.

Puja Generic Hindu term for "ritual," "devotion."

Purdah Muslim seclusion of women.

Qadr Arabic term for "glory."

Qur'an Muslim scripture, Muhammad's "Recital."

Rasul Prophet or Messenger (of Allah): Muhammad.

Realissimum The most real.

Realized eschatology View that the final things have already occurred, may be found (at least germinally) in the present.

Reification Making something a thing, overly objectifying.

Reincarnation The soul's being put in a new body after death.

Relational Concerning connections, ties, mutuality.

Religion State or processes of being bound to ultimate reality.

Res Latin for "thing," (physical) entity.

Rubrical Concerning a liturgical or ceremonial rule.

Sacrament Material form for a holy reality or action.

Sadhus People whom Hindus regard as holy or devout.

Samadhi Yogic term meaning deepest trance or self-possession.

Samsara Reality as tied to death and rebirth, as perceived and lived with less than full enlightenment.

Scripture Sacred, canonical writings.

Sensorium Faculty for sensing or experiencing.

Shamanic Concerning a shaman or expert in archaic techniques of ecstasy.

Shariah Muslim term for "teaching," "law," "guidance."

Shema Jewish "call" to monotheistic faith (Deuteronomy 6:4).

Shia Muslim "party" or school dominant in Iran.

Shiite Concerning Shia Islam.

Shirk Muslim term for "idolatry."

Skepticism   View that one must be convinced, needs proof.

Soma   Ritual and magical drink mentioned in Vedas; Greek term for "body."

Soteriological   Concerning salvation.

Spoudaios   Greek designation for a mature person made ripe and wise by experience.

Sufism   Devotional or mystical Islamic movement.

Sunni   Major Muslim party and othodoxy.

Superbia   Latin term meaning pride, excessive self-regard, or self-assertion.

Surah   Unit or chapter of the Qur'an.

Sutu   Sumerian kind of ration or measure.

Symbiosis   Living together, co-dwelling.

Syncretistic   Amalgamated, run together.

Synoptic   Able to be taken in at a single glance; the gospels of Matthew, Mark, and Luke.

Talmudic   Concerning the Talmud or main collection of post-biblical Jewish wisdom.

Taboo   Something forbidden, fenced off, as religiously dangerous.

Tao   "Way" or path through the cosmos.

Te   Chinese term for "virtue," "power."

Theocracy   Political regime in which secular and sacred are one.

Theosis   Greek term meaning divinization, grace as divine life.

Ti   Chinese God.

T'ien-tzu   Chinese heaven.

Torah   Jewish Teaching, Divine Guidance, Law.

Transcendence   State of going-beyond, being more-than-worldly.

Transmigration   The passage of the soul or spirit at death from one entity to another.

Trinity   Christian Father-Son-Spirit.

Upanishads   Hindu holy writings at the end of the Vedas that begin mystical speculation about ultimate reality.

Volk   People or social collectivity as a pseudosacral entity.

Wu-wei   Active inaction, not-doing.

Yang   Active, light, dry, male principle in Chinese dualism.

Yin   Passive, dark, wet, female principle in Chinese dualism.

Yoga   Discipline, especially that which is interior.

Yugas   Various "ages" in the Hindu cosmological scheme.

Annotated Bibliography

CHAPTER ONE: INTRODUCTION

Douglas, Mary, and Tipton, Steven M., eds. *Religion and America*. Boston: Beacon Press, 1983. Sociologically oriented essays on recent religious trends in the United States.

Hick, John. *Philosophy of Religion*. 3rd ed. Englewood Cliffs, N.J.: Prentice-Hall, 1983. A good, brief, representative survey of contemporary American philosophy's views of religious questions.

Streng, Frederick. *Understanding Religious Life*. 3rd ed. Belmont, Calif.: Wadsworth, 1985. A representative survey of the approaches to religion used in departments of religious studies.

Toynbee, Arnold. *Mankind and Mother Earth*. New York: Oxford University Press, 1976. A provocative and trustworthy overview of the whole of world history.

Wilson, John F. *Religion: A Preface*. Englewood Cliffs, N.J.: Prentice-Hall, 1982. A brief overview of the major traditions, stronger on the West than the East.

CHAPTER TWO: NONLITERATE PEOPLES

Collins, John J. *Primitive Religion*. Totowa, N.J.: Littlefield, Adams, 1978. A thorough, if somewhat schematic and dry, overview.

GILL, SAM D.   *Beyond the Primitive.* Englewood Cliffs, N.J.: Prentice-Hall, 1982.   A sympathetic view of nonliterate people that uses some of the best recent work in cultural anthropology.

HARNER, MICHAEL.   *The Way of the Shaman.* San Francisco: Harper & Row, Pub., 1980.   A fascinating personal interpretation of shamanic consciousness, disciplines, therapies, and the like.

JENSEN, ADOLF E.   *Myth and Cult Among Primitive Peoples.* Chicago: University of Chicago Press, 1973.   A somewhat dated but still fascinating interpretation that uses European notions of culture and focuses on fashioning ways of understanding the world.

TURNER, VICTOR.   *The Ritual Process.* Ithaca, N.Y.: Cornell University Press, 1977.   An illuminating study of ritual by a leading cultural anthropologist well rooted in traditional African cultures.

CHAPTER THREE: EARLY CIVILIZATIONS

ELIADE, MIRCEA.   *A History of Religious Ideas,* Vols. 1 and 2. Chicago: University of Chicago Press, 1978, 1982.   A full treatment of the major early cultures by the leading American historian of religion.

FRANKFORT, HENRI, et al.   *Before Philosophy.* Baltimore: Penguin, 1949.   The classic popular introduction to Ancient Near Eastern thought by leading scholars of the past generation.

FRYE, RICHARD.   *The Heritage of Persia.* New York: World Press, 1963.   A solid, dry, well-regarded, standard history.

GUTHRIE, W. K. C.   *The Greeks and Their Gods.* Boston: Beacon Press, 1955.   A good study of the popular religions of classical Greece.

RINGGREN, HELMER.   *Religions of the Ancient Near East.* Philadelphia: Westminster Press, 1973.   A reliable and informative introduction to Mesopotamian religion.

CHAPTER FOUR: INDIA

BASHAM, A.L.   *The Wonder That Was India.* New York: Grove Press, 1959.   An engaging, encyclopedic overview of Indian civilization before the coming of the Muslims.

CONZE, EDWARD.   *Buddhism: Its Essence and Development.* New York: Harper Torchbooks, 1959.   The standard brief introduction to Buddhist doctrinal developments.

ORGAN, TROY WILSON.   *Hinduism: Its Historical Development.* Woodbury, N.Y.: Barron's Educational Series, 1974.   A clear presentation of Indian religious history from prehistory to contemporary times.

ZAEHNER, R.C.   *Hinduism.* New York: Oxford University Press, 1966.   A solid treatment of the major concepts that have guided traditional Indian culture.

ZIMMER, HEINRICH.   *Philosophies of India.* Princeton, N.J.: Princeton University Press, 1969.   A thorough, if somewhat dry and demanding, treatment of the major Indian philosophico-religious schools of thought.

CHAPTER FIVE: CHINA

CHAN, WING-TSIT. *A Source Book in Chinese Philosophy.* Princeton, N.J.: Princeton University Press, 1963. A fine collection of representative texts from the major schools and thinkers throughout Chinese history.

EICHHORN, WERNER. *Chinese Civilization.* New York: Praeger, 1969. A thorough, reliable, standard, brief introductory overview.

KEIGHTLEY, DAVID N., ed. *The Origins of Chinese Civilization.* Berkeley: University of California Press, 1983. Environmental, cultural, linguistic, and political studies of the earliest Chinese eras.

THOMPSON, LAURENCE G. *The Chinese Religion: An Introduction.* 3rd ed. Belmont, Calif.: Wadsworth, 1979. A somewhat schematic overview of the whole that concentrates on Confucianism as the traditional orthodoxy.

THOMPSON, LAURENCE G. *The Chinese Way in Religion.* Encino, Calif.: Dickenson, 1973. A good collection of original sources that lays out the main representative religious emotions of the Chinese people throughout history.

CHAPTER SIX: GREECE

DIETRICH, B.C. *The Origins of Greek Religion.* New York: de Gruyter, 1974. A rather deep study of the beginnings in Crete and the Mycenaean age.

DODDS, E.R. *The Greeks and the Irrational.* Berkeley: University of California Press, 1966. A well-regarded study of the Dionysiac and other ecstatic cults.

JAEGER, WERNER. *Aristotle.* New York: Oxford University Press, 1962. A solid study by one of the leading classicists of the past generation.

MURRAY, GILBERT. *Five Stages of Greek Religion.* New York: Doubleday, 1955. A provocative schematization by a leading scholar of Greek tragedy.

ROSE, H.J. *A Handbook of Greek Mythology.* New York: Dutton, 1959. A useful reference that helps one keep the many stories about the Greek gods somewhat ordered.

CHAPTER SEVEN: JUDAISM

BOADT, LAWRENCE. *Reading the Old Testament.* New York: Paulist Press, 1984. A fine introductory text by a Christian scholar.

FINKLESTEIN, LOUIS, ed. *The Jews: Their History.* New York: Schocken, 1970. Essays covering the entire history of Judaism and suggesting its rich cultural and religious development.

NEUSNER, JACOB. *The Life of Torah.* Encino, Calif.: Dickenson, 1974. A good brief collection of readings that illustrate the range and development of Jewish religious experience.

SANDMEL, SAMUEL. *The Enjoyment of Scripture.* New York: Oxford University Press, 1972. A marvelously readable work by a respected biblical scholar that proves the thesis implicit in its title.

STEINSALTZ, ADIN.   *The Essential Talmud.* New York: Basic Books, 1976.   A good concise study of the history, structure, content, and method of the central source of guidance in traditional Judaism.

CHAPTER EIGHT: CHRISTIANITY

CARMODY, DENISE LARDNER, and CARMODY, JOHN TULLY.   *Christianity: An Intro-duction.* Belmont, Calif.: Wadsworth, 1983.   A basic overview in terms of essential doctrine, history, and contemporary developments.

CLEBSCH, WILLIAM A.   *Christianity in European History.* New York: Oxford Univer-sity Press, 1979.   A provocative sketch in terms of paradigmatic personality types that ruled in different periods and helped to define them.

FREND, W. H. C.   *The Rise of Christianity.* Philadelphia: Fortress Press, 1984.   A massive study of the first six centuries, when Christianity established its doc-trines and cultural viability.

SCHILLEBEECKX, EDWARD.   *Jesus.* New York: Seabury Press, 1979.   A powerful study focusing on the primacy of the historical Jesus and the synoptic gospels.

SCHMEMANN, ALEXANDER.   *The Historical Road of Eastern Orthodoxy.* Crestwood, N.Y.: St. Vladimir's Seminary Press, 1977.   An overview of the development of Eastern Christianity from New Testament to recent times.

CHAPTER NINE: ISLAM

ARBERRY, A. J.   *Aspects of Islamic Civilizaton.* Ann Arbor: University of Michigan Press, 1971.   A collection of primary sources that suggest the range and interests of traditional Muslim poetry, law, mysticism, and science.

CRAGG, KENNETH.   *The House of Islam.* 2d ed. Encino, Calif.: Dickenson, 1975.   A good undergraduate text that discusses the main doctrinal themes.

GEERTZ, CLIFFORD.   *Islam Observed.* Chicago: University of Chicago Press, 1968.   Brief studies of Moroccan and Indonesian Islam by a cultural anthropologist who writes brilliantly but demandingly.

RAHMAN, FAZLUR.   *Islam.* New York: Doubleday, 1968.   A solid, respected, histor-ical treatment.

WILLIAMS, JOHN ALDEN.   *Themes of Islamic Civilization.* Berkeley: University of Cal-ifornia Press, 1982.   Good selections dealing with the Muslim community, ruler, God, future messiah, warfare, and saints.

CHAPTER TEN: AFTER PHILOSOPHY AND REVELATION

BERMAN, MARSHALL.   *All That Is Solid Melts Into Air.* New York: Simon & Schuster, 1982.   A somewhat idiosyncratic treatment of modernity, with an interesting concentration on Russia, that suggests a massive loss of orientation and order.

FACKENHEIM, EMIL L.   *The Religious Dimensions in Hegel's Thought.* Boston: Beacon Press, 1967.   An insightful and sympathetic study of one of the most influen-tial modern philosophers.

JAKI, STANLEY L. *The Road of Science and the Ways to God.* Chicago: University of Chicago Press, 1978. The 1974–76 Gifford Lectures that treat the rise of modern science as dependent on Christian realistic assumptions.

KUHN, THOMAS S. *The Structure of Scientific Revolutions.* Chicago: University of Chicago Press, 1970. An influential interpretation of how modern science has moved forward in both normal times and times of radical theoretical shifts.

McMURTY, JOHN. *The Structure of Marx's Worldview.* Princeton, N.J.: Princeton University Press, 1978. A basic, thorough, brief study that lays out Marx's major ideas fairly evenhandedly.

CHAPTER ELEVEN: CONCLUSION

AMAREL, MARIANNE, et al. "The Arts and Humanities in America's Schools." *Daedalus* (Summer 1983). Essays that suggest the current state of culture at home.

LONERGAN, BERNARD. *Insight.* New York: Philosophical Library, 1957. A study of human understanding and metaphysics that largely supports Voegelin's historical analysis in terms of noetic and pneumatic differentiations leading to a critical realism.

McNEILL, WILLIAM H. *A World History.* 3rd ed. New York: Oxford University Press, 1979. A view of the whole without Voegelinian theoretical convictions.

NISHITANI, KEIJI. *Religion and Nothingness.* Berkeley: Univeristy of California Press, 1982. A view of religion quite different from that familiar to Westerners, written by a leading Japanese Buddhist philosopher.

WHITE, PATRICK. *The Vivesector.* New York: The Viking Press, 1970. A smashing novel by the Australian Nobel laureate that confirms Voegelin's convictions about the centrality of mysticism.

PRIMARY SOURCES BY ERIC VOEGELIN

Anamnesis. Notre Dame: University of Notre Dame Press, 1978. A collection of some of Voegelin's most important theoretical essays showing the depth and nuance of his interpretation of the classical noetic breakthrough.

From Enlightenment to Revolution. Durham, N.C.: Duke University Press, 1975. A portion of Voegelin's discarded history of political ideas that offers critical studies of major modern thinkers such as Comte and Marx.

The New Science of Politics. Chicago: University of Chicago Press, 1966. The Walgreen Lectures of 1951 that launched Voegelin's reputation in the United States and previewed such themes as the indebtedness of right order to experience of a transcendent God and the derailment of modernity through Gnosticism.

Order and History. Vols. 1–4. Baton Rouge: Louisiana State University Press, 1956–1974. Voegelin's masterwork, dealing with Israel, Greece, and the new multicentered analysis that he came to by 1974. Volume 4 is probably the best single piece of Voegeliniana, but also the most difficult.

Science, Politics, and Gnosticism. Chicago: Henry Regnery, 1968.   A brief study of the modern derailment, famous for calling Marx a deliberate swindler.

SECONDARY SOURCES ON ERIC VOEGELIN

KIRBY, JOHN, AND THOMPSON, WILLIAM, eds.   *Voegelin and the Theologian.* Toronto: Edwin Mellen, 1983.   Ten interpretative essays by and for Christian theologians.

LAWRENCE, FRED.   *The Beginning and the Beyond.* Chico, Calif.: Scholars Press, 1984.   Papers by and about Voegelin from the 1983 Gadamer and Voegelin Conference at Boston College sponsored by the Lonergan Workshop, especially interesting for the sympathetic critique of Voegelin's theory of consciousness by members of the Lonergan school.

MCKNIGHT, STEPHEN A.   *Eric Voegelin's Search for Order in History.* Baton Rouge: Louisiana State University Press, 1978.   Critical essays on various aspects of Voegelin's work occasioned by the publication of *Order and History*, Vol. 4 in 1974.

SANDOZ, ELLIS.   *The Voegelinian Revolution.* Baton Rouge: Louisiana State University Press, 1981.   Perhaps the best single introduction to Voegelin's thought, largely because of a most helpful biographical section that shows the consistency of Voegelin's interests and convictions, from student days to last years.

WEBB, EUGENE.   *Eric Voegelin: Philosopher of History.* Seattle: University of Washington Press, 1981.   A solid study of the main principles and conclusions of Voegelin's study of history.

ESTIMATED APPROXIMATE MEMBERSHIP OF WORLD'S RELIGIONS (in thousands)

Religion	North America	South America	Europe	Asia	Africa	Oceania	Total
Christianity	252,500	196,600	337,678	104,100	147,076	18,782	1,056,693
Roman Catholic	138,876	185,251	178,033	57,265	57,000	5,216	621,640
Eastern Orthodox	5,649	335	47,070	2,763	9,402	408	65,645
Protestant	107,935	10,993	112,577	44,071	80,675	13,158	369,408
Judaism	7,612	750	4,644	4,009	232	74	17,320
Islam	1,581	406	20,191	380,069	152,944	87	555,277
Zoroastrianism	2.75	2.6	14	224.4	.9	1	245.6
Shintoism	50	—	—	33,000	—	—	33,050
Taoism	33.25	12.975	13.5	20,500	.85	2.9	20,563.5
Confucianism	99.75	58.9	450.5	162,500	2.55	18.4	163,130
Buddhism	336.3	241.1	238.3	250,097	15	23.7	250,952
Hinduism	309.1	637.4	442.9	459,709	1,166	326.5	462,599
All Religions	262,483	198,709	363,672	1,414,207	301,436.5	19,315	2,559,821
Total Population	389,914	259,644	761,195	2,771,419	516,037	23,677	4,721,886

Index

DATE DUE

DEMCO 38-297